CW00705058

1 MONTH OF FREE READING

at

www.ForgottenBooks.com

By purchasing this book you are eligible for one month membership to ForgottenBooks.com, giving you unlimited access to our entire collection of over 1,000,000 titles via our web site and mobile apps.

To claim your free month visit:

www.forgottenbooks.com/free118212

ISBN 978-0-428-84067-9
PIBN 10118212

Forgotten Books is a registered trademark of FB &c Ltd.
Copyright © 2018 FB &c Ltd.
FB &c Ltd, Dalton House, 60 Windsor Avenue, London, SW19 2RR.
Company number 08720141. Registered in England and Wales.

For support please visit www.forgottenbooks.com

SKETCHES OF SERMONS

ON

CHRISTIAN MISSIONS.

ORIGINAL AND SELECTED.

Jabez Burns D.D.

BY THE AUTHOR OF

"FOUR HUNDRED SKETCHES AND SKELETONS OF SERMONS,"
"PULPIT CYCLOPEDIA," ETC., ETC.

"How shall they believe in Him of whom they have not heard? and how shall they hear without a preacher? and how shall they preach, except they be sent?"—ROM. x. 14, 15.

LONDON:

AYLOTT AND JONES, 8, PATERNOSTER ROW.

——

1845.

PREFACE.

THE subject of CHRISTIAN MISSIONS is emphatically identified with the age in which we live. Almost all sections
of the church of Christ are labouring in this cause; and
have sent forth heralds of mercy, to preach among the
heathen " the unsearchable riches of Christ."

Most ministers at home are necessarily often called upon
to preach and plead on behalf of the millions of benighted
Pagans, and to excite and sustain a missionary spirit among
their own people. The present work, therefore, is designed
as *suggestive* of themes and topics suited to these occasions.

For nearly fifty years men of decided talent and spiritual
excellence, have been preaching on this express subject in
our metropolis; and in the various large cities and towns
of this country, and the United States of America. From
these discourses most of the Sketches have been selected
and formed; and it is truly delightful to observe how
ministers of the Church of England, Wesleyans, Baptists,
Congregationalists, and Presbyterians, all enunciate the
same great and glorious truths, when advocating the momentous claims of a world which lieth in wickedness.

The selection of Sketches has been made irrespective of
the sect or party of the preacher; the end contemplated
being an exposition of the missionary spirit from some of
the most talented ministers of past and present times. It
is but justice to add, that the sketches by Methodist

ministers have been selected from sermons which have been reported in the *Wesleyan Preacher,* as but few sermons have been published by that most honoured and devoted class, whose missions stand forth a striking exhibition of the power of holy simplicity and Christian zeal.

, To have left out these sketches would have rendered the volume truly incomplete, and have exposed it to the charge of bigotted exclusiveness; and to have used the published works of Dr. A. Clarke, or Rev. R. Watson, might have subjected the publishers to legal proceedings. Therefore, deeming the reports of the Sermons in the main correct, Sketches have been arranged from them, which, it is believed, will not deteriorate from the well-known talent and popularity of those justly-celebrated preachers of the Cross.

It is scarcely necessary to add, that the Sketches without name are the productions of the compiler of this volume.

It has been deemed desirable to insert four Sketches on the subject of the Conversion of the Jews; and one specially addressed to children, whose exertions in the cause of Missions have of late been so strikingly exhibited. Trusting that the work may be useful in bringing, as it were, into one common focus, many rays of missionary light and truth, and that it may subserve, in some degree, the extension of the Saviour's kingdom in the world, it is respectfully commended to those who are labouring to hasten the predicted era when, as Jehovah of hosts hath sworn, "As truly as I live, all the earth shall be filled with the glory of the Lord!"

3, PORTEOUS ROAD,
  Paddington.

CONTENTS.

INDEX TO SCRIPTURE TEXTS.

INDEX TO PREACHERS FROM WHOM SKETCHES ARE GIVEN.

SKETCHES OF SERMONS,

ON

CHRISTIAN MISSIONS.

SKETCH I.

IGNORANCE OF THE HEATHEN, AND THE CONDUCT OF GOD TOWARDS THEM.

BY THE
REV. GREVILLE EWING, M.A., OF GLASGOW.*

"And the times of this ignorance God winked at; but now commandeth all men every where to repent: because he hath appointed a day in the which he will judge the world in righteousness by that man whom he hath ordained; whereof he hath given assurance unto all men, in that he hath raised him from the dead."—ACTS xvii. 30, 31.

THE words of our text, which were so well suited to introduce the doctrines of the Gospel to a heathen audience, may serve also to explain the motives of those who attempt to propagate those doctrines throughout the world; and, by the blessing of God, which we earnestly implore, a serious consideration of them may, at this time, animate and confirm our zeal in prosecuting the important object of our institution, as a Missionary Society.

* From a Sermon preached before the London Missionary Society, at Tottenham Court Chapel, May 12th, 1803.

B

In discoursing from them we shall consider,

I. THE IGNORANCE OF THE HEATHEN.

II. THE DIVINE PROCEDURE WITH REGARD TO IT.

III. THE REASON OF THIS PROCEDURE.

IV. THE EVIDENCE BY WHICH THIS REASON IS CONFIRMED.

I. LET US CONSIDER THE IGNORANCE OF THE HEATHEN. The charge of ignorance which the apostle brought home to his audience at Athens, is by no means to be understood as confined to them.   He speaks in general of the ignorance of the nations, and of times, or ages, during which that ignorance had been permitted to reign.   It is a truth which Divine revelation and universal history unite in attesting,

1. *That wherever men have not been blessed with the Holy Scriptures, they have, time immemorial, been grossly mistaken with respect to the character of God, the situation of man, the way of salvation, and the hopes and fears of a future state.*   These mistakes undoubtedly originate in that alienation of the heart from God, which followed as a consequence of the first transgression. Having offended the Almighty, fallen man did not like to retain Him in his knowledge; yet the fear of punishment, and probably the example of those whom God separated from the beginning for his service, prevented a total dereliction of worship.   But it is not by the idolatry alone of the heathen that their ignorance is betrayed.

2. *It is rendered at least equally conspicuous by that vain and deceitful philosophy, those "oppositions of science falsely so called," which in countries not blessed with the Gospel, (and in other countries also,) have been extolled as the utmost efforts of human understanding.*   What else do we learn from the jarring systems of the Epicureans

and Stoics, with whom the apostle, at Athens, was called to contend?

3. Further. *The ignorance of the heathen appears not only in the positive errors which they hold, but in their indifference, insensibility, and prejudice with regard to all things spiritual; while they are wholly occupied with worldly pursuits and sensual indulgence.* The superstition they have been accustomed to, they cherish with bigotted attachment; but they are unwilling to give ear to anything else of a religious kind. In them are verified the words of the apostle, " The natural man receiveth not the things of the Spirit of God; for they are foolishness unto him, neither can he know them, because they are spiritually discerned," 1 Cor. ii. 14.

II. LET US CONSIDER THE DIVINE PROCEDURE WITH REGARD TO THE IGNORANCE OF THE HEATHEN.

" The times of this ignorance God winked at, but now commandeth all men every where to repent." The word rendered " winked at," intimates nothing respecting the merits of the case; but seems simply to signify, the suspension of decisive measures, either in way of remedy, or of punishment. Thus, in Leviticus xx. 4, a similar phrase, which the Septuagint renders by the same word as that in the original of our text, is used to express the non-execution of punishment—" If the people of the land do any ways *hide their eyes* from the man, when he giveth of his seed unto Molech, and *kill him not.*" Again. In Deut. xxii. 1, it supposes the non-application of a remedy—" Thou shalt not see thy brother's ox or his sheep go astray, and *hide thyself from them:* thou shalt in any case *bring them again* unto thy brother." In our text, both uses of the word may be included. The apostle speaks of the Divine forbearance towards the heathen, during the ages with preceded the

gospel dispensation; neither cutting them off in their ignorance, nor yet immediately applying the effectual remedy.
His words may be illustrated by a parallel passage in Acts
xiv. 16, 17—"Who in times past suffered all nations to
walk in their own ways.   Nevertheless he left not himself
without witness, in that he did good, and gave us rain from
heaven, and fruitful seasons, filling our hearts with food
and gladness."

III. Let us consider the reason of this procedure
respecting the ignorance of the heathen.

1. *Perhaps heathen ignorance was permitted to continue so long, that the necessity of Divine revelation might
experimentally appear.*   " For after that in the wisdom of
God the world by wisdom knew not God, it pleased God
by the foolishness of preaching to save them that believe,"
1 Cor. i. 21.

2. *God did not approve of it.*   From the very beginning, a preparation was going on for removing that ignorance, by the blessed dispensation which now obtains.

IV. Let us consider the evidence by which the
reason for commanding men to repent is confirmed.

" He hath appointed a day in which he will judge the
world in righteousness by that man whom he hath ordained;
whereof he hath given assurance unto all men, in that he
hath raised him from the dead."

I. *The proof that God hath appointed a day of judgment to be executed by a Man, is the resurrection of that
Man from the dead.*   This proof is held out to all men; for
it forms an essential part of the gospel which is preached
to all.   " I delivered unto you first of all," says the apostle,
to the Corinthians, " that which I also received, how that
Christ died for our sins according to the Scriptures; and

that he was buried, and that he rose again the third day according to the Scriptures," I Cor. xv. 3, 4. These truths are intimately connected with the future judgment.

2. *The fact that Christ rose from the dead, is well fitted to excite universal attention.* The bare possibility of a resurrection from the dead, is a most interesting discovery to the human race. How much more, then, to hear that such an event has actually happened, and happened to one who is said to have " died for our sins," and to have promised his disciples a share of his glory!

3. *This fact is supported by evidence universally intelligible and convincing.* It depends not on vague tradition, on popular prejudice, or natural peculiarities; we have an authentic history of it, published in the holy Scriptures, containing the plain, consistent testimony of credible witnesses, who little expected what they saw; who, nevertheless, could not be deceived; who had no possible motive to deceive others; and whose success in preaching the gospel is a manifest token of the Divine favour sealing their veracity.

4. *This fact naturally confirms us in the belief of a future judgment, and of such a judgment as the gospel foretels.* It is an example of future life, of the reversal of iniquitous human decisions, and of victory to the righteous over every foe. It establishes the whole doctrine of atonement, the necessity and reasonableness of which are implied, even in the rites of pagan worship. It declares the man Christ Jesus to be the Son of God with power. It shows the acceptance of His sacrifice, and his ability " to save them to the uttermost that come unto God by him." When it is once admitted, that " Christ both died, and rose, and revived," it cannot be thought incredible that he should be " Lord both of the dead and living," Rom. xiv. 9;

that now he should be exalted to govern the universe, and to judge the quick and the dead at the great day.

The proof, then, which God hath given to all men of the judgment of the world, though not admitted by all, is sufficient for the conviction of all; and leaves those who reject it, without excuse: it is a striking, an apposite, an unanswerable proof. That judgment, again, is a most powerful reason at once for publishing and obeying the command to repent. That command is the grand display of Divine mercy to perishing men; and, however great and prevalent, and long borne with, their ignorance hath been, it is the revealed will of God, that now, at last, it should be effectually removed.

SKETCH II.

THE MORAL DIGNITY OF THE MISSIONARY ENTERPRIZE.

BY REV. F. WAYLAND, BOSTON, U.S.*

" The field is the world."—MATTHEW xiii. 38.

To show that the Missionary cause combines within itself the elements of all that is sublime in human purpose; nay, combines them in a loftier perfection than any other enter- prize which was ever linked with the destinies of man, will be our design. In prosecuting it, we shall direct your attention to the *grandeur of the object; the arduousness of its execution;* and *the nature of the means on which we rely for success.*

I. THE GRANDEUR OF THE OBJECT.

In the most enlarged sense of the term, " The field is the world !" Our design is radically to affect the temporal and eternal interests of the whole race of man.

1. We have surveyed this field *statistically*, and find that, of the eight hundred millions who inhabit our globe, but two hundred millions have *any* knowledge of the re- ligion of Jesus Christ. Of these, we are willing to allow that but one half are his real disciples; and that, therefore,

* From a Sermon delivered before the Boston " Baptist Foreign Mission Society," October 25, 1823.

there are seven of the eight hundred millions to whom the gospel must be sent.

2. *We have surveyed this field geographically.*

We have looked upon our own continent, (AMERICA,) and have seen that, with the exception of a narrow strip of thinly-settled country, from the Gulf of St. Lawrence to the mouth of the Mississippi, the whole of this new world lieth in wickedness. Hordes of ruthless savages roam the wilderness of the west; and men, almost as ignorant of the spirit of the gospel, are struggling for independence in the south.

We have looked over EUROPE, and behold there one nation putting forth her energies in the cause of evangelizing the world. We have looked for another such nation, but it is not to be found. A few others are beginning to awake: most of them, however, yet slumber.

We have looked over AFRICA, and have seen that upon one little portion, reclaimed from brutal idolatry by missionaries, the Sun of righteousness has shined. It is a land of Goshen, where they have light in their dwellings. Upon all the remainder of this vast continent, there broods a moral darkness, impervious as that which once veiled her own Egypt, on that prolonged and fearful night, when no man knew his brother, see Exod. x. 21—23.

We have looked upon ASIA, and have seen its northern nations, though under the government of a Christian prince, scarcely nominally Christian. On the west, it is spell-bound by Mohammedan delusion. To the south, from the Persian Gulf to the Sea of Kamschatka, including also its numberless islands—except where, here and there, a Syrian church, or a missionary station, twinkles amidst the gloom—the whole of this immense portion of the human race is sitting in the region and shadow of death.

3. *We have also made an estimate of the miseries of this world.* We have seen how, in many places, the human

mind, shackled by ignorance, and enfeebled by vice, has dwindled almost to the standard of a brute. Our indignation has kindled at hearing of men, immortal as ourselves, bowing down and worshipping a wandering beggar, or paying adoration to reptiles and to stones. Not only is intellect every where under the dominion of idolatry prostrated; beyond the boundaries of Christendom, on every side, " the dark places of the earth are full of the habitations of cruelty," Psa. lxxiv. 20.

4. *We have considered these beings as immortal, and candidates for an eternity of happiness or misery.* And we cannot avoid the belief, that they are exposed to eternal misery. To settle the question concerning their future destiny, it would only seem necessary to ask, What would be the character of that future state, in which those principles of heart, which the whole history of the heathen developes, were suffered to operate in their unrestrained malignity?

The object of the missionary enterprize embraces every child of Adam; it is vast as the race to whom its operations are of necessity limited. It would confer upon every individual on earth, all that intellectual or moral cultivation can bestow.

II. The missionary undertaking is arduous enough to call into action the noblest energies of man.

Its arduousness is explained in one word—" The field is the world!" Our object is to effect an entire moral revolution in the whole human race.

1. *Its arduousness then results, of necessity, from its magnitude.* This mighty revolution is to be effected not in a family, a tribe, or a nation; but in a world which " lieth in wickedness."

2. *We shall frequently interfere with the more sordid interests of men; and we expect them to increase the*

difficulties of our undertaking. We have to assault systems, venerable for their antiquity, and interwoven with every thing that is proud in a nation's history.

3. *This enterprise requires consummate wisdom in the missionary who goes abroad, as well as in those who manage the concerns of a Society at home.* He who goes forth unprotected to preach Christ to despotic or badly governed nations, must be "wise as serpents, and harmless as doves." With undeviating firmness upon every thing essential, he must combine the most yielding facility upon all that is unimportant. Great abilities are also required in him who conducts the mission at home. The missionary undertaking calls for perseverance: a perseverance of that character, which, having once formed its purpose, never wavers from it till death. This undertaking calls for self-denial of the highest and holiest character. Hence you see, this undertaking requires courage. But, above all, the missionary undertaking requires faith, in its holiest and sublimest exercise.

III. Let us consider the means by which the moral revolution is to be effected.

It is, in a word, by the preaching of Jesus Christ, and Him crucified. It is, by going forth and telling the lost children of men, that "God so loved the world, that he gave his only begotten Son, that whosoever believeth in him should not perish, but have everlasting life," John iii. 16; and by all the eloquence of such an appeal, to entreat them, for Christ's sake, to be reconciled unto God. This is the lever by which we believe the moral universe is to be raised; this is the instrument by which a sinful world is to be regenerated. Consider,

1. *The commanding simplicity of this means, devised by Omniscience, to effect a purpose so glorious.* This world

is to be restored to more than it lost by the fall, by the simple annunciation of the love of God in Christ Jesus. Here we behold means apparently the weakest, employed to effect the most magnificent of purposes.

2. *Contemplate the benevolence of these means.* In practice, the precepts of the gospel may be summed up in the simple command, " Thou shalt love the Lord thy God with all thy heart, and with all thy soul, and with all thy mind;—and thy neighbour as thyself," Matt. xxii. 37, 39.

3. *Consider the efficacy of these means.* The reasons which teach us to rely upon them with confidence, may be thus briefly stated—

(1.) We see that all which is really terrific in the misery of man, results from the disease of his moral nature. If this can be healed, man may be restored to happiness. Now, the gospel of Jesus Christ is the remedy devised by Omniscience, especially for this purpose; and, therefore, we do certainly know that it will inevitably succeed.

(2.) It is easy to be seen, that the universal obedience to the command, " Thou shalt love the Lord thy God with all thy heart, and with all thy soul, and with all thy mind; —and thy neighbour as thyself," would make this world a heaven.

(3.) The preaching of the cross of Christ is a remedy for the miseries of the fall which has been tested by the experience of eighteen hundred years; and has never, in a single instance, failed. Its efficacy has been proved by human being of all ages, from the lisping babe, to the sinner an hundred years old. All climates have witnessed its power. From the ice-bound cliffs of Greenland, to the banks of the voluptuous Ganges, the simple story of Christ crucified, has " turned men from darkness to light, and from the power of Satan unto God," Acts xxvi. 18.

(4.) We know, from the word of the living God, that it

will be successful, until this whole world has been redeemed from the effects of man's first disobedience—" For the earth shall be filled with the knowledge of the glory of the Lord, as the waters cover the sea," Hab. ii. 14.

APPLICATION.

Blessed be God, this is a work in which every one of us is permitted to do something. None so poor, none so weak, none so insignificant, but a place of action is assigned him; and the cause expects every man to do his duty. We observe, then—

1. You may assist in it by your prayers.

2. You may assist by your personal exertions. This cause requires a vigorous, persevering, universal, and systematic effort.

3. You may assist by your pecuniary contributions.

SKETCH III.

PAUL PREACHING AT ATHENS.

" Now while Paul waited for them at Athens, his spirit was stirred in him, when he saw the city wholly given to idolatry," etc.—ACTS xvii. 16—23.

PAUL had been driven out of Thessalonica by a rude mob of the baser sort; and from thence he had repaired to Berea, where the people gave him a fair and candid hearing. For " these were more noble than those in Thessalonica, in that they received the word with all readiness of mind, and searched the Scriptures daily, whether those things were so," Acts xvii. 11; the result was, " many of them believed," verse 12. But the persecuting Jews of Thessalonica pursued the apostle to Berea, and there also stirred up the people. It was deemed prudent, therefore, for Paul to leave Berea; and the brethren conducted him to Athens: here he waited until he should be joined by Silas and Timothy. Thus waiting, our text refers to the feelings and conduct of the apostle, " Now while Paul waited for them," etc. Observe,

I. THE DESCRIPTION GIVEN OF THE CITY OF ATHENS.

It may be well briefly to refer to its history. Athens was the most celebrated city of Greece. It was distinguished for the military talent, the learning, the eloquence, the luxury, and the politeness of its inhabitants. It was founded about 1,600 years before the Christian era; and was called Athens in honour of Minerva, who was chiefly worshipped there, and to whom the city was dedicated.   No city of antiquity was so celebrated for its warriors, statesmen, philosophers, sculptors, and poets.   Here was the celebrated ACROPOLIS, the glory of Grecian art: within this was deposited all that was most interesting in painting, sculpture, and architecture.   Here, also, was the PARTHENON, or Virgin Temple of Minerva, 217 feet in length, and 98 in breadth: within which was a statue of Minerva, a masterpiece of art, of ivory, 39 feet in height; and entirely covered with pure gold, to the value of £120,000 sterling.   Beside these, outside the walls, were the temples of THESEUS and JUPITER OLYMPIUS.   Three quarters of a mile to the north of the town, was the academy where Plato taught.   Here, also, was the Lyceum, where Aristotle diffused the light of science.   In addition to these was the AREOPAGUS.   This was an open building on an eminence, in the centre of the city, and was the court of the supreme judges of Athens, where they met to dispense justice, and enforce laws.   Here the judges held their court at midnight, that they might be less liable to distraction from surrounding objects.

Now, within this highly-educated city, the people were " wholly given to idolatry,"—full of idols.   On every side there were victims, temples, and altars.   Among these, there was one peculiar monument, or altar, which bore this strange inscription, " TO THE UNKNOWN GOD."   It is affirmed, on good historical testimony, that 600 years before Christ, the city was afflicted with a grievous pestilence. Epimenides took a number of sheep to the Areopagus, and then let them go whither they would; at the place where they halted, they were sacrificed, and the altar was erected " To the Unknown God."   Such, then, is a brief description of this celebrated city.   Notice,

II. THE FEELINGS WHICH A SURVEY OF THIS CITY PRO-
DUCED ON THE MIND OF THE APOSTLE. " His spirit was
stirred in him." His soul was agitated, greatly excited.

I. *It was stirred in him with jealousy for the Divine
glory.* Every idol and altar was a public dishonour to
the true God. Here senseless statues had possession, and
received. the homage of the thousands of this celebrated
city.

2. *It was stirred in him with compassionate indignation for human nature.* The feelings of compassion and
indignation are quite in accordance with each other : indignation against the evil, and compassion for the sinner.
Here human nature presented a singular appearance : intellectual, yet ignorant ; civilized, yea, polished, yet immersed in the senseless stupidity of idolatry. Behold those
lofty minds of Athens, those master spirits of their times
and country, yet bowing to idols.

3. *It was stirred up with intense anxiety for their
welfare and salvation.* Athens, after all, was the seat of
Satan. Its people were spell-bound. As an idolatrous
city, it was exposed to the displeasure and indignation of
heaven. The soul of the apostle was filled with deepest
solicitude for this dark, wicked, and infatuated people.
See Deut. v. 7, etc. ; xxvii. 15, etc. " Confounded be all
they that serve graven images, that boast themselves of
idols," Psa. xcvii. 7. Notice,

III. THE COURSE WHICH THE APOSTLE ADOPTED. " He
disputed in the synagogue with the Jews." That is, he
reasoned, etc.; endeavoured, by statement and argument,
to convince the people they were wrong. He did this with
the Jews who had a synagogue; with the devout or religious
people, and in the market-place; and he did this daily.
Observe,

1. *The apostle stood alone as a Christian minister, an apostle of the Nazarene.* The people were all idolatrous, except a few Jewish proselytes.

2. *The apostle grappled with the established errors of the place.* He did not say, I will be passive, and allow all to do as they please: he could not do this. Hence, we see all controversies and disputations are not wrong. Christ disputed and argued with the Jews, etc. So also the apostles; and so must we, with all the God-dishonouring enemies of truth.

3. *He made this his occupation, it was his daily work.* He was to be the light of Athens during his residence in it.

4. *He did this publicly.* " In the synagogue, and in the market." Wherever he could meet with a concourse of people, he felt for them, and argued with them, etc., concerning idolatry, and concerning the true God. Notice, then,

IV. THE OPPONENTS THE APOSTLE HAD TO ENCOUNTER.
We have previously referred to the intellectual celebrity of Athens; and, therefore, he had not to contend with a rude and maddened rabble, or bigoted Jews; but with highly cultivated minds, men of profound philosophical research. Certain of these philosophers, of two of the leading sects, encountered him.

1. *The Epicureans.* Epicurus, the founder of that sect, flourishes about 300 years before Christ. He represented the world as being formed by a fortuitous concourse of atoms, which met and united, and formed all things. He denied the doctrine of providence, or that the gods exercise any care about human beings. His principal sentiment was, that pleasure was the chief good. He evidently intended more the pleasures of the mind than of the body. His followers, however, were given to indolence, effeminacy,

and voluptuousness. Epicurus was a wonderful man for the age and country in which he lived, and was greatly admired for his endowments and virtues. He died in the seventy-second year of his age.

2. *The Stoics.* This was a sect of philosophers, of whom Zeno was the founder. They were so called, because he taught his disciples in an open portico, where he used to walk, and deliver his instructions. He taught, that there was only one Supreme Being; and that all things happened by *fatal necessity.* He held, that happiness consisted in obtaining a total insensibility to pain; and that a good man is always alike joyful, even under the greatest torture. Zeno lived until he was ninety-six years old, and died 264 years before Christ. Now, philosophers of these sects encountered Paul, " because he preached unto them Jesus, and the resurrection," ver. 18. How great a contrast between the Master of Paul, and the founders of these sects! How different his spirit, his maxims, his gospel, his life, his benefits! How strange to them the doctrine of the resurrection! In the soul's immortality many of the heathen philosophers believed; but a single conjecture is not to be found in the writings of all the pagans in the world, on the subject of the resurrection. This is one of the grand and glorious truths confined to the volume of eternal truth, and fully brought to light in the gospel.

V. The spirit which the Athenians evinced.

And here there is every thing to commend, for although Paul had come in direct collision with the tenets and the opinions of their distinguished philosophers, yet, with candour and respect, they gave the apostle an opportunity of stating fully and clearly the doctrines which he held. " May we know what this new doctrine, whereof thou speakest, is?" So they took him to the Areopagus, the seat of judicature, the highest and most dignified place within the city, and where thousands might hearken to the statements the apostle might make.   Here, within one of the most celebrated tribunals of the world, had the apostle Paul to stand, to declare among these Gentiles, " the unsearchable riches of Christ."   Observe,

VI. THE DISCOURSE WHICH THE APOSTLE DELIVERED.

Doubtless, we have but the analysis presented to our view.

1. *He refers to their superstitious veneration for idols.* " I perceive," etc.   Surely they could not be denominated an irreligious people, a reckless people; no, they carried their superstitious regards to the greatest possible extent. The city was full of temples, of idols, and altars.   To these they added one " To the unknown God."   How aptly did this exhibit their true and real character and condition.   To them the true God was unknown: they had learning, art, science, philosophy, etc.; yet they were without God.

2. *The apostle gave a striking representation of the true Jehovah.*   " Whom therefore ye ignorantly worship, him declare I unto you."

(1.) He declares him as the Creator of all things.

(2.) He declares his universal dominion and authority. " Lord of heaven and earth."

(3.) He declares the immensity of his nature. " Dwelleth not in temples made with hands."   That is, cannot be confined, not limited.

(4.) He declares his self-existence, and sufficiency.   He is not to be served, or " worshipped with men's hands." See also Psa. l. 7, etc.

(5.) He declares him the Fountain and Author of all life. " Giveth to all life, and breath, and all things."   Holds in his hands the breath of lives.

(6.) He declares him the universal parent of all men. " Hath made of one blood," etc.

(7.) He declares him to be the Disposer and Ruler of all events. " Hath determined the times before appointed," etc.

(8.) He declares unto them his omnipresence. He is " not far from every one of us."

(9.) He declares him the source of all our bounties. " In him we live, and move, and have our being."

(10.) He declares his spirituality, ver. 29.

(11.) He declares the forbearance and long-suffering of God, ver. 30. Did not punish, etc.

(12.) He declared the necessity of universal repentance. " But now commandeth all men every where to repent."

(13.) He declared the righteous judgment of all by Christ Jesus. " Whom God hath raised up," etc., ver. 31.

Notice,

VII. THE EFFECTS WHICH WERE PRODUCED.

1. *Some mocked.* Derided, as though he had spoken folly.

2. *Some deferred judgment, and agreed to hear again.*

3. *Some were converted.* " Howbeit certain men clave unto him, and believed "—one of the judges, several men, and Damaris.

APPLICATION.

Learn,

1. *The corruption and blindness of the human mind.* To give honour, etc., to stocks and stones—to idols.

2. *The insufficiency of the light of nature in matters of religion.* What can any nation or people have, that they had not? They had sun, moon, and stars. All the works of Deity were around them, etc. Yet by " wisdom they knew not God;" nay, all their science and literature were ineffectual here. Their poets and philosophers were all

strangers to God.   So it is with the heathen nations to this day.

3. *There is idolatry of heart, as well as of worship.* If Paul visited *this* metropolis, no such statues would arrest his eye, etc.   But every one who refuses God's authority, has a something enthroned, and that is their idol; and the love and service of that is idolatry.

4. *God demands the supreme homage of the mind, and affections of the heart.*   "Thou shalt have no other gods before me," Exod. xx. 3.   "Thou shalt love the Lord thy God with all thy heart," etc., Matt. xxii. 37.

5. *How thankful we should be for the gospel.*   How precious, how invaluable.   It will make you wise, holy, and happy.   Receive it cordially.

6. *Deeply feel for the perishing heathen.*   And let your compassionate solicitude lead you to zealous efforts for their salvation.

SKETCH IV.

CONTEMPLATION OF HEATHEN IDOLATRY, AN EXCITEMENT TO MISSIONARY ZEAL.

BY REV. RALPH WARDLAW, D.D.*

"Now when Paul waited for them at Athens, his spirit was stirred in him, when he saw the city wholly given to idolatry."—ACTS xvii. 16.

ATHENS stood pre-eminent, indeed, for the multitude of its deities; but, alas! it stood not alone. It was not a *city* merely that Paul had to contemplate as given to idolatry; but, with the exception of one little spot favoured of heaven as "the place which Jehovah had chosen, to put his name there," it was a *whole world*. And now, when eighteen centuries have passed away, does not the same heart-moving spectacle still, to a vast extent, present itself to the view? How very few, comparatively, of the tribes of our fallen and revolted race, have as yet "turned from their idols to serve the living and true God!" How immense the proportion of them that are still going astray after their dumb idols, even as they are led! It is true,—and let us record it with the liveliest feelings of delight and adoration, —the proportion is lessening. The true God is making his name glorious among the heathen. The idols he is abolishing. "The gods that made not the heavens and the earth, are perishing from off the earth, and from under

* From a Sermon, preached before the "London Missionary Society," at Surrey Chapel, May 13, 1818.

these heavens." The object of these annual meetings is to keep alive a missionary spirit, and to rouse it to still warmer and more active energy. It will not be found, I trust, unsuitable to this design, if we endeavour to show, with humble dependence upon the Divine blessing, how the survey of these idolatries is calculated to produce *indignant grief for the dishonour done by them to God; amazement at human weakness and folly; abhorrence of human impiety; and compassion for human wretchedness.*

I. The contemplation of heathen idolatries should excite indignant grief for the dishonour done to God.

This, I have no doubt, was the feeling which first stirred the spirit of the devout apostle of the Gentiles, when, looking around him, he contemplated the endless multiplicity of false deities, "the gods many, and lords many" of the Athenians, and, as he himself afterwards expresses it, "beheld their devotions."—In the altar inscribed "To THE UNKNOWN GOD," Acts xvii. 23, he had seen a melancholy acknowledgment of their ignorance. The only true God was the only God unknown. All the fabled deities were there, of heaven, and earth, and hell; but the one living God, whose peculiar honours were thus usurped and and alienated and abused, was not to be found. Not that Paul could have been gratified in His having a place amidst such a collection of falsehood, impurity, and folly. It would have been a vile affront to his infinite Majesty, to have been so associated, even if he had been placed at the head of their pantheon, and made their Jupiter Olympius. For, indeed, this Olympian Jove, the "mighty thunderer," the "father of gods and men," the "best and the greatest," was, in the actions ascribed to him by his deluded worshippers, the foulest and most infamous of the whole fabled fraternity.

Paul could not contemplate the prostrate honours of the infinite God with an unmoved and tranquil heart. He could not behold this world, which ought to have been one great temple to the exclusive worship of Jehovah, " whose he was, and whom he served," crowded with rival deities, the offspring of the depraved fancy of apostate creatures, with which the very thought of bringing Him, even for an instant, into comparison, makes the heart thrill and shudder, with detestation.

II. The contemplation of heathen idolatry may well fill us with amazement at the weakness and folly of the human mind.

Search the annals of our world, in every age and in every country, I question if you will find a more affecting and humbling exemplification of human imbecility, than that which is afforded by the history of idolatry. It is such, indeed, as we hardly know how to believe,—to be set down amidst the likenesses " to corruptible man, and to birds, and fourfooted beasts, and creeping things," Rom. i. 23, which form the immense museum of heathen mythology, one might be tempted to fancy, that some satirical defamer of our nature had been exhausting an inventive imagination to slander and to vilify it.

When Paul saw the wonderful results of human wisdom, and power, and skill, in the arts and sciences, in philosophy and literature, which existed in Athens in such profusion and splendour; when he beheld a people raised to the very pinnacle of eminence for all that was great and excellent in human attainments; and then viewed the same people, sunk in the abyss of ignorance and stupidity as to all that related to the higher concerns of God and of eternity, how striking! how affecting the contrast! Can we wonder that his " spirit was stirred in him?"

III. Paul's spirit was stirred in him, and the con-templation of heathen idolatry should stir ours, with abhorrence of human impiety.

Idolatry, like infidelity, has not been so much an error of the head as of the heart. Here it had its origin; here it still has " its power, and its seat, and its great authority." The head has been the dupe of the heart: the folly has sprung from the corruption; the infatuation of the judg-ment, from the depravation of the affections. The veil has not been upon the evidences themselves of the existence and perfections of God, but upon the hearts of his fallen crea-tures. The wretched votaries of idolatry are described as " walking in the vanity of their minds; having their under-standings darkened; being alienated from the life of God, through the ignorance that is in them, because of the blind-ness (or, rather, because of the hardness, or callousness*) of their hearts," Ephes. iv. 17, 18. To this source, even to the " carnal mind," which " is enmity against God," the philosophy of the Bible teaches us to trace the whole system, in all its varieties, of pagan idolatry: " They did not like to retain God in their knowledge," Rom. i. 28.

The origin of idolatry, then, is to be found in the aliena-tion of the heart from God; the unsuitableness of his cha-racter, to the depraved propensities of his fallen creatures, and the consequent desire to have a god " such a one as themselves, who will approve their sins." This view of the matter accords well with the characters of their " gods many, and lords many," 1 Cor. viii. 5, and with the nature of the worship with which they honoured them. The worship of their gods is such as might have been expected from their characters. Well are their superstitions deno-minated " abominable idolatries," 1 Pet. iv. 3. They consist, not merely of the most senseless fooleries and the wildest

* πορσιν—porosin.

extravagancies, but of the most disgusting impurities; the most licentious acts of intemperance, and the most iron-hearted cruelties.

IV. The contemplation of heathen idolatry ought to inspire compassion for human wretchedness.

I speak not at all, at present, of the wants and miseries of a savage life, destitute of the arts and sciences, and of the comforts and refinements of civilised society; because such miseries, and such wants, were evils unfelt at Athens. The mere man of the world would have looked on that far-famed city, as the emporium of all that was fitted to give dignity and happiness to men. But, in the midst of all this, the eye of the Christian philanthropist could not fail to discern a most melancholy want—a want, sufficient to throw a darkening shade over all the splendours of Athenian glory. The inhabitants of Athens, like those of Ephesus, were, in the eye of the "ambassador of Christ," without God, and having no hope in the world.

Do not your hearts bleed for them? When you think of the depth of their ignorance, and the enormity of their guilt; of their vain sacrifices, and their fruitless ablutions; their painful penances, their self-inflicted tortures and death; when you behold them with suppliant earnestness, crying for protection and deliverance to a thing which cannot help—falling down to the stock of a tree;—when you see them with an importunity worthy of a more rational service, repeating their cry from morning till noon, and from noon till evening; and, in the bitterness and frenzy of disappointed eagerness, " cutting themselves with lancets, till 'the blood gushed out upon them,"—and " there is neither voice, nor any to answer, nor any that regardeth," see 1 Kings xviii. 26—29; when you see them steeling their hearts against the meltings of nature, stopping their ears to

c

the pleadings of parental love, and " giving their first-born for their transgression, the fruit of their body for the sin of their soul," (Micah. vi. 1;) when you see them the wretched victims of a delusive hope, the dupes of a merciless and degrading superstition, devoting themselves to voluntary destruction—crushed beneath the ponderous wheel, or " sinking in the devouring flood, or more devouring flame"—Oh! does not a pang of pity go through your very souls for them? Are not your spirits stirred within you? Do not your bowels yearn over your kindred—over those, who are "bone of your bone, and flesh of your flesh," —for " God hath made of one blood all nations of men, for to dwell on all the face of the earth," Acts xvii. 26.

And, finally, without dwelling on the many particulars of wretchedness, which are suggested to our minds by such a description of personal and social character as we read in the beginning of the Epistle to the Romans, I think, my brethren, of your miserable fellow men in reference to an eternal world! I must now hasten to a close, by drawing from the subject some further practical improvement.

1. *All the sentiments and feelings which have been illustrated, ought to be principles of active and zealous exertion.*

2. *Let me, from this subject, endeavour to impress your minds with the necessity and value of Divine revelation.*

3. *The feelings expressed in the text, imply the opposite emotions of delight, in witnessing the contrary scene.*

If the spirit be " stirred" with indignant grief for the affront put upon the true God by the " abominable idolatries" of the heathen, it cannot fail to be stirred with exulting joy, when his alienated honours are restored; when the apostate sons of men " turn to God from idols, to serve the living and true God, and to wait for his Son from heaven," I Thess. i. 10.

4. *The guilt of idolatry, it is to be feared, attaches to many who little imagine that they are at all chargeable with anything of the kind.* Yes; there are many who may even, in contemplating the idolatries of the heathen, condemn and wonder and pity, without at all reflecting on the possibility of their being themselves in the same condemnation. You are not worshipping the host of heaven; you are not adoring deified men; you are not falling down to stocks and stones; you are not making to yourselves graven images, likenesses of things in heaven above, or in the earth beneath, or in the waters under the earth; and you conclude you are not idolaters. But what is the spirit of idolatry? Is it not the alienation of the heart from God? Is it not the withholding from him, and the giving to other objects, whatever they may be, that homage, and those affections, to which He alone is entitled? Every man's idol is that on which his heart is supremely set; and every heart in which JEHOVAH is not enthroned, is an idol's temple.

SKETCH V.

THE RECOLLECTION OF THE MISERIES OF A PAGAN CONDITION, A MOTIVE TO ZEAL IN THE MISSIONARY CAUSE.*

BY REV. GEORGE CLAYTON.

" Wherefore remember, that at that time ye were without Christ."
EPHES. ii. 11, 12.

ASSEMBLED as we are from all parts of the British empire, and indeed from all quarters of the globe; drawn together by one common object, and that the grandest which man can propose, or Deity achieve; urged forward by an impulse which, I trust, without presumption, may be pronounced similar, in some humble measure, to that which brought Jesus from the skies, and apostles and martyrs to the stake; it will be salutary to remember what we ourselves once were, in order that our motives may be invigorated, our resolutions confirmed, and our compassions awakened, in favour of those who are still " without God, and without hope in the world;" and whom we are determined, by the assistance and blessing of the Most High, to place on an equal footing with ourselves, in all the light and liberty and joy of which Christianity is the parent, and the source.

* Preached before the London Missionary Society, at Surrey Chapel, May 9th, 1821.

Let us consider,

I. The affecting condition which the text describes, " At that time ye were without Christ."

II. The duty of cherishing a distinct and constant remembrance of it.

III. The practical effects which ought to flow from such remembrance.

I. The affecting condition described : " At that time ye were without Christ."

It is quite clear that the reference in the text is to a state of unenlightened, unregenerated paganism, in which the Ephesians had been long immersed, and from which they had recently been delivered by the free and sovereign love of God, quickening them from a moral and spiritual death, and raising them " to sit together in heavenly places in Christ Jesus." In allusion to this period of heathenish darkness, the apostle says, " Remember, that at that time ye were without Christ;" and this short, but comprehensive delineation, contains in itself a finished picture of human wretchedness. We can conceive of no worse predicament for a rational, immortal, sinful, perishing being, than to be without Christ. Let us, then, trace the bearing and influence of this mournful deficiency upon the nature of man.

1. *Upon his understanding.*

And truly, my brethren, I know of nothing more deeply affecting than to contemplate the human intellect left to itself, and toiling, in its entangled march, through all the trackless labyrinths of speculative uncertainty; to behold a mind once adorned with the likeness of God, but now void of knowledge, spending its strength, wasting its energies, and wearing out its courage, in the anxious pursuit of that which satisfieth not; in spite of all that is intense in application, and profound in investigation, " ever learning, and never able to come to the knowledge of the truth," 2 Tim. vii. 7 ; panting towards the goal, but never reaching it ;—bewildered, deceived, disappointed, and " in endless mazes lost;"—this is, and must ever be the case, so long as men are without Christ.

2. *Consider this subject as it affects the conscience.*

" The whole world is guilty before God," Rom. iii. 19. Guilt is the parent of uneasiness; and though the cause may not be generally understood, the effect is manifest and undeniable. The apostle Paul expressly asserts the operation of conscience, even in minds unenlightened by the Christian revelation: " their conscience also bearing witness, and their thoughts the mean while accusing or else excusing one another," Rom. ii. 15. You have, in these words, a representation of the mental process which is the true cause of that inward disquietude which racks and convulses the moral world. Oh, there is a deep and festering wound in the conscience of every sinner, which no balm can reach, but the Balm of Gilead; no hand can heal, but that of the Physician who is there.

3. *As it affects the character.*

Where Christ is not, morality sheds but a dim, a feeble, and often a delusive ray. The fact, in its application to this part of the subject, is so fully established, and so perfectly ascertained, as to form an argument altogether irresistible. What were the Ephesians, the Corinthians, the Romans, the Cretans, as long as they were without Christ? " Earthly, sensual, devilish," James iii. 15. " Serving divers lusts and pleasures—hateful and hating one another" —" always liars, evil beasts, slow bellies," Titus iii. 3; i. 12. What is now the state of morals in unenlightened Africa? in unregenerated India? Why, blood toucheth blood; rapine and cruelty, oppression and violence, injustice and deceit, and all the hideous brood of unnatural abominations, exist and triumph.

4. *As it relates to the happiness of man in the present life.*

Without Christ, you leave man as a sufferer under all the unmitigated weight of trouble ; you leave him to grapple, unaided and unsustained, with the fierce and uncontrolable calamities of life, destitute of any alternative but a morbid sullenness of resentment, or an irritability which goads and chafes itself to death.

5. *We must, in justice to our subject, trace its operation on the civil and religious institutions of human society.*

All countries have found it expedient to form laws and governments for the safe and beneficial regulation of social intercourse; but, without the benign and salutary influence of Christianity, when has this object been secured?

Nor are the religious institutions of unenlightened nations in any degree better than their civil ordinances. The whole system of idolatrous worship, intended as it is to placate an offended Deity, only serves to offend him the more highly, and to leave the conscience really more heavily burdened, and more foully stained, instead of affording it relief. The various modes of propitiation resorted to, are alike impious and vain. The ablutions and the penances—the blood of bulls and goats—the immolation of human victims,—all proclaim the truth of the statement I have made; while they confess their own inadequacy to take away sin, or to satisfy the conscience.

6. *We must consider the relation of our subject to the immortal destiny of man.*

To live without Christ is dreadful; but, oh! what must it be to die without him? There is so much of overpowering solemnity in this view of the subject, that one is at a loss how to approach it. To all men " it is appointed once to die;" and all men need consolation (if ever) in a dying hour. But, alas! if, when the vail of the flesh is rent asunder, the mind can see no brightness beyond it, no solid ground of hope, no certain assurance of blessedness, the gloomy vail will be covered with a tenfold obscurity, and darkened with irremediable sadness.

II. THE DUTY OF CHERISHING A DISTINCT AND CONSTANT REMEMBRANCE OF THIS CONDITION.

1. *The light of reason, and the custom of mankind, are sufficient to show that we should cherish the grateful remembrance of eminent deliverances.*

All men have agreed in preserving the memory of the founders of states, the benefactors of their country, the heroes of the age. Hence pillars, statues, temples, trophies, and monuments, have been reared, as so many commemorative ensigns.

2. *The express direction of Holy Scripture.*

On the Jewish church such recollection was frequently and solemnly inculcated. Exod. xiii. 3, " And Moses said unto the people, Remember this day, in which ye came out from Egypt, out of the house of bondage; for by strength of hand the Lord brought you from this place." See also Deut. v. 15.

3. *We may appeal to the impulse of good feeling in every mind that is rightly, by which I mean religiously constituted.*

It will be found consonant to every dictate of ingenuous sensibility, that we should keep in abiding recollection the state of degradation and misery from which Divine grace has rescued us, whether individually, in our religious connexions, or in our national character. That man is chargeable with a brutish negligence, and must carry a heart of adamant in his bosom, who can erase from his mind the recollection of so great a benefit.

III. THE PRACTICAL EFFECTS WHICH SHOULD FLOW FROM THIS REMEMBRANCE.

1. *This recollection should be productive of deep humiliation and self-abasement.*

What pride studies to forget, humility delights to remember; whenever we are tempted to grow vain of our high distinctions, let us check the risings of self-esteem, and self-admiration, by considering what we once were—untutored barbarians, savage idolaters, fast bound in the fetters of a mental and moral slavery; yet, with maniac infatuation, dancing in our chains.

2. *This recollection should excite sentiments of the liveliest gratitude, for the happy change which has taken place in our condition.*

3. *This recollection should endear to us our native land, which the religion of Jesus has hallowed and blessed.*

From what a depth of abasement has Jesus Christ raised us!

> " I would not change my native land
> For rich Peru and all her gold :
> A nobler prize lies in my hand
> Than East or Western Indies hold."

The lines are fallen to us in pleasant places; yea, we have a goodly heritage!

4. *This recollection should engage us to demean ourselves in a manner answerable to the great change which, through the favour of God, has taken place in our moral situation.*

" The darkness is past, and the true light now shineth," 1 John ii. 8. As the " children of the light, and of the day," much is expected of us; let us, then, labour to profit to the utmost by the privileges we enjoy. In a word, let us cultivate personal piety, family religion, and social usefulness.

5. This recollection should excite in our bosoms, the tenderest compassion for those nations, who are yet without Christ, deeply plunged in all the miseries of which we have been hearing. It should generate pity for human souls, immortal souls, labouring under the infelicities of an unchristianized state.

Finally, *This recollection will supply the amplest justification of missionary efforts, and urge us forward in the prosecution of missionary labours.*

There is no objection brought against this species of active benevolence, which the case before us does not refute and annihilate. The attempt to convert the heathen is rational, scriptural, and must, by God's blessing be effectual. " Go ye, into all the world, and preach the gospel to every creature," Mark xvi. 15. Go, reveal " the mystery which was kept secret since the world began, but now is made manifest, and by the Scriptures of the prophets, according to the commandment of the everlasting God, made known to all nations for the obedience of faith," Rom. xvi. 25, 26.

SKETCH VI.

THE CERTAIN INCREASE OF THE GLORY AND KINGDOM OF JESUS.

BY REV. JOHN RYLAND, D.D., BRISTOL.

" He must increase."—JOHN iii. 30.

IT was not subject of regret to that burning and shining light, that his Lord should so greatly outshine him; he was willing to be concealed, or withdrawn, that the Saviour might shine forth with greater splendour. He had no wish that the manifestation of the Redeemer's glory should be delayed, that he himself might have the more time to shine, and that his disciples might rejoice in his light for a longer season. He was glad to recommend them to a more excellent teacher. He rejoiced greatly in the increasing discovery of the Divine glories of Jesus, and wished to direct every eye to behold " the Lamb of God." And, verily, this is the best and noblest ground of joy to all the friends of God and man. All other lights that have shined in the church, have soon arrived at their zenith, and have then declined and disappeared out of our hemisphere; but He, who is eminently " the light of the world," John viii. 12, *must still increase*, till this whole benighted globe is illuminated with His brightness; and He will be the light and glory of the upper world for ever.

I. IT IS PROPOSED TO CONSIDER THE NATURE OF THAT INCREASE, WHICH THE BAPTIST CONFIDENTLY EXPECTED SHOULD ATTEND HIS BLESSED LORD.

Doubtless, he principally refers to the manifestation of his spiritual glory, and to the establishment of his kingdom of grace. He could not intend an increase of worldly greatness, pomp, and power; for we know, by the subsequent history of the life of Christ, that he never possessed these objects of human ambition, while he abode on earth. They are things he never aspired after while here below; nor was it designed that he should attain them.

1. *It was announced, that "He must increase;"* and, lo! in the midst of poverty and reproach, of apparent weakness, and of cruel sufferings, Jesus exhibited an *increasing* display of Godlike fortitude and resolution; of spotless purity and rectitude; of infinite zeal for his Father's honour; and of the riches of grace and compassion for wretched ruined man. "He was numbered with transgressions" himself, that he might justify the ungodly, and make them associates with angels, and inheritors of celestial glory.

2. *On these transactions all the future increase of his kingdom absolutely depended.* But now the purchase of redemption has been completed, what shall prevent the Saviour from receiving his full reward? When his last sufferings were approaching, he said to Andrew and Philip, "The hour is come, that the Son of man should be glorified. Verily, verily, I say unto you, Except a corn of wheat fall into the ground and die, it abideth alone: but if it die, it bringeth forth much fruit," John xii. 23, 24.

3. *Well, then, might John the Baptist affirm, "He must increase," when he foresaw that his shameful death would be followed by so glorious a resurrection;* when He, who "was made a little lower than the angels, for the suffering of death," should be "crowned with glory and honour;" and after "he had by himself purged our sins, sat down on the right hand of the Majesty on high; being made so much better than the angels, as he hath by in-

heritance obtained a more excellent name than they," Heb. i. 3, 4.

4. *And how much more did the transactions of Pentecost justify this blessed prediction.* Then was so copious an effusion of the Spirit bestowed on the apostles, that they, who had lately hid themselves in secret chambers for fear of the Jews, were filled with courage and boldness, to testify to all the house of Israel, that the same Jesus whom they had crucified, was assuredly the Lord Messiah, Acts ii.

5. *The extensive donations of the Father to his incarnate Son had been long since recorded by David and Isaiah.* " Ask of me, and I shall give the heathen for thine inheritance, and the uttermost parts of the earth for thy possession."—" It is a light thing that thou shouldest be my servant, to raise up the tribes of Jacob, and to restore the preserved of Israel : I will also give thee for a light to the Gentiles, that thou mayest be my salvation unto the end of the earth," Psa. ii. 8 ; Isa. xlix. 6.

6. *That though the church below has not been always increasing in numbers, the Church above is continually increasing.* The gates of the New Jerusalem, which are never shut day nor night, are perpetually admitting some happy spirit, transported from a state of imperfection and conflict, to the perfection of holiness and bliss.

II. LET ME PROCEED TO LAY BEFORE YOU SOME CONSIDERATIONS WHICH MAY CONFIRM OUR . FAITH IN THE ASSURED EXPECTATION THAT HE MUST INCREASE.

(1.) I may briefly remark, before I specify the positive grounds of this conclusion, that it was not founded upon the prospect of his employing a military force to propagate his religion with the sword.

(2.) Nor was this expectation built upon the rank and influence of his adherents.

(3.) Nor is it on the multitude of Christ's genuine followers, in any period of time already past, that we ground our hope of his future increase.

(4.) We are far from building our hopes upon any flattering promises of worldly gain, and sensual indulgences, by which our Master would draw followers after him.

1. *Because he is the Son of God, in the highest and most absolute sense, and therefore heir of all things.* For, as John the Baptist observes, ver. 35, " The Father loveth the Son, and hath given all things into his hand."

2. *We are persuaded, therefore, that he must increase, because he hath all power to overcome every enemy that opposeth his blessed reign.* But " it hath pleased the Father that in him should all fulness dwell," Col. i. 19; and out of his fulness have all his people received, and grace for grace. Still shall his cause be carried on; nor will the blessed Spirit grow weary of his beloved work, in taking of the things of Christ, and revealing them to the souls of men.

3. *He must increase, for the decrees of heaven ascertain the great event.* God, that cannot lie, promised before the world began that eternal life should be imparted through him, to an innumerable multitude, who were chosen in him, and predestinated to the adoption of sons.

4. *A great part of Scripture consists of promises of the increase of the Messiah's kingdom, and it is evident that the season of their chief accomplishment is yet future.* See Isa. xl; lx.

5. *We conclude that Jesus must increase, since this world and all others were " made by him, and for him."* This earth especially had been made in vain, or had been used only as a place of punishment, had not the kingdom of grace been erected here by the glorious Immanuel. But here he has determined that " Mercy shall be built up for

ever"—not at the expense of righteousness, God forbid! but that " grace might reign through righteousness unto eternal life by Jesus Christ our Lord," Rom. v. 21. What inferences further shall we draw, my Christian brethren, from these premises?

(1.) Have they not abundant ground for joy and gratitude, who are decidedly on Christ's side? You, my dear brethren, were once aliens from the commonwealth of Israel; you were once enemies in your minds to the King of Zion!

(2.) How shall we all, my Christian friends, and especially we, my honoured fathers and brethren, who have been called unto the ministry of the word, be excited to activity and resolution in our Redeemer's cause. " He must increase;" and so he shall, whether we are faithful or not. But oh! what an honour, what a pleasure, will it be, to be employed as instruments in promoting his blessed kingdom!

(3.) Brethren! seek the increase of Christ's kingdom in your own souls. Let it be our daily prayer, " Thy kingdom come, thy will be done," in us, and by us.

(4.) And oh! let us seek the increase of his kingdom all around us, by the conversion of souls to God, by their being " turned from darkness to light, and from the power of Satan," to subjection to the Redeemer.

(5.) Nor let us confine our efforts, and much less our ardent prayers, to the increase of true godliness at home.

Finally,

Let all my hearers examine, whether they are yet the genuine subjects of Christ's kingdom. There can be no neutrality in this case: if we are not for him, we are against him. And oh! how awful will be the lot of them that oppose his government, and despise his grace!

SKETCH VII.

THE CHARACTER OF CHRIST'S CONQUESTS.

" Gird thy sword upon thy thigh, O most mighty, with thy glory and
thy majesty.   And in thy majesty ride prosperously because of truth and
meekness and righteousness; and thy right hand shall teach thee terrible
things. Thine arrows are sharp in the heart of the king's enemies; whereby
the people fall under thee."—PSA. xlv. 3—5.

THIS striking and beautiful psalm evidently refers to the
Messiah.   It is impossible, without doing the greatest violence to the glorious truths it contains, to apply it either to
Solomon, or to any other earthly sovereign.   This is evidently a poetical epithalamium, or song of congratulation,
before the marriage of some celebrated monarch.   The strain
exactly agrees with such compositions.   Three subjects are
introduced : 1, *The splendour of the bridegroom; 2, The
beauty of the bride; 3, The happy results arising from the
union.*   The glory of the bridegroom occupies the chief
part of the psalm.   He is praised for the comeliness of his
person,—the gracefulness of his address,—his triumphant
military exploits,—his righteous administration,—the lustre
of his renown,—and the magnificence of his court.   The
bride is celebrated for her high birth, her transcendant
beauty, her splendid and costly apparel, and her dignified
attendants.   The results arising from the union are these.
The marriage is to produce a race of princes, who are to
possess authority and dominion to the ends of the earth.
The name, too, of the king is to live through posterity, and
his renown to be as lasting as time itself.

Such is the beauty and richness of the psalm before us. It can apply to none but Jesus, who is " King of kings, and Lord of lords," and to whom the apostle applies the sixth verse, where he says, " But unto the Son he saith, Thy throne, O God, is for ever and ever," etc., Heb. i. 8. The psalmist was, doubtless, inspired to set forth the marriage of the Son of God with his redeemed church. A subject largely illustrated in the parables of the New Testament, and sustained in every part of the Divine word. That part which we have selected for our present contemplation, relates to the character of the bridegroom as a kingly conqueror, and shows the ardent interest the church takes in his triumphant career. Thus she says, " Gird thy sword," etc., Psa. xlv. 3, etc. Consider the *Person*, the *Cause*, the *Weapons*, and the *Triumphs of the Saviour*.

I. THE PERSON OF THE MESSIAH.

" He is a king." Distinguished for his glory, majesty, and might.

1. *His glory is that of supreme Deity.* " The glory of the only begotten," etc., John i. 14. Glory underived, supreme universal, everlasting. As the sun is the glory of the solar system, so Christ is the glory of the heaven of heavens.

2. *His majesty is that which involves the highest degree of royal authority.* Hence his throne is above every other. By him all principalities exist. By him kings reign, and princes decree justice, Prov. viii. 15. " King of kings." King of the whole earth; of the whole universe.

3. *Most mighty.* Powerful in the highest degree. Yet this is but a feeble illustration of his boundless power. One in whom power is concentrated; who has it in all its infinite and uncontrolable plenitude. So much so, that what is impossible to the most powerful of the angelic hosts, yea, impossible to all created powers, is easily effected by the

mere volition of His almighty mind. In creation, "He spake, and it was done," Psa. xiii. 9. In the days of his flesh, His word cured diseases, hushed tempests, expelled devils, and raised the dead.

II. The cause of Messiah.

His cause, or kingdom, is the very transcript of his own personal attributes and glory. His spiritual empire is based on the moral perfections of his own holy and blessed mind. Hence, the great end of redemption is, to bring our fallen world to reflect the glory of his moral excellence.

1. *It is the cause of truth.* Sin began in falsehood,— the whole empire of Satan is based upon this. Departure from the truth was the ruin of our world. Our first parents abode not in the truth. Hence Christ, in destroying the works of the devil, razes his fallacies, annihilates that which is tinsel, and presents God's truth for the reception of his lapsed and wretched creatures. Truth here, however, may be taken in its largest latitude: for reality, substance, knowledge. Christ is the truth of the gospel system. Truth, as it respects God, and man, and eternity.

2. *It is the cause of meekness.* And here we see its resemblance to its Author: Christ was eminently the meek one: "I am meek and lowly in heart," Matt. xi. 29. But the term meekness is to be taken in its most enlarged sense, for lowliness and humility. The cause of sin is the cause of pride and self-exaltation. To this Satan aspired. To this the first human transgressors aspired. This fills the carnal heart. It is the mental delusion of every sinner. Christ's kingdom is essentially connected with human abasement; prostration of the sinner. It covers the contrite with the garment of humility; brings man to a right estimate of himself and his deserts, and thus fits him to be a vessel of mercy.

3. *The cause of righteousness.* Christ is " THE LORD OUR RIGHTEOUSNESS," Jer. xxiii. 6. He came to set up a righteous dominion. Sin is unrighteousness,—robs God, —it is the refusal of Jehovah's claims, etc. This is the depravity of the spirit of man in its natural state. Christ's kingdom is a righteous kingdom. He came to turn men from their iniquities. He came to fulfil the prophecies and promises. To put God's laws into their hearts, etc. To give a right spirit,—so that they should walk in his statutes and ordinances to do them. By the gospel men are made righteous, and they work righteousness. Every kind of righteousness is included in the essential constitution of the kingdom of Christ. A right heart and life towards God, and also towards all mankind.

III. THE WEAPONS WHICH AS A WARRIOR HE WIELDS.

These are the sword and bow. In the sublime visions of the Apocalypse, Christ is represented with both of these weapons, Rev. i. 16, " And out of his mouth went a sharp two-edged sword." See also Rev. vi. 2, " And I saw, and behold a white horse: and he that sat on him had a bow; and a crown was given unto him: and he went forth conquering and to conquer." The Divine word is fitly represented by these weapons. Our text supposes Christ in a chariot of war, going forth into the midst of his enemies, using his two-edged sword, and directing his arrows in every direction. The word, or gospel, of Christ is both the sword and arrow. It slays, it pierces, it severs in two; or, like the arrow, it enters the vital part, produces anguish, bitterness, and death to sin. See Heb. iv. 12, " For the word of God is quick and powerful, and sharper than any two-edged sword, piercing even to the dividing asunder of soul and spirit," etc.

Two ends have to be effected,

1. *Conviction of sin.* A sense of it,—a desire for its removal, etc.

2. *The soul healed.* Comforted, and filled with joy and peace. Messiah's weapons produce both these effects: "The power of God to salvation," Rom. i. 16. Every way effectual: "Mighty through God to the pulling down of the strongholds" of sin and Satan, see 2 Cor. x.

IV. THE TRIUMPHS WHICH MESSIAH ACHIEVES. In the phraseology of the text,

1. *He rides prosperously.* As a man of war, he advances in his course. His holy crusade is successful: this is the promise, that "the pleasure of the Lord shall prosper in his hand," Isa. liii. 10. God has pronounced the mandate and fixed the decree, that to him every knee should bow. He therefore says, "Sit thou on my right hand, until I make thine enemies thy footstool," Psa. cx. 1.

2. *His right hand accomplishes wonderful things.* For so the word was originally rendered in our old Bibles. The history of Christianity is a history of the wonderful things which the right hand of Jesus has accomplished. It was wonderful that his cause lived in the midst of the opposition of earth and hell. Jews and pagans all laboured at exterminating it. But Christ's right hand sustained it; and, like the vessel on the lake of Galilee, it survived the storm; or, like the burning bush on Horeb's summit, it lived in the midst of flame. But it was more wonderful that this "stone cut out of the mountain" should overthrow all its opponents,—silence all adversaries,—triumph over all opposition,—and succeed every where in spite of earth and hell. His right hand effected wondrous things every where, where the gospel chariot won its widening way.

3. *His enemies subjugated fell under him.* Not by their destruction,—not as the victims of wrath and ven-

geance,—but as subdued in heart and converted in life, so as to be the devoted disciples of the Nazarene. Look at the three thousand Jews, Acts ii. 41; at Saul of Tarsus; at the jailor of Philippi, etc. Look to your own personal history, you, who have felt his conquering love, resisted no longer, hated no longer; but were compelled, by the force of truth and the power of grace, to exclaim, in the words of the poet,

> "I yield, I yield, I can hold out no more ;
> But sink, by dying love compelled,
> And own thee Conqueror."

Such are the triumphs the conquering Jesus obtains. We ask, by way of

APPLICATION.

1. Do you thus personally know the Saviour? Have you felt the power, the saving power of the gospel? Are you numbered with his loyal subjects, his devoted friends?

2. Are you fully committed to his cause? Do you consider his cause yours? is his glory your first consideration? Do you pray for this—live for this—labour for this? Will this apply to each and all of you? Let us consider the text,

3. As God's voice. He speaks and looks with intense interest and delight on the church. Oh yes! and the bride, too, longs for the blissful consummation. Do we, all and each? This, then, be our prayer: "Blessed be the Lord God of Israel, who only doeth wondrous things. And blessed be his glorious name for ever; and let the whole earth be filled with his glory; Amen, and Amen," Psa. lxxii. 18, 19.

SKETCH VIII.

MESSIAH'S FINAL TRIUMPH.

"I will overturn, overturn, overturn it; and it shall be no more, until he come whose right it is; and I will give it him."—EZEK. xxi. 27.

THE prophecy of the text has reference to the removal of the crown from the head of Zedekiah, and the vacancy in the royal line of David, which should not be filled up until the sceptre should be given into Christ's hands, whose true right it should be to reign. Now, all this was literally fulfilled, for the kingdom of Judah ceased not until Christ appeared, who was the root and offspring of David, and King of kings, and Lord of lords. But there is another version of the text which may be taken, and which is in perfect unison with the spirit of prophecy: that Jehovah has given universal empire to Jesus; that it is Christ's right to reign; and that God will overturn every obstacle and impediment until it be accomplished. Let these three topics, then, now engage our attention.

I. JEHOVAH HAS GIVEN UNIVERSAL EMPIRE TO JESUS.

A few citations from the oracles of truth will establish this. Psa. lxxii. 8—11; ii. 8; lxxxix. 27; Dan. vii. 14; Zech. ix. 10; Phil. ii. 10; Acts ii. 32, etc. It is evident from these truths that Christ's dominion is to embrace the whole world —every empire, kingdom, continent, and island. All people of every language, and colour, and tongue. His kingdom is to swallow up every other; and the kingdom that will not serve Him is to utterly perish. This blissful consummation was beheld in prophetic vision by John, Rev. xi. 15.

With this state of things will be associated universal righteousness, universal knowledge, universal peace, universal
bliss. We notice,

II. THAT IT IS CHRIST'S RIGHT THUS TO REIGN. "Whose
right it is." Now, this right of Jesus to reign supremely
and universally is founded,

1. *On his creative property in all things.* The apostle
says, Col. i. 16, " All things were made by him, and for
him." By his power, and for his glory. Satan is an
usurper—the world is alienated from its rightful Lord.
But the right of Christ remains unaffected and that right
he will demand and obtain.

2. *On his supreme authority as universal Lord.* He is
Lord of all, King of kings, etc. His majesty and glory
fill the heavens. His claims are as great as the universe.
As such, he has a right surely to the earth—to the whole
earth. This authority is seen in controlling all events, in
upholding all things, etc. In his infinite out-goings of
benevolence and love.

3. *He has a redeeming right.* He became incarnate,
he descended into it, he brought the light of heaven into
it, he gave his own life for it, he is the proprietor, etc.
Here, then, is a right, ratified with his precious blood.
And he redeemed it expressly that he might reign over it.
That he might be King, and King alone, that the diadem
might encircle his own brow. And thus, in the extension
of his kingdom, he is receiving his joy and reward. He
was willingly lifted up that he might draw all men unto
him, see John xii. 32.

III. GOD WILL OVERTURN EVERY OBSTACLE UNTIL THIS
BE EFFECTED. " I will overturn," etc. Now, in effecting
this glorious purpose, the works of the devil must be
destroyed, and the empire of sin totally overthrown.

Ignorance must give place to light, error to truth, sin to holiness. Satan must be driven from his strong-holds; and thus Jesus will enlarge his empire, and extend his domains. There are, however, four mighty impediments, which must be overthrown—entirely overturned.

1. *Paganism, and all its multifarious rites.* The idolatry of paganism, the superstitions of paganism, the cruelty of paganism. The very atmosphere of paganism is the smoke of the bottomless pit. Paganism, whether of the intellectual and metaphysical kind of the Hindoos, or of the rude and illiterate kind of the untutored tribes, must be overturned. Every pagan idol must be cast " to the moles and to the bats," etc. Every altar razed, and every temple desolated, see Isa. ii. 18—20.

2. *Mohammedanism in all its earthly gratifications.* Mohammedanism is a splendid admixture of adulterated truth and vulgar error. This must be overturned. The false prophet must be denounced and forsaken; the crescent must wane, and retire into oblivion before the power of the cross.

3. *Judaism, with its obsolete rites.* A system originally of God, but which consisted of types and shadows, which have long ago been ratified in Jesus, the great Substitute and Antitype. Eighteen hundred years ago that system lost its vitality; and Ichabod has been for ages written upon its rites, and services, and people—the glory has departed. The Jews are like persons who at eventide are looking for the rising sun; but every vestige of that shadowy economy must pass away, and all the relics of the scattered tribes be collected into the fold of Christ, see Rom. xi. 25.

4. *Antichristian Rome.* The papal hierarchy is evidently that man of sin to which the apostle alludes, who must be destroyed. This is evidently the mystical Babylon whose overthrow is certain. This is to be as a millstone

thrown into the depths of the sea, Rev. xviii. 20. Every
thing that exalteth itself against God, or attempts the
division of Christ's merits, must be consumed before the
brightness of Messiah's countenance, and the power of his
truth. But you ask, How will God overturn, etc.? Doubtless, his providence will subserve the purposes of his grace.
He may cause science and commerce to open a passage
for the message of truth. He may even overrule war, and
may allow the military hero to pioneer the ambassador of
peace. But he will do it by the power of the gospel of
truth. The doctrines of the cross are to effect it. " We
preach Christ crucified," etc. 1 Cor. i. 23. " Not by
might, nor by power," etc. The spiritual sword is the
word of God. He did this by the gospel in primitive
times. In bigoted Jerusalem, in idolatrous Athens, in
lascivious Corinth, in imperial Rome, and in these, then
rude islands of the sea. He is doing so now. Look at
the islands of the South Sea; look at Central Africa; look
on the shores of continental India; look into the interior
of Burmah: in one word, that which converts a blaspheming
Briton will save a Hindoo idolater, or savage American
Indian.

APPLICATION.

I. Are your sympathies and affections on the side of
Jesus? Does the subject inspire, inspirit you? Has it
your affections, prayers, influence, and help?

2. How necessary is devoted, concentrated effort. What
has to be achieved? make the calculation. We spoke of
Pagans, write down 482 millions; Mohammedans, 140
millions; Jews, 3 millions; then add, as disciples of Papal
Rome, 80 millions: total 705 millions. Is it not hopeless?
No—read the text. God has spoken it, etc.

3. Secure a personal interest in the gracious administration of Jesus.

D

SKETCH IX.

CHRIST'S COLLECTED FLOCK.

BY REV. TIMOTHY DWIGHT, D.D. L.L.D.,*

PRESIDENT OF YALE COLLEGE, U.S.

"And other sheep I have, which aie not of this fold: them also I must bring, and they shall hear my voice; and there shall be one fold, and one shepherd.—JOHN x. 16.

IN the text, after having displayed in his previous observations, a tenderness never exhibited by any other inhabitant of this world, Christ proceeds to inform us, that he had other sheep, besides those of which he had been speaking; that he must bring, or collect, them; and that the two flocks should constitute one—be sheltered by one fold, and led by one shepherd.

"Other sheep," says our Saviour, "I have." Other disciples, beside those of the Jewish nation, and the present age, I have belonging to my family. They exist among the Gentiles in this age; and will exist in every future period. "The gospel of the kingdom," which is to be preached in all nations, will every where find those who will cordially receive and obey its dictates; those, who in the exercise of a living and affectionate confidence, will hereafter give themselves up to me, and become mine. They are now mine, and were given to me from the beginning. "Them I must bring." To collect them from every

* From a Sermon before the American Board of Commissioners for Foreign Missions, delivered in Boston, U.S., Sep. 16, 1813.

part of the world is one of the greatest duties of my office; a part of the glorious work which my Father gave me to do, and I shall not leave it unaccomplished. " They shall hear my voice." When I call, they will know and acknowledge me as their Shepherd, and cheerfully obey the summons. " There shall be one fold :" a single church— a single assembly of my disciples; one in name; one in their character, their life, and their destination; and I, the good, the only Shepherd, will lead them. " They shall hunger no more, neither thirst any more; neither shall the sun light on them, nor any heat. For the Lamb which is in the midst of the throne shall feed them, and shall lead them unto living fountains of waters," Rev. vii. 16.

" Other sheep," saith our Saviour, " I have, which are not of this fold." The sheep which Christ then had were *Jews:* inhabitants of a single country, and living at that single period. Nay, they were a little flock gathered out of these. His other sheep, as he has taught us in his word, are a great multitude, which no man could number, of all nations, and kindreds, and people, and tongues; born in every future period; gathered out of every distant land, Rev. vii. 9. " Them also I must bring, and they shall hear my voice." He who took such effectual care of the little flock which followed him during his ministry, because it was their " Father's good pleasure to give them the kingdom," will be easily believed, when he informs us, that he must and will bring into his fold a multitude, by their number and character of such immeasurable importance. For this very end, he hath " ascended far above all heavens, that he might fill all things." For this very end, he is constituted Head over all things unto his church. This is the third great division of his employment as Mediator. The first, to teach the will of God for our salvation; the second, to expiate our sins; the third is to gather us into his heavenly kingdom.

I. WHAT THINGS ARE TO BE DONE FOR THE COMPLETION OF THIS END? I observe,

1. *The views of mankind concerning religious subjects, are to be extensively changed.*

It will not be questioned, that truth is invariably an object of the Divine complacency; and error of the Divine reprobation. As God rejoices in his works, so it is impossible that he should not be pleased with truth; which is only a declaration of the state of those works, of his agency in accomplishing them, and of his character displayed in that agency. Error, which falsifies all these things, must, with equal evidence, be odious to him. As little can it be questioned, that truth is the instrument through which we are sanctified, and made free from the bondage of corruption.

2. *A mighty change, also, must be wrought in the disposition of man.*

Whenever mankind shall be brought into the fold of Christ, will succeed that love to God, and to man, which is the fulfilling of the law; that repentance towards God, and that faith in the Redeemer, which are the primary obedience of the gospel. In the train of these great evangelical attributes, will follow the meek and lowly virtues of Christianity, which so extensively occupied the instructions, and so beautifully adorned the life of the Saviour: "Love, joy, peace, long-suffering, gentleness, goodness, faith, meekness, temperance," Gal. v. 22, 23; all, glorious fruits of the Spirit of grace—natives of heaven; and though for a time pilgrims in this world, yet destined to return to heaven again.

3. *The change will not be less in the conduct of men.*

Permit me, then, to observe, that the private conduct of men will experience a mighty and wonderful revolution. Truth, at the same time, will resume her empire over the tongue, the pen, and the press. Honesty also will control the dealings of men. In the same manner, will unkindness vanish from the habitations of mankind. The stranger will every where find a home, and the wanderer an asylum. Uncharitableness, also, between those who profess the religion of the Redeemer, will be found no more. Nor will the *public* conduct of mankind be less extensively inverted. On the bench, will be seen those, and those only, who shake their hands from holding bribes; stop their ears from hearing evil; and close their eyes from seeing blood. At the bar of justice, prisoners will cease to be found: the deserted jail will crumble into dust; and the gibbet will be known only in the tales of other times. Wars, also, will be no more.

Then religion will resume her proper station, and no longer be subordinated to pleasure, gain, and glory; to frantic scrambles about place and power, and the aggrandizement of wretches, who steal into office by flattery and falsehood, in order to riot on peculation. From heaven will she descend, clothed with a cloud: and a rainbow upon her head, her face as it were the sun, and her feet pillars of fire: in her hand she will hold a little book; and that book will be opened to the eyes of all nations of men, see Rev. x. 1, 2: on its pages they will read, in lines of light, " Now is come salvation and strength, and the kingdom of our God, and the power of his Christ. God himself will dwell among the great family of Adam, and be their God; and they shall be his people."

II. In what manner are these things to be done?

I answer, they are to be accomplished not by miracles, but by means. St. Paul has, in the most express and decisive terms, given us the law of procedure, by which the kingdom of God is to be established in every part of the habitable world. " How shall they call on him in whom they have not believed? and how shall they believe in him of whom they have not heard? and how shall they hear without a preacher? So then, faith cometh by hearing, and hearing by the word of God," Rom. x. 14—17.

(1.) Permit me to add, that those by whom these mighty things are to be done, are themselves to exhibit the spirit of the gospel as the great controlling principle of their conduct. Common sense has proverbially declared, and all experience uniformly proved, that precept without example is vain. To the intended objects of this beneficence, it would be worse than in vain. From men, who do not practice what they teach, instructions would be received, as the Mexicans received them from the Spaniards, only with contempt and indignation.

(2.) The process of this mighty work is, in this respect also, exactly marked out by St. Paul. "Salvation has come unto the Gentiles to provoke the Jews to jealousy;" or, as in the Greek, To excite them to emulation, Rom. xi. 11.

(3.) The casting away of the Jews is the reconciling of the world: the receiving of them will be to that same world life from the dead.

(4). It is hardly necessary to observe, that the measures which will produce these mighty effects upon the Jews, will have a similar efficacy wherever they are employed.

III. BY WHOM ARE THESE THINGS TO BE DONE?

This question admits but of one answer—on this subject there can be no debate: the time for doubt is past, the work is begun. Missionaries, already in great numbers, run to and fro, and knowledge is even now greatly increased. "The gospel of the kingdom" is already preached is Greenland, in Labrador, in Tartary, in Hindostan, in China, in New Holland, in the Isles of the Pacific Ocean, and the Caribbean Sea; in Southern America, and in the African deserts. The voice of salvation, the song of praise to

Jehovah, echoes already from the sides of Taurus, and trembles over the waves of the Ganges. The Bible has travelled round the globe.

In such an enterprize, all who engage in it must be united: if Christians do not unite their hearts and their hands, they will effectuate nothing. Solitary efforts will here be fruitless; divided efforts will be equally fruitless; clashing efforts will destroy each other. Learn,

1. *The work to which you are summoned is the work of God.* My brethren, it is the chief work of God, which has been announced to mankind; it is the end of this earthly creation; it is the end of this earthly providence; it is the glorious end of redemption.

2. *The present is the proper time for this glorious undertaking.* It is the proper time, as it is marked out by the spirit of prophecy.

3. *The necessity of this work irresistibly demands every practicable effort.* " The whole world," says St. John, speaking of his own time, " lieth in wickedness," 1 John v. 19. Lieth—for such is the indication of the original—as a man slain, lies weltering in his blood. How extensively is this strong picture a portrait of the world at this moment!

4. *The day in which these blessings are to be ushered in has arrived.* The day in which the mighty work will be seen in its full completion is at hand. We must labour, that those who come after us may enter into our labours. We must sow, and in due time, both we and our successors, if we sow bountifully, shall reap a Divine harvest. With every faithful endeavour of ours, the Spirit of grace will co-operate. " As the earth bringeth forth her bud, and as the garden causeth the things that are sown in it to spring forth; so the Lord God will cause righteousness and praise to spring forth before all the nations," Isa. lxi. 11.

SKETCH X.

PRAYER FOR THE COMING OF GOD'S KINGDOM.

BY REV. J. E. BEAUMONT, M.D.*

"Thy kingdom come."—MATT. vi. 10.

MAN is a selfish being since his fall. So much does selfishness cleave to human nature, that many philosophers have affirmed, that every human action is the product of self-love. This principle is so inwoven with our nature, so intwined with the very essence of our being, that it can only be subverted by a principle mightier than itself; and no principle mightier than itself has ever been found, except the principle that the gospel makes known — the principle of love : love to God, love to Christ. The gospel is the antidote to selfishness: its doctrines are all against selfishness; its facts are all opposed to selfishness; its precepts are all antagonists to selfishness; its very prayers are opposed to selfishness.

What a difference there is between the man that prays, and the man that never prays; between the infidel and the believer! The infidel would environ and smother and crush what we call, what we *believe*, what we *feel*, to be the truth. Yes, he accuses us by our folly, our fanaticism, and our enthusiasm, of turning the world upside down. He scoffs, raves, and ridicules our grand, benevolent,

---

* From a sermon delivered on behalf of the Wesleyan Missionary Society, in Southwark Chapel, London, April 27th, 1838.

majestic, heaven-planned enterprise. But how is it with the Christian—with the believer—with him to whom the kingdom of God has come with power? He longs for the diffusion of it; he prays that this kingdom may stretch far and wide. Observe,

I. The kingdom itself here referred to.

The phrase " *kingdom of God*" is like some other New Testament phrases, employed with some variety of signification—all the varities, however, having a common relation. Sometimes the expression " kingdom of God," implies the subjects of Christ's sceptre—the aggregate, the multitude of the " called, and faithful, and chosen;"—that part of them that are on earth: then it is called the kingdom of Christ in the world. At other times, that part which has arrived already in *heaven:* and then it is called, the kingdom of *glory.* In the passage before us, we are to understand that dominion, that holy dominion, which God is setting up in the human heart, in the human world, in and by the Messias: a kingdom of which all time, since its early dawn, hath been the duration, of which mankind are the subjects, of which salvation is the object, of which the glory of the triune God is the end.

I. *This kingdom is not a worldly kingdom.* And yet the Jews, among whom the Saviour dwelt when he was manifest in the flesh, expected such a kingdom at the hands of the Messias; and the apostles themselves were not free from this misleading, master delusion.

2. *This kingdom is constituted in the very person of the King himself.* Christ, like others, has waded to his empire through blood; but he has waded to his empire through no blood but the blood of his own heart. He fell himself to exalt us.

3. *This kingdom is a peaceable kingdom.* It is a

beneficent institution.   Its attributes are righteousness, peace, benevolence, integrity, purity, justice, charity.

4. *This kingdom admits of unlimited extension, of indefinite diffusion.* This kingdom shall spread and grow: it shall go out in this direction, and go forth in that; it shall traverse that region, and pass over the other; it shall go "from sea to sea, and from the river unto the ends of the earth,—men shall be blessed in him: all nations shall call him blessed," Psa. lxxii. 8, 17. The prophet Isaiah says, "The earth shall be full." Full! What is the meaning of *full?* "The earth shall be full." What! FULL? Yes, *full;* that is the word :—"The earth shall be full of the knowledge of the Lord, as the waters cover the sea," Isa. xi. 9.

5. *This kingdom of Christ will be of long duration.* Not like earthly kingdoms, which rise up, run forward, gain the zenith, and then decline, and their names pass away, and their memory is blotted out; not like these shall be the kingdom of Christ. This kingdom " lasts, like the sun it shall stand."

6. *The brightness of this kingdom is perpetually increasing.* Oh! I rejoice to think—I think it, I believe it —that there is not an hour in any day, in which some straggling rebel is not coming in to Christ, kissing his sceptre, and devoting himself to his service. The number of Christ's subjects is continually increasing; there is already a multitude before the throne that never can be withdrawn; and the successes that are going on upon earth are swelling that continually-accumulating amount of the first-born that is in heaven. Let us point out,

II. SOME GROUNDS ON WHICH THE PIOUS MAY LOOK AND PRAY FOR THE DIFFUSION OF THIS KINGDOM. Some of the grounds on which they may expect its universal diffusion.

1. *We are warranted in such an expectation, I may say, from all analogy.* Why does the moon spread her horns? Why, it is to fill them. Why does the sun rise above the horizon? It is that he may go on his march upward and onward till he gains his meridian altitude, and pours his vertical glory on the world below. Why is the corn deposited in the soil? It is that it may unwrap, that it may unfold itself—that, of that single seed, there may come a tree, the branches of which are for a lodgment of the birds, and a shadow for the beasts of the earth. Why does the rill steal silently from under the sod, wend its way among the grass and the pebbles, following its course onward and onward, enlarging its channel, rendering the fissure wider and wider for itself,—till at last, that little rill becomes a mighty river, bearing on its bosom, the riches of a nation, and feeding with its irrigations a nation's agriculture.

When shall the kingdom of Christ have no boundaries? Shall it always be in a state of minority? Shall Satan usurp all? Why, it is impossible that it should remain so. Christ MUST reign. Take it in the vigorous language of the apostle, in that passage in his first epistle to the Corinthians, where he says, xv. 25, " He must reign, till he hath put all enemies under his feet."

2. Again, *We are led to the same conclusion from the symbolical events of Jewish history.* Look, for a moment, at Egypt; and see the contest that went on between Moses and Aaron, and the magicians of Egypt. Moses was triumphant. So, in the contest between light and darkness, between truth and falsehood, between revelation and idolatry—light, truth, and revelation, shall win the day. So with respect to Dagon and the ark of the Lord. The idol being brought in juxtaposition with the ark of God, the ark retained its place, but the idol fell down prostrate, and was broken in pieces, 1 Sam. v.; and so surely, every other

idol shall be prostrated before our Immanuel. Passing from individual cases, take the general case—I mean, the contest about the land of Canaan; and as sure as the children of Israel took possession of that land according to the promise of God to their fathers, so surely the last stronghold of idolatry shall yield to the sceptre of Christ, and the whole earth shall be filled with His glory.

3. *I might say, that moral proportion requires that the kingdom of God should become thus glorious.* Christ must "see of the travail of his soul;" and oh! how millenially must his kingdom come, before his philanthropic heart shall say, " Enough! enough! that is all I look for: stop! stop! I shed my blood for no more!" We know that Jesus Christ by the grace of God tasted death for every man, Heb. ii. 9; and, having poured out his soul as an offering for the whole race, vast indeed must be his triumphs before he can say, " Enough! that is all: that completes the whole!"

4. *When we think of the energy which is employed in the diffusion of this kingdom,* our hopes rise, and our expectations rise.

III. POINT OUT SOME OF THE ENCOURAGING INTIMATIONS WHICH WE HAVE OF THE COMING OF THIS KINGDOM OF CHRIST.

1. *Look at the facilities which there are for it.* There never were such facilities since the apostles' time. We have colonies, great flourishing colonies, all over the globe, which are so many focal points whence the light is to radiate in every direction beyond them. We have swift-winged messengers to carry our missionaries and our Bibles to more distant lands; and, of all the ships that have left our shores, none surely have ever left them with more interest than those which have gone forth, manned with

missionaries, and freighted with Bibles : ship-loads of instrumentality with which to put back the frontier of idolatry.

2. *Besides the facilities for effort, there is, I think, rather more union of effort than there has been for ages.*

3. Then, again, *the success of effort* is also a most encouraging circumstance.

APPLICATION.

1. I cannot suppose that all, in this immense assembly, are yet the real, voluntary subjects and followers of the Lord Jesus Christ :—to that part of the congregation, therefore, I address myself. You, my fellow-sinners, are not far from the kingdom of Christ : yes, you are not far from it; you have heard the gospel. Oh! that this night the kingdom of God may come to you.

2. You who are the subjects of the kingdom of Christ, bear with me while I address one word to you. You have grace— seek for more grace: the reality and the experience of grace are one thing—the abundance of its communications is another. Oh, that great grace may rest on you all ! Amen.

SKETCH XI.

LOVE TO CHRIST THE ONLY TRUE MOTIVE
TO MISSIONARY EXERTION.

BY REV. LEGH RICHMOND, M.A.,*
RECTOR OF TURVEY, BEDFORDSHIRE.

" He saith to him again the second time, Simon, son of Jonas, lovest thou me? He saith unto him, Yea, Lord; thou knowest that I love thee. He saith unto him, Feed my sheep."—JOHN xxi. 16.

LOVE to Christ, in his person and offices, is inseparably connected with love to his people, and anxiety for the salvation of sinners. He who loveth God will love his brother also, 1 John iv. 21. It will be the prayer and desire of his heart, as it was of Paul's, that Israel may be saved. Hence, in a special manner, spring the solicitude and unwearied diligence of the pastoral office. That holy zeal for the increase of the Redeemer's kingdom, which is so essential a characteristic of the new creature, carries the man of God, whom love has devoted to this peculiar service, through dangers without number, that he may seek and save them that are ready to perish. He knows that the sheep of Christ must be fed. They are a flock purchased with blood. But they are " scattered upon the mountains, and no man gathereth them," Nahum iii. 18. The love of God is shed abroad in his own heart by the Holy Ghost,

* From a Sermon, delivered before the Society for Missions to Africa and to the East, May 23, 1809.

which is given unto him. Therefore, the shepherd cannot slumber. Awake to the call of love and duty, he hears his Master's voice, and flies to execute His commands.

I propose to consider,

I. THE NATURE AND DESIGN OF THE COMMISSION.

As Peter had thrice denied his Master, so Christ, in the most solemn yet affectionate manner, questioned him three times, whether indeed he loved him. "Simon, son of Jonas, lovest thou me?" The lately fallen, but now recovered sinner, loved much, because much had been forgiven him. He earnestly appealed to his Lord's omniscience, as a testimony to the sincerity and ardour of his love. "Yea, Lord, thou knowest that I love thee.—Lord, thou knowest all things; thou knowest that I love thee." On each repetition of these questions and replies, Jesus deliberately committed that most important charge to his care, as a means of proving the integrity of his profession, "Feed my sheep." It appears, therefore, that the words of Christ, in this memorable passage, exhibit very clearly the principles, duty, character, and conduct of the faithful shepherd of souls; and especially of the Christian Missionary.

I. *The Christian's love to Christ is his great motive to exertion.* The life which he lives in the flesh, he lives by the faith of the Son of God, who loved him, and gave himself for him, Gal. ii. 20.

2. *The commandment of Christ, to feed his flock, declares the nature and object of his labours.*

3. *The example of Christ himself, in his life and death, is the model and pattern for his imitation.* Thus enlightened, and warmed by the animating beams of the Sun of Righteousness, he lives to the glory of God, and finds by happy experience, that "His service is perfect freedom."

Henceforward, the life of this apostle was a continual comment upon the Redeemer's precept. We find him faithful and diligent in his office; with an unconquerable zeal endeavouring to instruct the ignorant, bring back the wandering, strengthen the weak, confirm the strong, reclaim the vicious, and turn many to righteousness. He took all opportunities of declaring the glad tidings of salvation to perishing sinners. With holy patience and perseverance he endured all conflicts and trials, surmounted every difficulty and opposition, so that he might plant and propagate the Christian faith.

II. The application of the commandment to feed the sheep of Christ, as it respects the heathen nations at present, and our exertions in order to their conversion.

1. *Who are comprehended under this term, sheep?* " Ye my flock, the flock of my pasture, are men, and I am your God, saith the Lord God," Ezekiel xxxiv. 31. The flock committed to the apostle's care, consisted of yet unconverted Jews and unconverted heathen, who should, through preaching of the word, become disciples, and believe in the name of Christ. But this promise, said St. Peter to the Jews, " is unto you, and to your children, and to all that are afar off, even as many as the Lord our God shall call," Acts ii. 39. And again, addressing the Gentiles afterwards, at Joppa, " God is no respecter of persons; but in every nation, he that feareth him, and worketh righteousness, is accepted with him," Acts x. 34, 35.

2. *Why ought these sheep to be thus fed?* The positive injunctions of Christ to his apostles, as to the propagation of the truth, give the most direct and unanswerable reply to this question; and in no instance is the appeal made so powerfully to the Christian's affections, as in that

related in the text : " Lovest thou me ?"—" Feed my sheep."

But, taking the question in another point of view, I should say, when speaking of the heathen, that they ought to be taught the Word of life, because we have no warrant whatsoever from the Scriptures for concluding that they will be saved without the knowledge of Christ.

3. *We are next led to consider, when is this great duty of sending missionaries among the heathen to be under-taken?*

To this inquiry, I would unequivocally answer, Now ! " Behold, *now* is the accepted time; behold, *now* is the day of salvation," 2 Cor. vi. 2. Go *now*, and proclaim Christ as a light to the Gentiles, and a salvation unto the end of the earth. Of late years, a great increase of gospel light and knowledge has been diffused throughout this country in particular. Protestants have not at the present period of time, as our forefathers had, to contend with the papists, almost for very existence. The growing attention of serious Christians, to the fulfilment of prophecy, as it concerns the downfall of popery, the restoration of the Jews, the conversion of the Gentiles, and the approach of the millenium, all of which are intimately connected with missionary plans, seem to mark the present as a signal period for exertion. I would not here omit to notice that happy consummation of the wishes of the pious and humane in the abolition of the slave trade.

4. *The next subject of inquiry is, By whom ought the sheep of Christ among the heathen to be fed?*

Evidently, by those who themselves know the joyful sound. The visible churches of Christ are, by their principle and constitution, missionary bodies, from whose bosom holy emissaries should continually come forth to propagate the faith of Christ among the heathen. Is it asked, By whom, individually and personally, are the sheep of Christ to be fed among the heathen? Who shall be your missionaries?—The shepherds, whom you set apart to this honourable labour of feeding and nourishing souls for Christ, must be men who love Christ for the salvation which he hath wrought in their own souls—men who feel in themselves the working of the Spirit of Christ, mortifying the works of the flesh and their earthly members, and drawing up their minds to high and heavenly things. They must be men, not of warmth and zeal alone, but of solidity, patience, and perseverance; men who, like their Lord, can endure the contradiction of sinners, Heb. xii. 3.

5. *Wherewith ought the sheep of Christ to be fed? With the declaration of what truths are we to labour for the conversion of the heathen?*

In answer to this question, there must be one reply,—preach Christ, as a free, full, perfect, and all-sufficient Saviour, to the greatest of sinners. The sheep of Christ, whether at home or abroad, will hear and know their own good Shepherd's voice, and none other. Proclaim, as from the house top, that " God commendeth his love towards us, in that, while we were yet sinners, Christ died for us," Rom. v. 8; and thus accomplished that wonder of men and angels, " that God might be just, and yet the justifier of him which believeth in Jesus," Rom. iii. 26. Preach to them, the blood of Christ—its atoning and its cleansing power; preach to them, the perfect righteousness of Christ, as alone acceptable in the sight of God; preach to them, free justification by faith in what Christ suffered, and what Christ fulfilled in their stead; unfold to them, the mysteries of the covenant of peace, made in heaven for man; and the unsearchable riches of Christ, so freely therein provided for man's redemption;—set before them the purity of the Divine law—contrast it with the heinousness of their sins, and the pollution of their nature. Hence prove to them, that " Except a man be born of water and of the Spirit. he cannot enter into the kingdom of God," John iii. 3

Johannes, the Mahikander Indian, at one of the meetings which the brethren held for pastoral conversation and inquiry into the state of the congregations, related the occasion of his conversion in the following manner, in consequence of their speaking with one another about the method of preaching to the heathen.

" Brethren, I have been a heathen, and have grown old amongst them; therefore, I know very well how it is with the heathen, and how they think. A preacher once came to us, desiring to instruct us, and began by proving to us that there was a God. On which we said to him: ' Well, and dost thou think we are ignorant of that? Now, go back again to the place from whence thou camest.'

" Then another preacher came, and began to instruct us, saying, ' You must not steal, nor drink too much, nor lie, nor lead wicked lives.' We answered him: ' Fool that thou art! Dost thou think that we do not know that? Go and learn it first thyself, and teach the people whom thou belongest to, not to do those things;—for who are greater drunkards, or thieves, or liars, than thine own people?' Thus we sent him away also.

" Some time after this, Christian Henry, one of the brethren, came to me into my hut, and sat down by me. The contents of his discourse to me were nearly these: ' I am come to thee in the name of the Lord of Heaven and Earth. He sends me to acquaint thee, that he would gladly save thee, and make thee happy, and deliver thee from the miserable state in which thou liest at present. To this end he became a man, gave his life a ransom for man, and shed his blood for man. All that believe in the name of this Jesus obtain the forgiveness of sin. To all them that receive him by faith, he giveth power to become the sons of God. The Holy Spirit dwelleth in their hearts; and they are made free, through the blood of Christ, from the slavery and dominion of sin. And though thou art the chief of sinners, yet, if thou prayest to the Father in his name, and believest in him as a sacrifice for thy sins, thou shalt be heard, and saved; and he will give thee a crown of life, and thou shalt live with him in heaven for ever.'

" When he had finished his discourse, he lay down upon a board in my hut, fatigued by his journey, and fell into a sound sleep. I thought within myself: ' What manner of man is this? There he lies, and sleeps so sweetly. I might kill him, and throw him out into the forest,—and who would regard it? But he is unconcerned.—This cannot be a bad man: he fears no evil, not even from us, who are so savage; but sleeps comfortably, and places his life in our hands.'

" However, I could not forget his words; they constantly recurred to my mind. Even though I went to sleep, yet I dreamed of the blood which Christ had shed for us. I thought, ' This is very strange, and quite different from what I have ever heard.' So I went and interpreted Christian Henry's words to the other Indians.

" Thus, through the grace of God, an awakening took place among us. I tell you, therefore, brethren," said he, " preach to the heathen, Christ and his blood, his sufferings and death, if you would have your words to gain entrance amongst them; if you would wish to produce a blessing among them."*

APPLICATION.

I beseech you to hear me, while I propose a few cousiderations to your attention.

* Loskiel's " History of the Mission of the United Brethren among the Indians of North America."

1. Consider the state of the world, its empires, nations, kindreds, and tribes.

2. Again, consider the state of the church; and, if you love Christ, feed his sheep.

3. Consider, also, what the church shall be in the days to come.

4. Again, consider your own privileges; and, if you love Christ, feed his sheep.

Are you Christians? How came this? Did no man cross the seas, to teach your forefathers wisdom? Did no missionary brave the perils of a journey among your heathen ancestors, because he loved the sheep of Christ? Yea, brethren, through a blessing on missionary exertions, Christ visited Britain. He had a fold here; and he sent some faithful shepherd to gather the scattered sheep into it. Go, then, and feed the sheep of Christ, as you yourselves have been fed.

SKETCH XII.

NO CESSATION OF THE GREAT WORK.

"Why should the work cease?"—Neh. vi. 3.

Nehemiah was engaged in building the dilapidated walls of Zion. To this work he was called of God, and for its execution he was qualified from on high. But, during its progress, he had to contend with many difficulties. He had to encounter hostile foes; he had to resist the craft of secret opponents; and he had to contend with the formality of professed friends. He was possessed with a most magnanimous spirit, and he nobly persevered.

To some solicitations to discuss the engagements on which he had entered, he replied, " I am doing a great work, so that I cannot come down." And then' said, in the language of the text, " Why should the work cease?"

As Christians, we are connected with a greater work than that of Nehemiah—the work of building the spiritual temple of God, and the evangelization of the world. This work is God's work of saving men, and extending his glorious kingdom in the world—the work of true and vital religion; and which is designed to overthrow the kingdom of darkness, and fill the whole earth with the Divine glory.

Now, this work has been set up in our world from the announcement of the first promise of mercy to our fallen parents. It has been identified with all ages and dispensations. Like a golden thread, it ran through all the families of the pious antediluvians, and through all the godly tribes of Israel. It was exhibited among all the patriotic and devout, during the long line of prophets. It burst forth with peculiar energy during the labours of the Baptist. It shone with meridian splendour in Judea, during the labours of the Redeemer. It went forth with irresistible power in the apostolic age; and has been handed down to us, and is living and blessing men wherever the evangelical truths of the gospel are known. In reference to this work we intend to apply the text, and ask—" Why should the work cease?" We shall,

I. Assign some reasons why this work should not cease.

II. Show the interest and concern we should manifest in it.

I. Assign some reasons why this work should not cease.

1. *Because of its moral grandeur.* Every work of God is grand in itself. Every department is so; but not all in equal degree. The work of saving souls is the most exalted and the greatest of all the Divine works. As such, it occupies a pre-eminence in the sacred volume. As such, God is represented as being especially interested in it. It is the work of God's arm, and the work of his heart. He spoke the universe into being; but to save men there were councils, covenants, dispensations, promises, oaths, blood! This work deeply interests and powerfully agitates the three worlds. It is a work which includes all time, and equally all eternity : surely such a work should not cease!

2. *Because of its gracious character.* We might assent to the cessation of displays of mere power. We should rejoice in the cessation of exhibitions of judgment and

wrath.   We hail the subsiding of the waters of the deluge; we hail the termination of the plagues of Egypt; we hail the ceasing of the storm, the rumblings of the earthquake, the descent of the fiery lava.   We rejoice when the sword of war finds its peaceful scabbard.   But the work of God is one of grace—of favour to guilty man—compassion to the ungodly—mercy to the wretched.   This work announces eyesight to the blind, health to the diseased, liberty to the captive, riches to the poor, joy to the mourner, salvation to the lost, heaven to the guilty.   The emblem of this work is the rainbow, spanning our world with its arch of peace and mercy.   So long as there is one unsaved sinner this work should not cease.

3. *Because of its elevating influences.*   This work is one of emphatic exaltation.   It humanizes the savage; intellectualizes the ignorant; purifies the unholy; and subordinates the animal man to mind, and to moral power. It ennobles its possessor, it lifts up " out of the mire and clay," etc.   It transforms the thorn into a fig-tree, the lion to a lamb, the vulture into a dove, the sinner into a saint, the curse into a blessing.   It is this work that has exalted our little sea-girt isle to be the glory of all lands, and the spiritual Goshen of the world.

4. *Because as this work progresses the work of hell and Satan declines.*   If this work of light cease, darkness will prevail.   If this work of truth cease, error will abound. If this work of liberty cease, tyranny and oppression and slavery will be extended.   If this work of purity cease, corruption and profligacy will triumph.   If this work of heaven cease, then death and hell will have the accursed ascendancy.

5. *Because of its comprehensive and benevolent designs.* The religion of the cross is destined to be the religion of the world.

(1.) It is adapted to the world, and nowhere does it refuse to thrive. It is for man—man every where—in every condition, and of every colour and tongue.

(2.) It is sent to the world: not to this city or country alone, but for the world. "Go ye into all the world, and preach the gospel to every creature," Mark xvi. 15. It is to be preached among all nations, etc.

(3.) It is to be succeeded by the setting up of the reign of universal righteousness, peace, and blessedness. As yet little has been done for the great mass of our species. As yet, how much has to be done in our world. Read the annals of savage ferocity, gross idolatry, and pagan cruelty in distant lands; and the fearful accounts of crime, ignorance, and irreligion at home. Do we not, then, deprecate the idea that " the work should cease?" If we desire its continuance and progress notice,

II. THE INTEREST AND CONCERN WE SHOULD MANIFEST IN THIS WORK.

It may be said this is the work of truth, and must live; of God, and must prevail; of holiness, and must spread: so it is. But there are certain things connected with it worthy of especial observation.

1. *That though it is a Divine work, yet it is connected with human instrumentality.* God could carry on this work by miraculous power; but it is not his will to do so. He has set up an instrumentality for the accomplishment of the object. That instrumentality is his *church.* (1.) The church, by its ministers, deacons, and members. (2.) The church in its ordinances, means, and influence. (3.) The church, by its example, truth, and compassion.—By these the work is to be sustained, perpetuated, diffused. God will effect his councils by, and through, and not without these. Then the church must know its duty, feel its

E

responsibility, and discharge its energies rightly, if the work is not to cease.

2. *Though the work must progress generally, it may cease partially.* This work once flourished in Jerusalem, in Ephesus, in Corinth, in Antioch, in Rome, etc. It once flourished in Italy, Arabia, and Samaria. How fearfully has it ceased in many of these places—ceased for ages upon ages. So we see it, in reference to towns and churches in our own land. How many sanctuaries, scattered through the land, in which the pure doctrines of the cross were once proclaimed; where our puritan fathers lived and laboured —where crowded auditories of holy men were being trained for immortality: but another gospel now echoes from those pulpits. The congregation, in most instances, have been scattered, and " Ichabod" written on their walls—the glory is departed.

We doubt not the general progress of the truth, but locally and partially it may cease. Then our concern and labour must be that the work cease not in our own churches and neighbourhoods, or we lose the power of conveying the tidings of salvation to the distant heathen. And however great the obligations to send the gospel abroad— *Home* must not be forgotten. It must be our anxiety, labour, and prayer, that both in this, and other lands, the work may not cease.

3. *That the work may flourish around us, it is indispensable that it should prosper within us.* The real prosperity of a church is the true spiritual prosperity of each member. If each one is religiously advancing, then the work is going on. It will give us the interest, the desire, and the power of usefulness. By the spiritual prosperity of each, the whole have a moral influence which the world cannot resist: let each be truly the Lord's, and every one will labour for the general work.

(1.) There will be no apathy in the church, for a sleeping church cannot awaken the world.

(2.) There will be no formalism in the church, for a formal church cannot spiritualize a locality.

(3.) There will be no indolence in the church, for an idle church cannot do God's arduous and difficult work.

(4.) There will be no covetousness in the church; for covetousness is the freezing of the waters — the icebergs that interrupt the vessel of mercy on her voyage of salvation.

4. *That the work may not cease a spirit of glowing zeal and activity must animate every department of the church.* Zeal and diligence and self-denial, like that of Nehemiah. Let those who occupy the temples of Zion as her watchmen, " Cry aloud," etc. " Preach the word; be instant in season, out of season; reprove, rebuke, exhort with all long-suffering and doctrine," 2 Tim. iv. 2. Let them immolate their entire selves on the altar of the Saviour's service. Let those who are the spiritual judges in Israel—who serve tables, and assist in the oversight and rule in the church—be men of uncompromising fidelity, burning ardour and Christian affection. Let fathers and mothers in Israel, cherish a praying and fervid spirit of consecratedness to the institutions of religion, cherish a delightful attachment to those means which will extend the kingdom of the Lord Jesus, both at home and abroad.

Let every member be a worker—" Labour" must be the watch-word of Zion; " Activity" her motto; " Zeal" her spirit; " Truth" her ammunition; and clad in the habiliments of " love," she must go forth with her illustrious Head " conquering, and to conquer," Rev. vi. 2.

APPLICATION.

1. Who are for the work going on? More and more—more than ever, etc. Who are ready—willing—able? " Who will come to the help of the Lord?" etc, Judg. v. 23.

2. Think of your obligations to God and his people. Let gratitude, filial piety, etc. If the work had ceased forty years ago, you would have been unenlightened, unsaved, etc. How much you owe to the work!

3. Think of the day in which we live. Unprecedented for activity, and liberal and benevolent institutions. Then shall the work cease in this day? in this country? in Christ's church? Oh no! The vote, the declaration, the vow is— " It shall not cease!"

Finally—What are you doing that the work may not cease? Review your exertions and influence for the last twelve months. In what sphere? to what extent? Put it down on paper: compare it with the labours of prophets, apostles, etc. With those of your forefathers. With those of some around you. Ask, " If all did just so much and no more would it succeed, or cease?" Do this with the light of eternal things surrounding you—with the day of judgment in prospect; and so do it, as God will do it, when he shall examine every one of you, and render to all " according to their works," Rev. xx. 13.

SKETCH XIII.

THE QUESTION OF CHRISTIAN MISSIONS STATED AND EXPLAINED.

BY REV. R. WINTER HAMILTON, D.D.*

"I am come to send fire on the earth; and what will I, if it be already kindled? But I have a baptism to be baptized with; and how am I straitened till it be accomplished!"—LUKE xii. 49, 50.

THE impassioned exclamations of the Redeemer, prefixed to this discourse, admirably agree to our design. There is a good in his religion worthy of any hazard and any expense. The exclamations are conceived under this impression of the case. He contemplates nothing but the evolution of that good, by the propagation of that religion.

Missions, we avow, may "bring fire on the earth;" so did the incarnation of Christ; and what would He but that it should kindle? Missions will assuredly task the spirit of exertion and self-devotement to the utmost; but so did the ends of the Saviour's work. For the acquisition of those ends he was impetuous to yield to the ineffable exertions and sacrifices demanded of him; and, as he approached the awful scene of sore amazement and heaviness, of sorrow unto death, (Mark xiv. 33, 34), of the cup and of the cross, he " set his face steadfastly" to it; and was mysteriously constrained for the catastrophe! That cannot be fanatical in the disciple, which is heroic in the Master; nor extravagant in the servant, which is magnanimous in the Lord.

* From a Sermon in reference to the persecutions in the West India Colonies, delivered in August, 1824.

I. The mission of Christ was undertaken for the most important ends.

There must have been some prospective benefit to draw forth such breathings, and to awaken such desires. A prospective benefit which awaited the close of his sojourn on earth, and had been made conditional on his death. It was not impatience of suffering; it was not regret that he had interposed, which imbued his mind with those anxieties, and wrung from it those importunities. He longed " to cease from his works," because upon his death alone could he realize the conception of his mind, and grasp the purpose of his heart. He, therefore, anticipated the agony of the garden, as one looking for a spoil; and waited for the darkness that came over the land, when he was crucified, " more than they who wait for the morning." Let us produce some of these ends.

I. *To present an atonement to the Divine government for the sin of man.*

What an end was this! To make peace between God and man! To bind heaven and earth in amity! Instead of casting down the glorious high throne of the everlasting King under the feet of man, to capacitate man to draw nigh to its footstool here, and to entitle him to sit down amidst its splendours hereafter—a throne of grace, accessible now; a throne of glory, inheritable for ever!

> —— " Jesus' blood through earth and skies,
> Mercy, free, boundless mercy cries!"

2. *To overthrow the rebellious power which had usurped the dominion of this world.*

Four thousand years witnessed the preparation and muster for this struggle; and at last He appeared. " Of the people there was none with me," Isa. lxiii. 3. It was not a combat to be shared—His single arm must win it. Nor was it a combat whose grapple was for mortal eye, whose shock was for mortal ear. He returned from it with his trophies. He had stained all his raiment.—His fury, it upheld him, Isa. lxiii. 3—5. He had destroyed the works of the devil : " that through death he might destroy him that had the power of death, that is the devil," Heb. ii. 14. And we may chant as we " walk about" the cross, and "go round about" it, He hath " spoiled principalities and powers, he made a show of them openly, triumphing over them in it," Col. ii. 15.

3. *The redemption of innumerable multitudes of our race 'from the consequences of their apostacy.*

Redemption may sometimes be used much in the same sense as atonement, but its stricter meaning will not suffer this use. As atonement associates itself with the idea of government, it must have a *general* aspect ; as redemption identifies itself with that of purchase, it must have a particular one. Redemption is of persons, not of blessings ; and may be considered that application of the atonement which purchases us as " the church of the Lord." What an end is again proposed in this redemption! What is a soul ? What is the multitude of these souls ? What is their rescue from sin, death, and hell ? " None can by any means redeem his brother, nor give to God a ransom for him ; for the redemption of their soul is precious, and it ceaseth for ever," Psa. xlix. 7, 8.

4. *The 'formal assumption and complete discharge of his mediatorial characters.*

One of the most distinguished of these is his priesthood. Some have asserted that he could not be a priest until he died. At least, until then he reminds us more of a victim. If a priest, in any acceptation, he was never seen engaged in his highest rites, or arrayed in his costliest vestments. An inspired writer has decided, " if he were on earth, he should not be a priest," Heb. viii. 4. But now he ministers in " the holiest of all." His empire, as King, is founded in death. His sword did not flesh itself in his foes, but clave his own heart. His march to dominion was not cut through his enemies, but he waded to it in his own blood.

5. *The effusion of his Spirit as essential to the promotion of his cause, and accumulation of his church.* All power in heaven and earth was, for the first time, wielded by him, to stamp the missionary law with indelible authority.

With these ends we are zealously determined that our missions shall coincide. We would dislodge the crude and monstrous conceptions of the Divine government which invariably obtain in the absence of Christianity, by the exhibition of the atonement. We would expose the foul usurpation, which has for so long a period arrogantly held and fiercely tyrannized over our nature.

We would proclaim the redemption of souls. The missionary is the herald of universal deliverance. We would exalt the Lord Jesus in all the mediatorial offices, with which he is invested for the salvation of man. We would remember, through all the steps of this work, that the Holy Spirit alone can endue our agents with power, and crown their labours with success.

II. THESE ENDS COULD ALONE BE PROSECUTED AT A MOST PAINFUL EXPENSE.

By " sending fire on the earth," the Saviour appears to intend some evils, which would accompany the propagation of his religion; evils not chargeable upon its constitution, but yet contingent upon its progress. He anticipated these, and forewarned his followers of them.

1. *We cannot conceal the fact, that Christianity may affect political systems.*

He who " rebuked kings" for the sake of his ancient church, will never long endure any state of things unfavourable to his people, or prejudicial to his cause. He "will overturn, overturn, overturn it; until he come whose right it is," Ezek. xxi. 27. Kings and kingdoms are very little matters, in comparison with His glory, and nothing in opposition to it.

2. *It is further admitted that Christianity must produce a variety of innovations.*

Christianity went forth with the torch of extermination. It rendered its " anger with fury" against all that resisted it; and its " rebuke with flames of fire," Isa. lxvi. 15. It, by the very process of fire, transformed all things into itself. The interested and bigoted beheld the conversion with alarm. All was yielded to the flame. Nothing was proof against its intensity, nothing sufficient to check its progress. We may easily conceive of the inconvenience of such an innovating principle. What excitement of new ideas! What disturbance of immemorial customs! The mind of some bewildered! the craft of more in danger! " No small stir about that way!" " These that have turned the world upside down!" Acts xix. 23; xvii. 6.

3. *Very unnatural divisions in society have apparently been fomented by Christianity.*

When it is really understood and truly felt, it constitutes the very balm of life. By it " shall all the families of the earth be blessed," Gen. xxviii. 14. But yet, in its course, many of these ties are severed. The converted child, once folded in the kindest embrace, now finds his parents more cruel than the sea-monster; and becomes a stranger with his brethren, and an alien unto his mother's children.

4. *Christianity must be viewed in connexion with those persecutions which it has experienced.*

Persecution will always endeavour to disguise itself under forms of piety, or enactments of law, or impositions of necessity. He, therefore, whose name, faith, and church, were to be the very lures and marks to this persecuting rage, openly declared that he " came to send fire on the earth." He knew that the fire thus kindled, would prove the ordeal to his followers,—" try every man's work of what sort it is." He announced it from the first that none might think it " strange concerning the fiery trial."

5. *Christianity has drawn forth some acts, on the part of its adversaries, which have more effectually exposed the depravity of human nature than any other occasion could have admitted.*

The doctrine of the cross can never be understood with indifference. No man can comprehend it, and be neutral. It elicits our inner man, it defines emotions which were vague, and bodies forth conceptions which were immature. It is a " sign which shall be spoken against;—that the thoughts of many hearts may be revealed." It has a point to repel, as well as one to attract. It is a stumbling-block and foolishness. The offence of the cross cannot cease.

6. *The religion of Jesus Christ has very frequently been perverted to designs most estranged from its character, and abhorrent to its spirit.*

The most successful antagonists of this religion are they who plead its authority, and retain its name. The anti-christian power grew insensibly out of it. "That Wicked," " That man of sin," is revealed from his nativity, 2 Thess. ii. 3, 8. And to what more general abuses has Christianity been desecrated! What hypocrisy has it served to favour! What ambition to desolate! What sensuality to riot! What avarice to grab! What superstition to dote! What bigotry to hoodwink! What despotism to oppress! On its stock, what earthly scions have been grafted! what infernal fruits have been plucked! Hence all the tricks of priestly jugglers—all the plots of wily statesmen—all the persecutions of blood-thirsty monarchs! The religion of

Christ has ever been pretext and screen! In this additional manner the Son of God " sent fire on the earth.".

7. *The augmentation of moral responsibility has necessarily attended the establishment of Christianity.*

Every hearer of the gospel, from the moment " the kingdom of God" comes nigh to him, enters a far more critical probation, and must abide by a far more fearful issue. The " sweet savour of Christ" is to them who perish, "the savour of death unto death," 2 Cor. ii. 15, 16. They must, if disobedient, await " a sorer punishment."

III. The importance of these ends justified the vast expense necessary to their acquisition.

That certain evils, or disadvantages, when intrinsically considered, are contingent on the progress of the gospel we have allowed; but never would the Saviour have " sent fire on the earth," and even willed it to kindle, had he not been persuaded that all which was intended by the figure, would be absorbed in a glorious and infinite superabundance of blessings. Whatever be the evils, then, arising out of the constitution of Christianity, or attendant on its progress, we think " our light affliction, which is but for a moment, worketh for us a far more exceeding and eternal weight of glory," 2 Cor. iv. 17. They are more apparent than real, more contingent than fundamental, and infinitely countervailed. And, as figured by that " fire sent on the earth," so far from reflecting on the character and religion of Christ, they illustrate the majesty of the one, and the stability of the other. In the first place, the Saviour treats those disadvantages as diminutive : " I am come to send fire on the earth." But when he alludes to these sufferings, he cannot regard them so indifferently. He therefore put them into contrast and opposition : " But I have a baptism to be baptized with." As to the fire, he heeds it not: " What will I, if it be already kindled?" But as to the baptism it engrosses him : " How am I straitened till it be accomplished!" The oracle which foretold that his soul should be made " an offering for sin," also announced, " He shall see of the travail of his soul, and shall be satisfied," Isa. liii. 10, 11. That satisfaction must pervade the vast capacity of his mind, must answer the long suspense of his ambition, and must ascend the infinite scale of his desert. This was " the joy which was set before him," and in whose prospect " he endured the cross, despising the shame," Heb. xii. 2. We ask not what vesture can be too splendid for the form, that the purple mockery insulted; what diadem too glorious for the brow, the thorny coronet lacerated;—but what must be the delight, most exquisite and boundless, which reconciles him to all his endurances and conflicts : which prompts him to bear his crucifixion-wounds, as the scars of His noblest triumph, and centres of His brightest glory!

APPLICATION.

1. Here, then, we find an apology for our warmest zeal and firmest courage, in extending Christianity. We but imbibe the spirit and follow the steps of our Exampler.

2. And here, too, we learn that this unconquerable temper, this inexpressible ardour, is of the first importance in every department of missions. Nothing half-hearted should be betrayed in our institutions at home, or efforts abroad.

3. In this spirit of unshrinking courage, and unabating ardour, let us proceed. We carry the commission of Him who " came to send fire on the earth." We may blow the flame, we may spread the conflagration; what will he, if it be already kindled? All must yield to the gospel of Christ, or be consumed by its progress.

SKETCH XIV.

THE FIELDS WHITE TO HARVEST.

BY REV. DANIEL WILSON, D.D.,

BISHOP OF CALCUTTA.*

" Say not ye, There are yet four months, and then cometh harvest? behold, I say unto you, Lift up your eyes, and look on the fields; for they
are white already to harvest. And he that reapeth receiveth wages, and
gathereth fruit unto life eternal: that both he that soweth and he that
reapeth may rejoice together."—JOHN iv. 35, 36.

THE text was spoken when the disciples, during the absence of the Samaritan woman, had urged to partake of
the provisions which they had procured. Our Lord, in
reply to their solicitations, described his ardent zeal for the
salvation of souls, which the prospect of instructing the
Samaritans had excited, as supplying the want of bodily
food: " My meat is to do the will of Him that sent me,
and to finish His work," ver. 34. And then he addressed
them in the words of the text, with the design of leading
their minds from the natural harvest, which was still four
months distant, and of which they had probably been discoursing as they passed through the fields, just springing with
the tender blade, to a spiritual harvest, which was already
ripe for the sickle; and to excite them, after his example, to
that activity in teaching and saving mankind, which the hus-
bandman manifests when the corn is ready for the garner.

· The spirit of the passage, then, is obviously to animate
the reaper to enter into the harvest, from the consideration
of the ripeness of the whitening grain. And it will therefore

* Preached on behalf of the Church Missionary Society, 1817.

afford me an occasion of bringing before you various motives to redoubled efforts in the cause of missions, now
that opportunities of diffusing the gospel are opening upon
us from every quarter. In considering this subject, as
represented by the striking image of my text, we must
look first at the aspect of the fields; and, secondly, at the
encouragements to the reaper.

I. WE MUST LOOK AT THE ASPECT OF THE FIELDS.

When our Lord uttered these words, he had immediate
respect to the Samaritans. It wanted, at that time, four
months to the harvest of the earth. But, if the disciples
would " lift up their eyes, and look on the fields," across
which the inhabitants of Sychar were hastening at the
tidings of the woman, and whom our Saviour probably
pointed at with his finger when he spake, they would
behold a spiritual harvest, not merely shooting up its early
blade, but now ripe for their labour ; they would see
people coming with eagerness, to hear and receive the
doctrine of salvation.

Our Lord had respect also, in this language, to the general
state of the Jewish nation, and of the world. The time of
God's mercy was then near. The faith of the pious servants
of God among the Jews, had welcomed the " Consolation
of Israel." The general expectation of the people was fixed
on His character and doctrine. But the whole civilized
world was also, in a considerable measure, in a like state.
Thus things were ripening for the harvest ; and the apostles
were soon to go forth as reapers into that vastly more
extensive field of labour.

The spirit of our Lord's address, however, is applicable
generally to all periods of the church, when the providence
of God concurs with his grace, to present remarkable opportunities for diffusing the gospel. For when facilities

are afforded for disseminating Divine truth; when these facilities are embraced with suitable activity on the part of the spiritual church; and when, above all, a disposition to inquire into Christianity appears among the heathen nations, then the fields may be said to stand loaded with corn, demanding the hand of the reaper. For, if you cast your eye over the different parts of the heathen world, you will find,

1. *That in most places there is evidently a preparation in the minds of both Pagans and Mohammedans for receiving the servants of Christ.*

In the vast continent of India—the most promising scene for missionary labour—we are credibly informed by those who have been eye-witnesses of what they relate, that the native mind is obviously opening to receive the gospel.

In Persia, on the one side of India; and in China on the other—opportunities have offered for extending the knowledge of the word of God.

If, from hence, we pass to the countless islands of the Southern Ocean, it is peculiarly animating to read the accounts of what the providence and grace of God are effecting in those newly-discovered regions. In some of them, large bodies of men have renounced their idols; and received the doctrine of salvation.

The immense territory of New Holland also, and the neighbouring islands of New Zealand—the latter under our own Society—are opening to the Christian Teacher.

I will not detain you by particularising what is doing in the two American continents, and the West Indies; but I will merely stop, and ask whether this rapid view, which we have taken, be not highly encouraging to redoubled exertion? But it may here be asked,

2. *What are the peculiar advantages which pious and zealous Christians in Britain enjoy for extending the gospel.*

Here, then, I would first inquire, whether the circumstance of so large a part of the heathen world being subject to the British sceptre, or bordering on its possessions, be not, in itself, a remarkable advantage to our cause. Where can you look, from 100 degrees in the remote West, to Norfolk Island, in the East; or from the Shetlands in the North, to 33 degrees South of the Line: that is, over 270 degrees of longitude, and 94 of latitude, or nearly 20,000 miles, by 6 or 7,000, without seeing parts of that dominion which God has entrusted to this Protestant country? Why is it that such large and important additions have been made to its territory during the last few years—additions which would, of themselves, constitute a great empire?

3. *But the disposition among the heathen to receive the gospel, and the facilities which we possess for diffusing it, would be insufficient, unless the activity of the spiritual church were awake to improve the occasion.* This is, then, the third point, which marks the present period, and contributes to make up the aspect of the ripened field.

By the spiritual church, I mean the invisible and mystical body of true Christians in this country, who hold Christ as the Head, are vitally united to him by his Spirit, and obey his laws; though they may differ in minor points of doctrine and discipline. This body is diligently occupying the post assigned to it. Christians, of almost every class, are exerting their efforts to seize the golden opportunity. Various Societies have been formed—correspondences opened with suitable persons abroad—information circulated at home—appeals made to the public conscience—and missionary stations selected and occupied in heathen countries.

II. ENCOURAGEMENTS HELD OUT TO THE REAPERS.

These encouragements, then, we shall now proceed further to consider, after we have first explained the nature of the labour with which they are connected. The labour of the spiritual reaper consists in preaching the gospel of Christ to perishing sinners; and in achieving those services, and enduring those privations, which, in a heathen country, are inseparable from so arduous an employment.

His main duty is, to set before men the doctrine of the cross of Christ, in all its bearings. This is the appointed means of gathering in the spiritual harvest.

But, great as is the toil of such devoted servants of Christ, the encouragement held out to them is more than commensurate.—" He that reapeth receiveth wages, and gathereth fruit to life eternal: that both he that soweth and he that reapeth may rejoice together."

1. *The important good, which the Christian missionary effects, is, that he gathers fruit to life eternal.*

And what an inspiring motive is this! If the earthly harvest-man is animated by the thought, that he is collecting the blessing of the year, and gathering fruit for the support of temporal life; how much more will the spiritual reaper be cheered by the reflection, that every soul which he is the means of turning from the error of his ways, is fruit gathered to life eternal! But this is not all.

2. *The abundant reward which awaits him, when the toil is finished, is a further incentive to persevering labour.*

" He that reapeth receiveth wages,"—not indeed of merit,—for he is, at last, but an unprofitable servant: all that he has done, which has been good, has come from the grace of God,—but of Divine mercy; wages that his Lord has engaged to give after the harvest is over, which will bear a proportion to the measure of the work done, and to which he is encouraged to look forward, to support and animate him when ready, through sloth and self-indulgence, to faint under his toil; that thus, like Moses, he may endure, " having respect unto the recompense of the reward." Great is his reward in heaven. When he rests from his labours, his works do follow him, Rev. xiv. 13.

His wages are sure. All who have joined in the work shall partake of the reward. They may differ from one another in abilities and education, and cast of mind; in opinion on smaller matters, in the extent of the stations allotted them, and in the success granted to their labours: but they shall all hear, at last, those blessed words, "Well done! good and faithful servant: thou hast been faithful over a few things, I will make thee ruler over many things: enter thou into the joy of thy Lord," Matt. xxv. 21. With this joy the reaper's reward is connected; for, together with his wages, he shall have a peculiar satisfaction and triumph. "He that soweth and he that reapeth shall rejoice together."

(1.) This common joy *began* when the holy apostles, having finished their labours, were taken to receive their reward. Then the patriarchs and prophets, who had been sowing for so many ages, joined them in the strain of triumph, at the gathering in of the first evangelical harvest.

(2.) This joy has been *increasing*, as the several sowers and reapers, in different ages of the New Testament church, have been taken to their eternal rest.

(3.) It will be *completed* when all the church shall meet before the throne; when the mystery of Christ shall be finished; when God shall have accomplished the number of his elect, and have hastened his kingdom.

APPLICATION.

If such, then, be the encouragement to us to enter on those fields, which we have seen to be white for harvest, it remains only, in drawing to conclusion, that, according to the command of our Saviour, we "lift up our eyes, and look on the fields," and apply ourselves without delay to the work.

1. " Behold, I say unto you, Lift up your eyes, and look on the fields"—shows the necessity of rousing men from their torpor, and directing them to the actual state of mankind.

2. And shall not these emotions of surprise and pleasure lead you to redoubled exertion? Will you not enter into the fields? Did ever such an exuberant crop wave over the lands? Was ever our Protestant church invited to such a scene of labour? And, surely, that church, the glory of the Reformation, will not be backward in such a crisis!

3. But for these ends we must be led, as our Saviour in another and similar passage instructs us, to fervent prayer to the Lord of the harvest, who is so abundantly able to prosper our endeavour. He can send forth the labourers. He can qualify them for the work. He can sustain them under their fatigue, cheer them when they faint, grant them success, and bestow on them their reward. He can do all this for us; while, without this mighty aid, our utmost efforts must fail.

4. Nor is it a slight recommendation of the measures to which your attention is now called, that zealous exertions in behalf of missions, accompanied with the spirit prayer—of habitual, fervent supplication to God, for our own and all other Societies engaged in this great design—will also have the happy effect of materially furthering our own salvation. No one can touch this sacred cause, much less engage in it with a spirit of prayer, but it will promote his individual piety!

SKETCH XV.

THE TRIUMPHS OF THE GOSPEL.

" Now thanks be unto God, who always causeth us to triumph in Christ."
2 Cor. ii. 14.

Our text evidently refers to the triumphant entry of heroes
into their native kingdoms, or chief cities, after the attainment of some splendid victory.   On such occasions the
spectacle was of the most imposing kind.   The conqueror,
either led on horseback, or seated in a triumphal car, was
met by the great, the illustrious, and the fair; and conducted
through the gates with unusual magnificence and rejoicing.
In some cases, deposed monarchs, or captains and great
men taken in battle, were dragged at the conqueror's
chariot; and often the spoils taken from the foe were
exhibited to the admiring gaze of countless thousands.

Whole volumes have been written on these pageant
scenes; and historians have vied with each other in setting
them forth with all the adornments of a gaudy rhetoric, or
vivid, glowing eloquence.

Now, the apostle compares the success of himself and
fellow apostles to ancient conquerors; and, in the language
of impassioned ardour, exclaims, " Now thanks be unto
God," etc. Consider, in reference to the gospel, the achievements obtained; contrast them with the victories of the
warrior; and then urge to a holy and pious exultation in
God.   " Now thanks be unto God, who always causeth us
to triumph in Christ."   In reference to a preached gospel
observe,

I. The victories achieved.

Triumph implies conflict, and supposes its successful termination. By the preaching of the gospel by the apostle:—

1. *The gospel triumphed over the prejudices of Judaism.* The Jews had a Divine system of religion—a system from God; attested by miracles; identified with heavenly interpositions; established by prophets; and diffusing a holy light and heavenly halo around their nation. To this system they were devotedly attached : indeed, to it they had an idolatrous veneration. Abraham was the father of their nation; Moses their law-giver; Samuel and Isaiah their prophets; David their poet; Solomon their legislator; the Oracles their directory. But they gave a temporal explanation to the writings of their seers, and expected a Messiah of worldly dignity and warlike prowess. They were looking for secular blessings, and an earthly kingdom. Hence their moral unpreparedness for the Son of God—their dislike, hatred, oppression, persecution, and putting Him to death.

All thinking persons know the power of prejudice, and especially when it is associated with blighted hopes and keen disappointments. This was the case with the Jews; yet, even over this barrier, which seemed impassable, did the gospel triumph: three thousand of these prejudiced Jews were enlightened, converted, and saved under one discourse. Oh! think of such a multitude being disarmed, overcome, and added to the kingdom of Jesus, even in the city of his death. And of these, untold thousands were afterwards the humble, adoring disciples of the cross.

2. *The gospel triumphed over the various and multifarious systems of Paganism.* The gentile world had its systems of religion and philosophy. Many of these were ancient; established by law, and sanctified by custom. In some instances, human industry was identified with their

temples and worship. Most of these systems pandered to the vices of the people; and were so decorated by art, and so connected with the pleasures of sense, that they presented many attractions to the mass of the people.— But the gospel triumphed over these.

At Ephesus, a holy host was rescued from the worship of Diana; and in Athens, crowded with altars; in Corinth, in Antioch, and in Rome, the churches of the Messiah were founded and established, and men were turned from dumb idols to the service of the pure and living God.

3. *The gospel triumphed over the corruptions and lives of mankind.* The gospel not only encountered error and idolatry, but depravity and sin—depraved hearts and corrupt lives. Interwoven with the systems of Pagan religion and philosophy were the most disgusting and odious vices— vices which were unblushingly practised, and so horrible, that the apostle only feebly hints at them in the first chapter of his epistle to the Romans. Now, if it were something great and glorious for the gospel to triumph over the darkness of the understanding, and the errors of the judgment, how much more over the passions of the heart, and the corruptions of the life. Read 1 Cor. vi. 9, etc.

4. *The gospel triumphed over the love of self and the world.* In the early ages of Christianity, men had more to do than change their religion, and alter their creed. They had to do this by the most comprehensive self-denial, and often the sacrifice of all things. They had to set at defiance human laws, and oppose themselves to fines, confiscations, imprisonment, and even death! A converted wife had to lose the affections and support of her Pagan husband, and perhaps endure the scorn of her own offspring. In fact, all was to be forsaken for Christ and his kingdom; yet the natural attachment to the enjoyments of this world, the still closer attachment to friends, and the innate love

of life, were all too feeble to stay the triumphs of the cross; and despite these fearful obstacles, the apostle could exclaim, " Now thanks be unto God," etc. Let us,

II. CONTRAST THESE TRIUMPHS WITH THE VICTORIES OF ANCIENT WARRIORS. Do this—

1. *In the agents sent forth.* Contrast an ambitious, worldly, cruel hero, with the humble, spiritual, and 'benevolent apostles of Jesus. Pride, lust, and cruelty, are the traits in the one; meekness, virtue, and philanthropy, the features in the others. Do this—

2. *In the weapons employed.* In the one case, the sword, the arrow, the spear, the battering ram ; in the other, the torch of truth, the message of mercy, and moral suasion. The one appears with his implements of death, and his garments died in blood ; in the others, " How beautiful upon the mountains," etc., Isa. hi. 7. See the warrior, with the instruments of death, on the battle field ; and then see Paul on Mars' Hill, with the truth of heaven and the gospel of mercy.

3. *In the results that followed.* The warrior may be traced as to his work of woe, by the footsteps of blood, by the groanings of the wounded; by the putrescence of the air, tainted with the slain ; by the desolated country, the sacked city, the burning dwellings, the frenzied widows, and desolated orphans. Over the field of the warrior is the vulture hovering for his prey, or the marauding wild beast snuffing his food. The triumphs of the cross are succeeded by the diffusion of knowledge, the communication of joy, the extension of civilization, the prosperity of commerce, domestic felicity, and the true blessedness of the world.

" Blessings abound where'er He reigns," etc.

Human warfare degrades, blights, curses, and enkindles hell upon earth. The triumph of the gospel elevates, sanctifies, blesses, and brings down the reign of heaven to earth. Surely, then, we may proceed,

III. To URGE TO A HOLY AND DEVOUT EXULTATION IN GOD. " Now thanks be unto God," etc. Observe,

1. *The object of our exultation*—"GOD." The Author of the Christian system. It is " The glorious gospel of the blessed God," 1 Tim. i. 11,—full of God ; and, therefore, all its efficiency redounds to His glory.

2. *The nature of the exultation.* " Now thanks be unto God, who always causeth us to triumph in Christ." The highest, most earnest thanks, etc. : the ascriptions of the lip, the homage of the mind, the gratitude of the heart, and the service of the life—all and each of these, we must express : " Now thanks be unto God," etc.

3. *The extent of this exultation.*

(1.) As to persons. The whole church, every believer : ministers, deacons, members.

(2.) As to duration. Thanks now, and through all time; and thanks in heaven, and through all eternity.

APPLICATION.

1. The gospel yet triumphs — at home and abroad. How cheering the reports from the servants of Jesus in India, Burmah, Africa, New Zealand, the West Indies, etc.

2. To these triumphs many here are infinitely indebted. To the influence of religion you owe your respectability in life, your preservation from ten thousand perils, and blessings and enjoyments beyond enumeration.

3. To extend these triumphs should be the design and effort of all. Every Christian should possess the missionary spirit, and employ his influence in extending the gospel of the Lord Jesus Christ. The church of Christ, in its collective character, should be one united and catholic missionary association.

SKETCH XVI.

THE SPIRITUAL TEMPLE, ERECTED BY THE HANDS OF GENTITES.

BY REV. JAMES BODEN, OF SHEFFIELD.

"And they that are far off shall come and build in the temple of the Lord."
ZECH. vi. 15.

I SHALL not detain your attention by attempting any critical remarks on the important contents of this chapter. I think I may venture to assume, that in the person of Joshua, and the building of the temple, this context contains a very clear prediction and type of one infinitely greater than the Jewish high priest, or the material temple of God. This text unquestionably refers to the times of the gospel: and under this dispensation of grace, we observe,

I. GOD HAS DETERMINED ON THE ERECTION OF A SPIRITUAL TEMPLE. And that,

II. IN THE EXECUTION OF THIS DESIGN, HE WILL EMPLOY SUCH AS HAVE BEEN STRANGERS, AND FOREIGNERS, AND AFAR OFF.

I. GOD HAS DETERMINED ON THE ERECTION OF A SPIRITUAL TEMPLE.

1. *This temple is the gospel Church.* The church of God is represented, by the prophets and apostles, as a sacred building, of which the temple at Jerusalem, built a

* From a Sermon preached before the London Missionary Society, at the Tabernacle, Moorfields, May 10th, 1815.

F

thousand years before the Christian era, was a striking type, or figure. Isaiah, under the inspiration of heaven, and wrapt into future times, says, "And it shall come to pass in the last days, that the mountain of the LORD's house shall be established in the top of the mountains, and shall be exalted above the hills; and all nations shall flow unto it," Isa. ii. 2. The apostle adopts the same language, and perpetuates the same illustration. "Ye are built upon the foundation of the apostles and prophets, Jesus Christ himself being the chief corner stone; in whom all the building fitly framed together groweth unto an holy temple in the Lord: in whom ye also are builded together for a habitation of God through the Spirit," Eph. ii. 20—22

2. *This temple is the peculiar residence of the Almighty.* But here a difficulty seems to arise. Will "the high and lofty One that inhabiteth eternity, whose name is Holy," whom "the heaven and heaven of heavens cannot contain;" will God, in very deed, dwell with men on the earth? He will; for he hath said, "I will dwell in them, and walk in them; and I will be their God, and they shall be my people," 2 Cor. vi. 16; and "where two or three are met together in my name, there am I in the midst of them to bless them," Matt. xviii. 20. "The Lord hath chosen Zion; he hath desired it for his habitation. This is my rest for ever: here will I dwell; for I have desired it."

3. *The gospel temple is of large extent.* Ezekiel's prophetic temple by its immense dimensions, greater than the whole city of Jerusalem, prefigured the universal and truly Catholic church, which was to be collected at that period, when the knowledge of the Lord shall cover the earth, "and all flesh shall see the salvation of God."

4. *Extraordinary magnificence and beauty distinguish the dwelling of God.* Solomon's temple was the most superb and finished material structure the sun ever saw;

but the grandeur of the Jewish sanctuary was only a shadow of the celestial glory of the Christian temple. The church of the living God is purified with the blood of the Lamb, covered with the magnificent righteousness of her Redeemer, and adorned with those heavenly graces and good works, which are ornaments after the style of the upper world. Her glory is not indeed appreciated by the rules of worldly wisdom. No; her symmetry and beautiful proportions are confusion; and those splendours of holiness with which God has invested her, are deformity to the carnal eye. But soon the reproach of Zion shall be rolled away for ever. Then God will proclaim, "Arise, shine; for thy light is come, and the glory of the Lord is risen upon thee. For, behold, the darkness shall cover the earth, and gross darkness the people: but the Lord shall arise upon thee, and his glory shall be seen upon thee. And the Gentiles shall come to the light, and kings to the brightness of thy rising," Isa. lx. 1—3.

5. *The plan of this temple was formed by infinite wisdom.* The first master-builders in the Christian church plainly asserted and proved, that the gospel which was preached by them, was not after the corrupt taste of man; neither did they receive it of men; neither were they taught it, but by the revelation of Jesus Christ, Gal. i. 12. The Christian temple is a spiritual edifice, composed of living stones, prepared, collected, and united according to His purpose, "who worketh all things after the counsel of his own will;—wherein he hath abounded toward us in all wisdom and prudence," Eph. i. 8, 11.

6. *This sacred temple is reared under the immediate agency of God the Saviour.* Jehovah incarnate claims the church as his own house, and as the erection of his own hand. It is the language of prophecy, "The Lord shall build up Zion," Psa. cii. 16. It is the assertion

of our Saviour, " Upon this rock I will build my church,"
Matt. xvi. 18. Christ builds his church, not by his instruction and example merely ;—so the apostles were labourers with God ;—but by his omnipresent energy, and
by the efficient power of his Holy Spirit.

7. *The temple of the Lord is placed on a sure foundation.* The foundation answers to the extent, the grandeur,
and the elevation of the superstructure. To provide the
foundation, God claims as his own exclusive act : " Behold, I lay in Zion for a foundation a stone, a tried stone,
a precious corner stone, a sure foundation," Isa. xxviii. 16.
This scripture is quoted by Peter, and applied to the Lord
Jesus Christ, whom he calls, " a living stone, disallowed
indeed of men, but chosen of God, and precious," 1 Pet. ii. 4.

8. *The completion of this temple is reserved for the world
of glory.* The trenches are dug, the corner stone is laid,
and we see the basement already rising to view ; yet much,
very much, still remains to be done. But the plummet is
in the hands of our Divine Zerubbabel : " His hands have
laid the foundations of this house ; his hands also shall
finish it ;—and he shall bring forth the head stone thereof
with shoutings, crying, Grace, grace unto it," Zech. iv. 9, 7.

II. In the execution of this design, God will employ such as have been strangers, and afar off.

1. *By those afar off, are to be understood the Gentile
nations*, as contradistinguished from the community of
Israel. The admission of the Gentiles to this honourable
work was plainly intimated at the erection of the first and
second temple in Jerusalem. Solomon was zealously
assisted in his great undertaking by Hiram, king of Tyre,
and his subjects, the Sidonians ; and all the Gentile strangers
in the land of Israel were put in a state of requisition on
the memorable occasion.

2. *The first stones in the gospel temple were laid by the hands of Jewish master-builders.* Christ himself, a greater than Solomon, and the true Zerubbabel, was of the seed of Abraham, according to the flesh. The apostles were all Jews; and on account of their eminent services at the commencement of the gospel era, the church is represented. as having "twelve foundations, and in them the names of the twelve apostles of the Lamb," Rev. xxi. 14.

3. *The incorporation of the Jews with the Christian church, is to be accomplished by Gentile instrumentality.*

APPLICATION.

I. In consequence of this promise, you are met here this day. Were you not once numbered with those who are afar off, though now brought nigh?

2. The extension of this temple to all nations, is to crown your exertions, and those of your gentile fellow-labourers. Can any doubt be entertained whether God designs to make Missionary Societies engines to move the world? How far have the concentric circles already extended from this centre? Are they not extending every year?

3. Have we not lately heard that some who were afar off, dwelling even on the extreme verge of humanity, are already enrolled among the builders? I trust, before many years have elapsed, your sight and your souls will be cheered, your zeal and your exertions will be excited, under missionary sermons, by Hottentot, Hindoo, or Chinese ministers of the gospel.

I will only add, let the bounties of Providence; the necessities of a perishing world; and, above all, the dying love of Jesus, constrain your hearts, and direct your contributions. Amen.

SKETCH XVII.

ENCOURAGEMENT TO PERSEVERANCE IN MISSIONARY EXERTIONS.

BY REV. JOHN HYATT.*

" As the rain cometh down, and the snow from heaven, and returneth not thither, but watereth the earth, and maketh it bring forth and bud, that it may give seed to the sower, and bread to the eater : so shall my word be that goeth forth out of my mouth: it shall not return unto me void, but it shall accomplish that which I please, and it shall prosper in the thing whereto I sent it.—ISAIAH lv. 10, 11.

HOPE of success imparts energy to the mind, whilst it has to contend with opposition and difficulties, in the pursuit of any grand object.   If a man of enterprise possess assurance that he shall succeed, nothing can intimidate and compel him to relinquish his pursuit; assurance of success in the issue makes him bold and fearless in the face of a thousand opponents and dangers.

My Christian brethren, the object that has long engaged your attention, and called forth your energies, is infinitely important.   In its pursuit, your faith and patience have been exercised; yet you have not despaired of success— nor will you despair.   While you expect that the labours of your missionaries, amongst the idolatrous gentiles, will be crowned with the blessing of Almighty God, you do not expect " a new thing in the earth."

* From a Sermon, preached before the London Missionary Society, at Tottenham Court Chapel, May 11, 1815.

The gospel of Jesus, preached by feeble men, has made the brazen front of superstition blush; it has rivetted the eye of philosophers to the Redeemer's cross; it has demolished idols and their temples, and taught idolaters to worship " the only true God" in an acceptable manner.

The analogy between the rain in the natural world, and the word of God in the moral world, is the doctrine of the text. We propose to consider four things, in which they are analogous.

I. Both exhibit the sovereignty of Jehovah. Two things exhibit the sovereignty of Jehovah in the rain that cometh down from heaven.

I. *The time of its descent.* The earth is not watered with rain by chance. All the works of the infinite Creator are constantly subject to his control; the different elements which He hath created, are all under a law which they cannot possibly violate. He " giveth rain, and fruitful seasons." He " prepareth rain for the earth," Psa. cxlvii. 8. Every shower of rain depends upon His sovereign pleasure. None but God can raise the clouds—none but He can discharge their contents.

The time when God sends his word to any of the human race, displays his sovereignty. He gave his word to the Jews, and preserved it amongst them for ages; whilst he left the Gentiles in gross darkness, and gave them up to abominable idolatry.

2. *The place upon which the rain descends,* exhibits the sovereignty of the Supreme Being. The clouds, whose contents water the earth, are not driven by chance; they steer their course according to the will of God : they are, indeed, driven by the wind; but the wind is controlled by the Almighty Creator, " who maketh the clouds His chariot, who walketh upon the wings of the wind," Psa. civ. 3.

The sovereignty of Jehovah is displayed in the place to which he sends his word. He sends it to one place, and not to another. One part of the moral world is fertilized by the influence of the gospel, and another remains waste. One part is a garden, producing abundance of the fruits of righteousness; another is a wilderness, abounding with noxious weeds and thistles.

II. BOTH THE RAIN IN THE NATURAL WORLD, AND THE WORD OF GOD IN THE MORAL WORLD, ARE EFFICIENT IN THEIR INFLUENCE.

The great and glorious Governor of the universe doeth nothing in vain : all His works praise him. He gathereth the waters into clouds—conducts them by the wind to the place of their destiny—discharges their contents, and waters the earth, " Nor lets the drops descend in vain." God employs the rain as a means to an end; and whatever means he employs must be efficient to produce the end he designs. We are not astonished at the efficiency of the rain, when we consider the power by which it is employed.

God sends not the gospel to any place in vain: "It shall prosper in the thing whereto I sent it," is His positive and merciful declaration. Both the rain in the natural world, and the gospel in the moral world, *must* be efficient in their influence. The efficiency of both is promised, and the promises of Jehovah shall assuredly be accomplished. The promises of God insure the continuance, the promulgation, and the success of his word in the world, till time shall expire. The gospel must prosper, and effect what its eternal Author hath purposed. Its success cannot possibly be prevented. "Many shall run to and fro, and knowledge shall be increased," Dan. xii. 4. The way of God shall " be known upon earth: his saving health among all nations."

III. Both the rain in the natural world, and the word of God in the moral world, are advantageous in their effects.

The rain promotes vegetation; it causeth " the earth to bring forth and bud." It is the means of producing much that is ornamental, to delight man; and much that is essential to his support. The earth produces innumerable blessings for our use; not one of which could be produced without rain. We enjoy the fruits of the rain in the bread we eat, the beverage we drink, and the clothing we wear.

The effects which are produced by the gospel are both ornamental and useful. When the word of God, accompanied by the influence of the Holy Ghost, savingly operates upon any part of the moral world, how beautiful is its face!—how advantageous are its effects! The gospel transforms mankind, that were counterparts of Satan, into the lovely image of the Son of God. Odiousness is exchanged for beauty—injuriousness gives place to utility; the hateful fruits of the flesh, are supplanted by the admirable fruits of the Spirit. The wilderness is turned into a blooming paradise. The indolent, become industrious; the revengeful, become kind and affectionate; the licentious, become chaste; the proud, become humble; the covetous, become liberal; and the worshippers of dumb idols, worship the God of heaven and earth in spirit and in truth. The gospel binds mankind in fraternal bonds, and they live together in peace and harmony.

IV. The effects of the rain in the natural world, and of the gospel in the moral world, display the glory of the Divine perfections.

The beautiful scenery of nature displays the glory of the eternal Creator. Impressions of his infinite perfections appear upon every bud—every blossom—every blade of grass—every ear of corn.   In every part of the vegetable world, the glory of illimitable power, infinite wisdom, and boundless goodness shines.   The glory of God is visible in every thing that is produced by the rain, " from the cedar that is in Lebanon, even to the hyssop that springeth out of the wall."

> " Nature with open volume stands,
>   And spreads her Maker's praise abroad ;
> And every labour of His hands,
>   Shows something worthy of a God."

Infinitely more of the Divine glory is seen upon the face of the moral world, transformed by the influence of the gospel.   How effulgent is the glory that shines in the marvellous change that is produced in the mind of man in regeneration, and in the various fruits of holiness that adorn his life.   The glory of Jehovah shines in the existence of an angel; but that glory is eclipsed, when a sinner, saved by grace, united to Christ, and devoted to the pursuit of holiness and heaven,—is placed at his side.

APPLICATION.

1. The gospel cannot be preached altogether in vain. Wherever the Almighty designs to send it, he designs to produce the most glorious effects by its instrumentality.

2. The extent of the success of the gospel is determined. " It shall," saith Jehovah, " accomplish that which I please, and it shall prosper in the thing whereto I sent it."

3. When the word of God is widely diffusing, we may reasonably encourage hope, that much good will be done.

4. The genuine influence of Christianity will produce an ardent concern for the salvation of the heathen.   What Christian can place before his imagination, hundreds of millions of the human family, enslaved by Satan, and paying

senseless adoration to images, and not feel pity and compassion excited in his bosom towards them?

5. We live at an eventful period: the history of the present age will be read by millions that are unborn, with joyful astonishment.

6. We shall shortly quit this world. We all must die; but the cause of missions will live and flourish. It is the cause, of all others, most dear to God. It is the cause which a gracious Providence hath fostered in all ages. It is the cause whose success a race of holy prophets foretold and anticipated. It is the cause for which a noble army of martyrs cheerfully consented to expire in flames. It is the cause for which the Son of God agonized and died. It is the cause that will bring the largest revenue of glory to the triune Jehovah—AND MUST PROSPER! "O LORD, I beseech thee, send NOW prosperity!" What individual is there in this vast assembly that is not disposed to add a hearty—AMEN!

SKETCH XVIII.

MARY'S MEMORIAL.

BY REV. W. MOORHOUSE, OF HUDDERSFIELD.*

" And Jesus said, Let her alone; why trouble ye her? she hath wrought a good work on me."—MARK xiv. 6.

WE presume not to say, that this text is the most pertinent of all others upon the present occasion; yet, it is hoped, it will appear, in the sequel, not so foreign to the subject of our missionary meeting as some might imagine. The design in bringing it forward, is to urge the force of an amiable example of love and zeal in the weaker sex, and to animate all our hearts in the work before us. O that I might be so happy as to advance anything upon the subject, which might give this sermon a right to the title of Mary's memorial!

With a view, in some small degree, to accomplish this end, there are four things included in the text to which we must attend.

I. THE PROBABLE MOTIVES.

II. A FEW OBVIOUS CIRCUMSTANCES WHICH ATTENDED THIS GOOD WORK.

III. THE OBJECT UPON WHOM IT TERMINATED.

IV. THE TESTIMONY OF THE IMPARTIAL, INFALLIBLE, JUDGE.—" She hath wrought a good work on me."

I. THE PROBABLE MOTIVES OF THE GOOD WORK.

I call them probable, not because they are altogether

* Preached before the Missionary Society, at Surrey Chapel, May 10, 1797.

doubtful, but because they are not expressed; and we should always speak cautiously where there is not sufficient authority to be positive. However, let it be remembered by all, that there is one thing, which, in every age, in every nation, in every individual, is essential to a good work in the sense of our text.

1. *A new heart.* That Mary was blessed with this best of blessings we have sufficient reason to conclude from what Jesus said of her in another place, " One thing is needful: and Mary hath chosen that good part, which shall not be taken away from her," Luke x. 42.

2. *The second probable motive of the good work spoken of in the text is love.* Love, that native of the celestial world, which is like the impulsive cause of all mechanical motion. Love, that tender exotic, so little known in this dark, disordered world, moved all the powers of Mary's expanded soul in this good work. The strength and effects of this passion are incredible! What is too hard for love to do, or endure, for the beloved object! Without love, what is zeal but wildfire! devotion, only splendid hypocrisy! My dear hearers, it is owing to a deficiency in this, that the heathen world has been so long and so shamefully neglected by those called Christians.

3. *Gratitude was a motive, not less probable in Mary's good work than the foregoing.* If any were to ask, what gratitude is? my answer should be, it is a pleasing sensation of the mind, excited by the soul being pressed with an inexpressible sense of high obligation to an object, for favours received. Mary knew Christ—for what end he was come into this lower world: she knew what He had done, and what he would do for her. How shall she show her thankful sense of benefits and blessings so great, so undeserved? Like Abigail, laying her present at David's feet, she brings forth the best she had in this world; and, with

her whole heart, bestowed it upon him whom her soul loved, and to whom she had such transcendant obligations.

II. WE NOW COME TO TAKE NOTICE OF A FEW OBVIOUS CIRCUMSTANCES WHICH ATTENDED THIS GOOD WORK.

1. *It was public.* Have any of you, my friends, been ashamed of being active in promoting the missionary business? Be ashamed of your shame; and, from this day, cast away your cowardice, and consider it as a peculiar honour to appear the zealous supporters of such a cause.

2. *It was liberal, nay, profuse.* The passage tells us, the ointment was very costly. I trust you will excuse me for not giving you a particular description of all the articles which constituted the odoriferous composition. Let us, for the present, be content with Judas' estimate: he said " it might have been sold for more than three hundred pence," Mark xiv. 5. The usual way of calculating the value of different coins, gives the Roman penny at rather more than sevenpence halfpenny, sterling; according to this calculation, the ointment was worth near ten pounds: perhaps a great part of her living; as much, or more, for her to give, than if some rich Jew had given ten thousand guineas.

3. *It was performed in due time.* Had Mary brought her box when Christ had got into heaven, though it had been ten times the value, it would not have availed—she would have lost all. Many good works lose nine-tenths of their value by being too late. The apostolic rule is, " That they which have believed in God might be careful to maintain good works," Titus iii. 8. Critics frequently render it, " to *go before* in good works." We have but too few; but here is one instance:—Mary goes before, or is in due time in her labour of love.

4. *Mary made her little temporalities answer the greatest and the noblest ends.* It is said, Psa. cxv. 16, that the

Creator "hath given the earth to the children of men."
For what purposes are we to suppose that property is given
to all, or any of us? To ornament mortal, dying bodies?
To feed the follies of fancy—to foster the pride óf the
heart; or, to amuse the possessor with counting over his
gold, and feasting his eyes by gazing upon it? Oh, no!
God gives the good things of this world for the noblest
ends; and those ends are specified both in the Old and
New Testaments. "Honour the Lord with thy substance,
and with the firstfruits of all thine increase," Prov. iii. 9.
This brings us to the general proposition.

III. THE OBJECT UPON WHOM THIS GOOD WORK TERMI-
NATED. On this our text is very express: "She hath
wrought a good work on me."

Too many religious and generous acts terminate in self;
and the end they are intended to answer is, to gain a little
of that airy bubble, "the honour that cometh of men."
Remember Mary's object—it was to make Christ "a sweet-
smelling savour;" and, as she is said to anoint him for his
burial, it is probable that she intended it to signify that
even in the grave his body should breathe a sweet odour,
without seeing the least taint of corruption. Here learn,
the true and laudable object of all well-intended missions,
viz., to make known to a perishing world the efficiency
and glory of the sacrifice of the Lord Jesus Christ;—the
very same which Paul had in view, when he went forth into
the dark regions of the gentile nations, as will abundantly
appear from the following passage, "For we preach not
ourselves, but Christ Jesus the Lord; and ourselves your
servants for Jesus' sake," 2 Cor. iv. 5.

Actions terminate on Jesus Christ, though mediately,
when they are calculated to increase his family; and, of
course, the universal sacrifice of praise and thanksgiving

ought daily to be presented unto him.   The prophetic
pen informs us, " Daily shall he be praised;" and if any
ask, By whom? the same author tells us, "All nations
shall call him blessed," Psa. xxii. 15, 17.   This brings us
to the last proposition.

IV. THE TESTIMONY OF THE IMPARTIAL AND INFALLIBLE
JUDGE WHO SPEAKS IN OUR TEXT.   " She hath wrought a
good work on me."

It gives me pleasure to say, the Judge is impartial and
infallible; and that he is such, all must admit who believe
revelation.   An earthly judge may be impartial, but not
infallible ; nor does the latter unavoidably secure the
former; but in Mary's Judge, "the Judge of all the earth,"
both meet, and for ever abide.   He sees all motives, and
will pronounce just judgment in all cases, temporal or
spiritual, between man and man, or between man and God.
This is well on various accounts, especially two, upon each
of which I would beg leave a moment to dwell.

1. *It is well because there are so many bad actions in
this world, which at first sight appear good, by which men
of great penetration have been deceived.*

2. *This necessity will appear still greater, by considering how many good actions have appeared the very
reverse in the eyes of spectators.*

The judgment formed upon Mary's good work, by some
of the company, may serve as one striking instance.   Some
may judge you sincere, but pity your weakness; others
may ascribe it to your pride and vanity, declaring it all a
whim—enthusiastic zeal: a work for which you have no
Divine authority, etc.   Care not for any or all of these
reflections.   Your Judge liveth; and, we trust, as he is
perfectly acquainted with your work, so he will, in due
time, say of it, " Ye have wrought a good work for me."

APPLICATION.

1. Suffer me, in the name of the Lord, to entreat all, Look well to your motives! You see it is love to Christ, more than the ointment, which makes the work good and honourable. Dread self-seeking as a deadly enemy, which will taint and spoil the whole.

2. Let all see that Christ puts a high value upon small matters done to him and his followers. When love and gratitude give energy to their abilities, a cup of cold water shall not lose its reward, Mark ix. 41.

3. Again. We learn, from this passage, that carnal, ungodly men think all is lost that is laid out for Christ's honour and interest in the world.

4. Once more. We take it for granted, that most of those present are ready to say, the conversion of the heathen is a very desirable object.

Think, oh! think, how inconsistent, how awful, how dreadful, to appear anxious for the conversion of infidels, and yourselves in an unconverted state—your own souls in danger of everlasting perdition! Suppose you saw a man exerting all his power to assist his neighbour, whose house was on fire; and, at the same moment, his own was in flames, and his family in the utmost hazard; and yet he takes no thought for them, nor makes any attempt for their relief. What would you think of him? You might commend his good-will to his neighbour, but all would condemn his shameful negligence to his dearest relatives!

SKETCH XIX.

THE CHARACTER AND WORK OF THE MESSIAH.

BY THE HON. AND REV. G. T. NOEL, M.A.,*
VICAR OF RAINHAM, KENT.

"Behold, my servant shall deal prudently, He shall be exalted, and extolled, and be very high.   As many were astonished at thee; his visage was so marred more than any man, and his form more than the sons of men: so shall he sprinkle many nations; the kings shall shut their mouths at him: for that which had not been told them shall they see; and that which they had not heard shall they consider."—ISAIAH lii. 13—15.

THREE subjects principally claim our attention in this prophetic record:—The introduction of Christianity into the world, by the mysterious sufferings of its Divine Founder; its complete diffusion over the earth; and the process by which that diffusion will apparently be accomplished.   Each of these points is full of momentous interest.   Let us, then, briefly advert to—

I. THE INTRODUCTION OF CHRISTIANITY INTO THE WORLD, BY THE MYSTERIOUS SUFFERINGS OF ITS DIVINE FOUNDER.

" Behold, my servant!—Many were astonished at thee: his visage was so marred more than any man, and his form more than the sons of men."

This " astonishment of many" evidently refers to the inconsistency apparent, between the high pretensions and the

* From a Sermon, preached at St. Bride's, Fleet Street, May 3, 1819, before the Church Missionary Society.

depressed condition of this Servant of God.   He had been
foretold as "the Desire of all nations," Hag. ii. 7.; the
Shiloh, unto whom should be the gathering of the people,
Gen. xlix. 10; the Ruler, who should come forth from
Judah, to sit upon the throne of David; upon whose
shoulders the government should be laid—and as, emphatically, the "Wonderful" and the "Counsellor," Isa. ix. 6, 7.
A sordid and earthly interpretation had enshrined these
promises in the hearts of the Jewish nation.   The Jewish
patriot hailed, in expectation, the brilliant hour in which
the Messiah should break to shivers the chains which held
his country in subjection to the Roman yoke; while the
man of narrow and selfish ambition, rejoiced in the vision
which gleamed before his eyes, when the descendants of
Abraham should hold dominion over the prostrate nations
of the world.

When, therefore, the Saviour of the world appeared in
the lowly garb of the son of the carpenter of Nazareth;
when he shunned every effort for personal aggrandizement;
when he resisted every popular movement to advance his
regal claims; when he put forth his power, only to heal the
diseased, and to comfort the wretched; when, with a humility which knew no parallel, and with a sympathy which
evinced no exclusion, he constantly mingled with the
meanest and most despised of his countrymen;—then the
mortified expectations of the Jewish rulers burst with
tremendous efficacy on his devoted head.

The evidence, in favour of his high claims, was speedily
examined, and as speedily rejected.   That evidence was
indeed strong, and clear, and palpable.   His character was
unimpeached; his benevolence was diffusive; his power
was undeniable.   "Never man spake like this man;" and,
"It was never so seen in Israel," John vii. 46; Matt. ix. 33.
The accents of his lips had more than once controlled the

swellings of the deep, and startled the inhabitants of the dead. " He saved others !" was the testimony extorted from his enemies at his dying hour. But the union, in his destiny, of power and of suffering—of dignity and contempt—of riches to others, and of poverty to himself,—was the source of astonishment to many. In this destiny, the exhibition of every moral beauty was blended with the exhibition of every form of terror and distress. Angels looked on, and wondered, and adored.

In truth, the plan of Christianity, with its introduction into the world, is far above the calculations of human sagacity. It proved, accordingly, " to the Jews a stumbling-block, and to the Greeks foolishness ;" nevertheless, to him who believeth, it has ever proved, and it will still prove to be, " Christ the power of God, and the wisdom of God," 1 Cor. i. 23, 24. Let us notice,

II. The declaration of the prophet with regard to the universal diffusion of the religion of Christ on the earth. " My servant shall deal prudently. He shall be exalted, and extolled, and be very high."

1. The expression, "*He shall deal prudently,*" is, in the margin, translated, "*He shall prosper;*" and thus the whole clause is declarative of the same truth—the triumph and success of the Son of God. If many were astonished at his humiliation, a far greater number shall be astonished at his exaltation.

2. *This grand and glorious achievement he effected by means that came not within the range of mortal discernment.* It was by death, that he conquered Death. It was by a perfect obedience in action and in suffering, that he became the second Adam—the spiritual Head of a new and happier race. He " was delivered for our offences, and raised again for our justification," Rom. iv. 25; and

thus revived from the dead, He shortly " divided the spoil with the strong." He planted his religion in the earth, opposed by hostile scorn, and relentless malice, and despotic power. In a few years, the banner of the cross waved upon the conquered fortresses of Paganism ; and enlisted under its folds, the great and mighty of the earth. Yet no earthly weapon had been raised in its defence. The cause of Christ achieved its victories by its own inherent power. It was resistless by its truth, and by the silent operation of the Spirit of truth. Its adherents were, indeed, strong ; but it was in faith, and purity, and charity. Thus the Servant of God prospered, and was extolled, and became very high.

3. *But his reign on the earth is yet very limited, and his conquests incomplete.* " There remaineth yet much land to be possessed." Five-sixths of the millions of the human race are still the prey of idolatry or of imposture ; and the ancient people of God are still the outcasts from His favour, and the victims of unbelief. It stands recorded in characters, which no lapse of years can ever erase : " It is a light thing that thou shouldest be my servant to raise up the tribes of Jacob, and to restore the preserved of Israel : I will also give thee for a light to the Gentiles, that thou mayest be my salvation unto the end of the earth," Isa. xlix. 6. We proceed to inquire,

III. WHAT WE MAY GATHER FROM THIS PROPHETIC ACCOUNT RESPECTING THE PROCESS BY WHICH THE KINGDOM OF THE MESSIAH SHALL THUS BE FULLY AND FINALLY ESTABLISHED.

Now, it is declared, " As many were astonished at thee : so shall he sprinkle many nations ; the kings shall shut their mouths at Him : for that which had not been told them shall they see ; and that which they had not heard shall they consider." This passage of Scripture is pregnant with information, as to the PROCESS by which Christianity shall advance to her sacred and ultimate dominion. We are led to infer,

1. *That there shall be a wide dispersion of Divine knowledge over heathen and Mohammedan nations ;* for men cannot see or consider that which is not first presented to their notice. If, then, they shall see and consider that which in former times had not been told them, it follows, that a wide dissemination of Divine knowledge shall take place in the earth. Connect together missionary exertions and the translations of the Scriptures and the education of the young,—connect these with the growing and heavenly sympathy which is dilating itself in the human heart; and say, whether or not, a mighty machinery is at work, directed by God himself, and impelled by the very movements of the Almighty Hand! Let us turn again to the prophetic record: " That which had not been told them shall they see ; and that which they had not heard shall they consider.'' That is,

2. *The nations shall fix their anxious attention on the truths declared to them.* And let me ask, Is there no symptom of the approaching reign of Christ, of this very character, now before our eyes? If the servants of God are becoming active in the cause of their adorable Lord, is no corresponding emotion manifesting itself on the part of the heathen? If the fertilizing dews are beginning to fall from heaven, are there no thirsty lands panting for the shower? Surely, the reports from pagan nations are of the most cheering kind. On every hand there is, more or less, a shaking of old opinions. The kingdom of Satan is dividing against itself.—Nor shall success be long unseen ; for mark again the encouraging statement of the prophet, " The kings shall shut their mouths at him,"—

3. *Impressed with holy awe, they shall assume the atti-*

tude of abasement and submission. I apprehend, that the expression, " the kings shall shut their mouths at him," implies, the submission of whole nations, here represented by kings; for, as the reception of Christianity on the part of the rulers of a country, requires the overthrow of every system of religious polity previously established; such a reception publicly made, implies, more or less, the submission of the mass of the people. Enlightened by the Divine Spirit, they shall at length " behold the Lamb of God," slain to take away " the sins of the world." They shall recognize his righteous claims; they shall receive his law; they shall trust in his grace; they shall bow to his sway. But who can adequately unfold His ultimate and glorious triumph, when

4. *He shall forgive their iniquities and sanctify their hearts?* For, " He shall sprinkle many nations;" that is, in allusion to the aspersions under the law, by which the people were sanctified, the Son of God shall apply to the souls of regenerated multitudes, the blood of His great atonement, and the sacred influences of his Holy Spirit. " Then a nation shall be born in a day." Then the conquests of the Redeemer shall be visible and splendid. Thus shall adoring millions be washed in the blood of Jesus, and shall be presented holy unto the Lord. " Men shall be blessed in him : all nations shall call him blessed," Psa. lxxii. 17.

APPLICATION.

Let me then—1. Suggest to you, in special allusion to the success of our missionary cause, the importance of conducting all our measures in a spirit of prayer.

2. Let us be diligent in the cultivation of personal godliness. Let us, in very deed and spirit, each draw nearer daily to heaven, while labouring to do the work of heaven in the world !

3. Let us cherish a warmer sentiment of gratitude for the gift of the gospel. What a theme is here for gratitude! what an argument for praise! " Who made thee to differ from another? and what hast thou that thou didst not receive?" 1 Cor. iv. 7. Oh! let it be our care to value and improve our mercies. May the blessing never be withdrawn! May the light never be extinguished!

4. But, once more, in reference to this great cause, it seems to be of essential importance, that we cherish a spirit of Christian union and mutual charity. Oh! it is reserved for the glory of the latter days, to merge minuter differences in those grand questions which are the heart and life-blood of the Christian cause—dear to one church as to another, because dear to God, and essential to the repose of man. Then " Ephraim shall not vex Judah, and Judah shall not vex Ephraim," Isa. xi. 13. And truly, it has been pleasant, during the progress of these few last years, to watch the orient leaves of this blessed " unity of the spirit, in the bond of peace;" and to hail them as the harbingers of a brighter day.

Let us solemnly and deliberately cultivate a spirit of tenderness and compassion toward the heathen. Let their actual situation often rest on our remembrance, and have a place in our prayers.

SKETCH XX.

HINDERANCES TO THE SPREAD OF THE GOSPEL.

BY REV. LEONARD WOODS, D.D.*

" For Zion's sake will I not hold my peace, and for Jerusalem's sake I will not rest, until the righteousness thereof go forth as brightness, and the salvation thereof as a lamp that burneth. And the Gentiles shall see thy righteousness, and all kings thy glory."—ISAIAH lxii. 1, 2.

SUCH was the love which the evangelical prophet felt for Jerusalem, and such his desire that its glory might be extended. It was a desire which gave him no rest; but prompted him to incessant labour and prayer for the accomplishment of its object. Desires similar to this have been felt, and similar efforts made, by the faithful servants of God, from age to age, for the propagation of the Christian religion. Since the commencement of the present century, the spread of Christianity has been a subject of growing interest to the friends of religion. Good men have been excited in an unusual degree, to unite their efforts and prayers for the enlargement of the church. The God of heaven has shown, by the promises of his word, and the dispensations of his providence, that he regards this object with the highest favour; and that it is his unalterable purpose, that " the earth shall be filled with his glory." It would certainly be reasonable to expect that the cause of Christianity, thus aided and supported, would soon prevail through the world; that the reign of righteousness and peace would speedily be extended " from the rising of the sun unto the going down thereof." And it becomes a subject of serious inquiry, Why this is not the case? Why

* From a Sermon delivered before the American Board of Commissioners for Foreign Missions, Newhaven, Connecticut, (U. S.), Oct. 5, 1831.

G

has not this blessed cause, which is eminently the cause of God, become universally triumphant?

Our particular inquiry is, What obstacles to the conversion of the world are found among those, who, in different ways, are enlisted in the cause of foreign missions?

I. THE DEFECT OF OUR CHRISTIAN CHARACTER, OR THE WANT OF A HIGHER DEGREE OF HOLINESS.

Before Him who searcheth the heart, "and knoweth all things," and in whose sight " the heavens are not clean;" we must, every one of us, be filled with shame and self-abhorence, and penitently cry out, Behold! I am vile; what shall I answer?

That this imperfection of our Christian character must prove a great hinderance to the success of the cause we are endeavouring to promote, appears from the very nature of that cause. It is the cause of holiness. It is the inward, invisible machinery, (if I may so call it,) which gives efficiency to the external means. It is the spiritual, devont, fervent action of a purified heart, which exerts the most certain and powerful influence in promoting the salvation of men. Who can estimate the amount of good which twelve men, possessing the character of the twelve apostles, might accomplish at the present day?

II. THIS UNHAPPY EFFECT MUST RESULT IN A STILL HIGHER DEGREE, FROM THE DIRECT INDULGENCE OF AFFECTIONS WHICH ARE SELFISH AND EARTHLY.

Selfish, earthly· affections aim at a selfish, earthly interest. But the spread of the gospel through the world is a benevolent and spiritual interest. These two interests are directly opposite to each other; and the dispositions and efforts which are suited to the one are not suited to the other. If worldly and selfish passions prevail in any considerable degree, they will have a visible influence.

III. THE ADVANCEMENT OF CHRIST'S KINGDOM IS ES-
SENTIALLY HINDERED BY DIVISION AND STRIFE AMONG HIS
FOLLOWERS.

The cause of missions must be promoted by the *united*
exertions of ministers and Christians. There is, on the
contrary, too often displayed a clashing of influence. The
efforts actually made for the cause of Christ by one part,
will be more or less resisted, and their good effect prevented, by the counter efforts of another part.

IV. WE MAY HINDER THE CAUSE OF MISSIONS BY THE
UNNECESSARY EXCITEMENT OF POPULAR PREJUDICE.

The missionary enterprise must fail of success, without
the cordial affection and support of the Christian community. It essentially needs the aid of their efforts, contributions, and prayers. Now, if those who are intrusted
with the sacred interests of missions, are chargeable with
any misconduct, or any manifest indiscretion; such misconduct or indiscretion proclaimed, as it will be, in the
ears of the public, may cool the affections, excite prejudices,
and prevent the contributions and prayers of thousands.

V. WE HINDER THE SPREAD OF THE GOSPEL, SO FAR AS
WE FALL SHORT IN OUR DUTY IN REGARD TO THE BENE-
VOLENT USE OF PROPERTY.

Just in proportion to the magnitude and excellence of
the object, should be our liberality in contributing of our
substance for its promotion.

Brethren, suffer me to speak freely. The Christian community has of late years been waking up, in a measure,
to better views in regard to the proper value and use of
money; and many examples have been exhibited of a very
honourable liberality in contributing to benevolent objects.
But is not the prevailing, practical sentiment still very far

below the right standard? Can it be that men of wealth make the cause of Christ their great object, when they generally give it so small a proportion of their substance? The only remaining obstacle to the spread of the gospel which I shall mention, is,

VI. THE WANT OF A PROPER FEELING AND ACKNOWLEDGMENT OF OUR DEPENDANCE ON GOD FOR THE SUCCESS OF OUR EFFORTS.

There is nothing which stands in more direct opposition to the truth, than the spirit of pride and self-dependance. For whatever importance we may attach to our own efforts in the work of evangelizing the world, and whatever good we may expect from the faithful labours of missionaries; yet all success comes from God. In the most favourable circumstances, therefore, nothing can be effectually done to bring men into the kingdom of Christ, except by the special operation of God.

APPLICATION.

1. We have now seen what are the obstacles to the accomplishment of the great and excellent work we have undertaken. Let us keep these obstacles out of the way, and the religion of Christ will soon make rapid progress.

Finally. Let us never forget that it is owing to the grace of God, that the cause of Christianity, with so many obstacles in its way, has made such progress in the world. Is it not rather a matter of wonder, that this light of the world has not been totally extinguished, than that it does not shine more brightly? Is it not a miracle of Divine power, that religion maintains a place in the world, and is making any progress, when there is so much to oppose it, even among its friends? Let, then, the pride of man be abased; let every high thought be brought low, and let God alone be exalted.

SKETCH XXI.

THE FULNESS OF THE TIMES.

BY REV. JOHN HEY, OF BRISTOL.*

"That in the dispensation of the fulness of times he might gather together in one all things in Christ, both which are in heaven, and which are on earth; even in him.—EPH. i. 10.

In the discussion of this subject, our thoughts will be employed, firstly, in meditating on the important period specified in the text; and, secondly, on that glorious work which will be accomplished during the same.

I. THE IMPORTANT PERIOD SPECIFIED IN THE TEXT.

The apostle calls it, "The dispensation of the fulness of times;" by which he intends, a marvellous season of grace, which has not yet taken place—at least, in the fullest sense of the words. To discover the import, strength, and beauty of these expressions, we must fix our attention,

1. *On the times referred to.* The Bible speaks of various times: such as, times appointed, times predicted, " times or the seasons, which the Father hath put in his own power," Acts i. 7.

(1.) We read of times of ignorance. Our world has been most awfully afflicted with times of mental obscurity: " Darkness shall cover the earth, and gross darkness the people," Isa. lx. 2.

* From a Sermon, preached at the Tabernacle, September 23, 1795, before the London Missionary Society.

(2.) A time of error and general defection from the primitive faith. The author of the second Epistle to the Thessalonians, describes this event in the predictive language of "falling away," 2 Thes. ii. 3. This almost universal declension had a surprising effect on the professors of Christianity, and produced an astonishing alteration both in the state and the appearance of things; for from this alarming apostacy resulted—

(3.) A time of awful superstition. The most ridiculous, not to say blasphemous modes of worship, were now invented; an almost endless train of contemptible, unmeaning, and useless ceremonies, were introduced into the pretended worship of God.

(4.) A time of tremendous persecution began under the reign of the papal beast. This persecution raged with unabating fury for several ages.

(5.) The time of the glorious Reformation. This was a time of joy and prosperity to the church of God. Truth now began to shine in its native lustre and beauty.

(6.) We are now brought to that period referred to in the text. We have glanced at times of almost every description: times of ignorance, defection, superstition, persecution, light, and reformation; at length we are arrived at the period called "the fulness of times!" God, "who worketh all things after the counsel of his own will," hath, in his unerring wisdom, given permission to new and false prophets—sin and hell, popes and devils—to exert their utmost rage and influence in opposition to his cause and interest in the world. And now, to confound these mighty adversaries of his church, he will bring on, in the end of those times, a dispensation of incomparable glory. This is styled in our text, "The dispensation of the fulness of times." This thought introduces the subsequent part of the subject:—

II. THAT GLORIOUS WORK WHICH WILL BE ACCOMPLISHED
DURING THIS WONDERFUL DISPENSATION.

The nature of this work is expressed under the idea of
gathering " together in one all things in Christ," etc.; viz.,
to incorporate in one body, or unite in one complete system,
all things in heaven and on earth. This presupposes that
a disunion and disagreement have taken place between the
various ranks of beings which God hath made. Several
considerations unite to corroborate this idea. But, notwithstanding these awful breaches, the Lord JEHOVAH will fulfil
his gracious purpose, to " gather together in one all things
in Christ, both which are in heaven and which are on
earth."

(1.) When the apostle asserts, that God will "gather together in one all things in Christ," he means, that all things
in creation, together with every event of Divine Providence
and effect of sovereign grace, are, and will be, so connected,
as to compose one grand system of universal economy; in
which all the perfections of Deity will shine forth with ineffable splendour and glory.

(2.) The inhabitants of different climes, customs, colours,
habits, and pursuits, both in Christian and Pagan lands,
shall be united in one large society under the genial influence of gospel grace, so that " there shall be one fold,
and one shepherd," John x. 16.

(3.) These words may signify farther, that human and
angelic intelligences will be associated in harmony and love.
Our adorable Immanuel has informed us, that the time will
come, when the millions of redeemed men shall be as the
angels of God in heaven, Matt. xxii. 30. The grand instrument by which this amazing work will be accomplished,
is the glorious gospel of God our Saviour. All things are
to be gathered together in Christ, even in Him; viz., in
his name, through his mediation, and by his power. The

great commission with which the heralds of salvation are invested, is to go and preach repentance and remission of sins, in Immanuel's name, among all nations. To inform them, " that God was (and still is) in Christ, reconciling the world unto himself, not imputing their trespasses unto them," 2 Cor. v. 19.

There are weighty reasons to be assigned, why this important work will be effected by the instrumentality of the gospel of Christ.

1. *It is superior to all other systems.* The superiority of the Christian system appears,

(1.) In the excellency of its doctrines. They are remarkably perspicuous, simple, and plain; though, at the same time, inconceivably sublime.

(2.) In the glory of its promises. It ensures to all who embrace it, inviolable security, strong consolation, and ample support under all the trials of the present state. It promises hope and joy in death; and beyond the grave, " an inheritance, incorruptible and undefiled, and that fadeth not away," 1 Pet. i. 4.

(3.) In the purity of its precepts. The threatenings contained in the Bible render it a fit instrument for converting the heathen.

2. *The success which has heretofore attended the preaching of the gospel, evinces it to be the proper instrument for the conversion of mankind.*

3. *Our expectations, as to the spread and prevalence of the gospel, are greatly encouraged by the promises which the Divine Father has made to his incarnate Son.* " Ask of me, and I shall give thee the heathen for thine inheritance, and the uttermost parts of the earth for thy possession." " It is a light thing that thou shouldest be my servant to raise up the tribes of Jacob, and to restore the preserved of Israel: I will also give thee for a light to the Gentiles,

that thou mayest be my salvation unto the end of the earth,"
Psa. ii. 8; Isa. xlix. 6. Can everlasting veracity fail to
accomplish such promises as these? No! "Till heaven
and earth pass, one jot or one tittle shall in no wise pass
from the law, till all be fulfilled," Matt. v. 18.

APPLICATION.

1. From a review of what has passed under our notice
at this time, we may derive encouragement as to our present momentous undertaking. That Arm which stands
engaged to bring salvation to the heathen, is omnipotent.
He that hath promised to gather the outcasts of the people
is JEHOVAH, and his designs cannot fail. "He is the Rock,
his work is perfect," Deut. xxxii. 4.

2. But with all this encouragement, let us not forget
our province, as to a vigorous, diligent, and persevering use
of means. The means are now before us; and that important plan, by which our active endeavours will be regu-
lated, is now formed.

3. In order to animate our minds and stimulate our
efforts, we ought to contemplate the delightful effects which
will result from our united exertions, when succeeded by
the blessing of God!

What a pleasing change now takes place! How different the aspect of those countries where the gospel hath
come with invincible energy. The seed of life is sown—
heavenly dews descend upon it—it takes root—springs
forth, and produces " some thirty, and some sixty, and some
an hundredfold," Mark iv. 8.

SKETCH XXII.

IMPREGNABLE SECURITY OF ISRAEL & GOD'S WONDROUS DOINGS ON THEIR BEHALF.

" Surely there is no enchantment against Jacob, neither is there any divination against Israel : according to this time it shall be said of Jacob and of Israel, What hath God wrought !"—NUMBERS xxiii. 23.

BALAK, king of the Moabites, anxious to rid himself of the children of Israel, whose tents were now pitched in the plains around him, sent for Balaam, that he might curse them.   It is evident that the spirit of true prophecy rested on this individual; but influenced by the love of sordid gain, he lent himself to Balak, and endeavoured to do his bidding.   God placed a variety of hinderances in his way, that he might return to the path of rectitude, and not attempt the execution of Balak's commission.   But, blinded by avarice, he went on and on, until God allowed his own infatuations to have the ascendancy, so that he became the miserable victim of his own worldliness.   But though willing to do Balak's work, yet, when the time came, he was impelled, by the Spirit of God, to predict of Israel the most glorious things.   Instead of declaring evil, he proclaimed the enrapturing prophecy recorded in Numb. xxiii. 8, etc.

A second attempt elicited the declaration in verses 18— 24: the conclusion of which is the subject of our present discourse.   How true is the text of Israel of old!   No evil spirit of enchantment could affect them.   No spirit of divination injure them.   The magicians of Egypt could mimic Moses, but only in adding to the misery of the Egyptians: but neither earth nor hell can injure those who "trust in the Lord: he is their help and their shield," Psa. cxv. 9. Applying our text to the children of God, consider,

I. THE TRUTH AFFIRMED. "Surely there is no enchantment against Jacob," etc.

II. THE EXCLAMATION UTTERED.

I. THE TRUTH AFFIRMED. "Surely there is no enchantment," etc. We enter not into the discussion, how far men may have had power from Satan to "enchant," to "divine," or to "curse" others. But we abide by the text, that there is no such thing against the cause and people of God. Hell is opposed to the cause of God; and united with it are the wicked powers of earth. They have the disposition, the will, the purpose, and may make the attempt to injure the church; but their efforts must fail—their plots must be frustrated—their attacks must be powerless.

Yet sometimes they have been able to harrass, and vex, and torture the people of God. Sometimes, they have apparently succeeded and triumphed; but really and eventually they must be frustrated. "For surely there is no enchantment," etc. Now, the certainty of this may be inferred,

1. *Because the counsels of God are more than sufficient to baffle the designs and plots of hell.*

We would not array human skill and tact against the wiles and stratagems of the devil. But the security of the church depends on the counsels of God: on the infinite wisdom of the Most High. He knows how to frustrate the devices of evil, and how to deliver those who trust in his name. His eyes are open to the thoughts and plots of the wicked; and hell has no covering before Him. Hence, he is the Watcher and Keeper of Israel, and neither slumbers nor sleeps, Psa. cxxi. 4.

2. *Because the power of Jehovah is ever effectual in thwarting the attacks of the enemies of his people.*

Divine wisdom and omniscience is united with resistless power. His mandate gave being to the universe: " He spake, and it was done: he commanded, and it stood fast," Psa. xxxiii. 9. The volition of his own mind and will, would overwhelm the fallen spirits with confusion and terror. All created power is mere impotency before him : how, then, can the powers of evil ruin the church, and over-throw the cause of the Eternal?

3. *Because Divine goodness is more than enough to counteract the malevolence of our foes.*

The wisdom and power of God are combined with im-measurable love. The institutions of the church are those of God's heart. His people are as the apple of his eye, Deut. xxxii. 10. " Behold, I have graven thee on the palms of my hands," Isa. xlix. 16. He has covenanted with them, to sustain, to keep, to preserve, to deliver, to glorify them. " Surely there is no enchantment against Jacob, neither is there any divination against Israel."

4. *The resources of God are more than adequate to render all the means of the church's enemies abortive.*

The enemy can combine various elements of evil—the wrath and power of fallen legions, craft and subtility; the wealth and influence of the world, the fascinations of earth, etc.; and all these have successively been employed. But all resources are Jehovah's: the angels of His presence, the stars of heaven, the sun and the moon; storms, and winds, and tempest; earthquakes, pestilence, and famine; locusts, and even flies, can effect his bidding. " Surely the wrath of man shall praise thee : the remainder of wrath shalt thou restrain," Psa. lxxvi. 10. On these grounds, we may well say, " Surely there is no enchantment," etc.

II. THE EXCLAMATION UTTERED.—" According to this time it shall be said of Jacob and of Israel," etc.

1. *What is to be said?* "What hath God wrought!" All deliverances are to be traced up to God. Agents are to be observed, but God only praised : God alone is to have the glory, as he has had the real work of delivering his people. This is to keep up our dependence on God. This is to inspire with adoration and praise. This is to keep human nature in its right place.

Not what Moses did in Egypt, or Joshua, or Gideon, or David, or the apostles, or the first martyrs, or the reformers, or Wesley, or Whitfield; but " What hath GOD wrought!" There is a tendency to lose sight of God, or to make God secondary; but it ought ever to be—" What hath God wrought!"

2. *Who are to say it?* Sometimes even enemies have said it. Balaam was forced to see it, and in the text to speak it.

(1.) It should be said especially by the ministers of the gospel: they are to draw attention to the doings of Jehovah; they are to extol the Lord, to celebrate the works of his hand, to speak of the glory of his kingdom, and talk of his power, Psa. cxlv. 10, etc.

(2.) It should be said by all the pious. Parents to their children—teachers to their pupils—Christians to one another. Thus the psalmist (lxxvii. 11,) " I will remember the works of the Lord," etc.; and thus the prophet Isaiah exclaims, (xii. 4, etc.,) " Praise the Lord," etc.

3. *When should it be said?*

(1.) It should be said in times of depression, as the means of consolation. However low, or destitute, or afflicted, yet so it has often been—that God has " remembered us in our low estate : for his mercy endureth for ever," Psa. cxxxvi. 23.

(2.) In times of great exertion, as an incitement to perseverance. Hope cheers, and renews with vigour for the toil. Never forget that the success is certain. Your efforts must avail,—" Surely," etc.

(3.) In times of great success, to give tone to our exultations. We then have former days brought to our remembrance. Thus reminded of God's doings of old, with grateful, rapturous joy we exclaim, " What hath God wrought!"

(4.) It will be reiterated in the world of the beatified for ever. There they will see, in one beautiful series, the doings of God—behold the golden chain entire. There the philosophy of Providence will be elucidated, and its harmony with redemption made clear as with letters of light.

APPLICATION.

1. Our text may apply to many as to their Christian experience before God. " Remember all the way which the Lord thy God led thee," etc., Deut. viii. 2.

2. The text is appropriate to Christian missions. What enemies, difficulties, and discouragements have been overcome and surmounted. Well may we exclaim, " What hath God wrought!" Let India—the islands of the South Sea—the deserts of Africa—the West Indies—New Zealand, etc., all testify.

3. Let God ever be exalted for the blessings we enjoy; and for all the good done in us, and by us.

SKETCH XXIII.

THE LIGHT OF THE GENTILES.

BY REV. W. B. COLLYER, D.D.*

"A light to lighten the Gentiles."—LUKE ii. 32.

WE shall endeavour to explain the import of the text, and to apply its testimony to missionary exertions. In explaining its import, we shall discover that the character of Jesus is represented under the image of "Light;" that the subjects of his influences are "the Gentiles;" and that the result of these things taken together, or, in other words, his manifestation to the world, is universal illumination— for he rises upon the nations to lighten them. In applying this testimony to missionary exertions, we shall find that it explains the principles upon which they are founded; and evinces that they proceed from nature, reason, humanity, patriotism, and religion. We shall be induced to examine the encouragements which this testimony affords; and shall find that they arise from revelation, from experience, and from existing circumstances. This is the ground on which we wish to prove that Missionary Societies are worthy your countenance and support, by showing that the work is of God, and that the heart and the understanding alike pay homage to its excellence.

I. WE SHALL ENDEAVOUR TO EXPLAIN THE IMPORT OF THE TEXT, "A light to lighten the Gentiles." Observe,

* Preached before the Missionary Society, at Surrey Chapel, May 9, 1810.

1. *The character of Jesus is exhibited under the image of " light."*   A more appropriate and more beautiful symbol could not have been selected, whether it be applied to the Saviour himself, or to his influence on the world.   In both these cases it is employed in the text, and in both of them it will be necessary to examine the figure.   Light is the most glorious of all the creatures of God ; and is, therefore, a singularly appropriate image in reference to the uncreated glory of the Son of God.   If, therefore, light convey to the mind an idea of glory, it is a fit emblem of Him, " by whom all things were created, that are in heaven, and that are in earth, visible and invisible, whether they be thrones, or dominions, or principalities, or powers :· all things were created by him, and for him : and he is before all things, and by him all things consist," Col. i. 16.

(1.) Among the properties of light, are penetration and universality.   It is said of the sun, " His going forth is from the end of the heaven, and his circuit unto the ends of it : and there is nothing hid from the heat thereof," Psa. xix. 6.   Light would have been an inappropriate image, in reference to Christ, had he not intended to illuminate the world.   Not to a district, nor to an empire, nor to one quarter of the globe, does that glorious boon of heaven—light—confine its influences.   It visits all in their turn—it burns within the torrid zone, and. reaches the dark and distant poles : it proceeds with gradual, yet inconceivable speed, in its restless career, till it has enlightened the whole.

(2.) Light is a source of comfort.   " Truly the light is sweet, and a pleasant thing it is for the eyes to behold the sun," Eccl. xi. 7.

(3.) Another quality of light, is purity.   It is this which renders it a fit emblem of Deity ; and which induced the apostle John to say, " God is light, and in him is no darkness at all," 1 John i. 5.

2. *The subjects of his influences, " The Gentiles."*
The original word signifies no more than *nations*, literally,
both in the Old and New Testaments. The confinement
of the oracles of truth to the Jewish people, caused nations
and heathen, or people who knew not the true God, to
be considered synonymous. Our English word heathen, is
derived from the word employed in the text: so that the
object of Missionary Societies is one of the express objects of the incarnation of our Lord; and the subjects of
his influences, promised in the text, are those who have
excited, at this time, your Christian sympathy.

3. *The result of the manifestation of Christ to the world,
will be universal illumination.* He rises upon the nations
" to lighten" them. The state of mankind, considered as
destitute of this light, is a state of most deplorable darkness. We include in this figurative expression, the absence
of knowledge and of comfort. They that live " without
God," of necessity live " without hope." The text pro-
poses a remedy as wide as the disease, and promises deliverance from this state of darkness and misery, while it
preaches Christ as " a light to lighten the Gentiles."

II. To APPLY ITS TESTIMONY TO MISSIONARY EXERTIONS,
OF WHICH WE HAVE NOT ENTIRELY LOST SIGHT IN THE
EXPOSITION.

1. *Let us examine the principles on which they are
founded.* These are of the highest order; and from them
the greatest effects may be anticipated.

(1.) They are founded in nature. As man is a compound
being, his actions are generally the result of many principles, bearing, at the same time, upon one point. This is
the fact relative to the exertions this day examined; and
it is at present our business to analyze and to arrange these,
that by viewing them separately, we may be able to

appreciate them as a whole. It is a principle of nature, that the same cause should produce the same effects. Whoever sincerely loves the Saviour, will feel a proportionate attachment to his laws, his people, and his interests. He cannot sit down indifferent to the last, any more than he can consent to break the first.

(2.) Missionary exertions are founded on the purest principles of reason. It is consistent with right reason, to connect means with the end. This Society has been charged with enthusiasm in what? That they expect the universal diffusion of religious knowledge? No such thing! This point is so generally admitted, that it appears impossible to hold the Bible, and to doubt the fact. In what, then, consists their enthusiasm? That they have embodied their faith in the adoption of those means which have received the sanction of all ages; and, having done so, that they wait not without hope, but with patient and chastened expectation, the success of their labours, and the fulfilment of the Divine promise. But, it is objected, that right reason always employs means proportionate to the end. What means could be deemed proportionate to such an end? Nothing less than Omniscience could draw a plan completely adequate to such a design; and nothing less than Omnipotence could execute it. The first has been done, and the last is gradually performing by the Deity himself. In the meanwhile, he employs, for the execution of all his purposes, human instruments; and we shall hereafter prove, that the means adopted by this Society are of his own ordination.

(3.) Missionary exertions are founded on the purest principles of humanity. We have described the world as in a state of deplorable ignorance and pollution. The consequences are bitter and inevitable. The empire of sin, must be an empire broken up by the ploughshare of calamity. The tyranny of moral evil is felt in the riot of wide-wasting sorrow, and the victories of unsparing death.

(4.) Missionary exertions are founded on the purest principles of patriotism. What lover of his country does not desire to see her the leader of this great work—the reformation of mankind, and the subversion of depravity? When God gave Jerusalem to desolation, it was not while she was " very zealous," or, in modern language, very enthusiastic " for the Lord of hosts;" but when she ceased to feel an interest in His cause, and when she sunk into the most criminal indifference. Religious lethargy precedes national ruin ; patriotism, therefore, calls for the support of religious zeal.

(5.) Missionary exertions are founded on the purest principles of religion. Religion adopts and influences all the springs of action which we have named, and all the properties of the human mind of every description. Religion directs the will, mollifies the passions, regulates the affections. Religion fosters the feelings of nature, guides the researches of reason, elicits the charities of humanity, kindles the fire of patriotism, while her own honour is singularly concerned in this great cause. As her name has been borrowed by ambition and superstition, it is time for her to discover herself in her native majesty. When the Druid slew a man and a brother in the consecrated circle, he called his murderous act a religious rite. The wretched Indian, who lays himself down to be crushed to death' under the car of some idol, thinks he is paying homage to religion. But real religion urges the use of all the means which reason points out, and stimulates all the sympathies which nature, or humanity, or patriotism acknowledge.

2. *The considerations by which we are encouraged.*

(1.) Missionary exertions are encouraged by revelation. We will not at this time, in making our appeal " to the law and to the testimony," recapitulate those sublime predictions, and those numerous promises, which relate to the final triumph of Jesus over all his adversaries, and the universal extension of his kingdom—passages which have been so largely produced, and so ably discussed on these occasions. One shall suffice : " The kingdoms of this world are become the kingdoms of our Lord, and of his Christ; and he shall reign for ever and ever," Rev. xi. 15.

(2.) Missionary exertions are encouraged by experience. The lapse of years lays the adversaries of Christianity dead at its foot; while it has acquired vigour from that which impairs every thing earthly, and received evidences from the destroying hand which sweeps into oblivion every record of this world.

(3.) Missionary exertions are encouraged, further, by existing circumstances,—by the existing circumstances of the Society. We are not ashamed to appeal to its influence at home, and abroad; and to call upon its adversaries to examine what it has actually effected. But what have you done abroad? Is there occasion to ask this question? Look at our reports, and the publication of our transactions: Is it nothing to maintain missionaries in so many remote parts of the world? Is it nothing to acquire languages, not reduced to any grammatical standard, so as to address the heathen in their own tongues? Is it nothing to have their children catechised weekly, and instructed in the fundamental principles of Christianity? Is it nothing to receive Hottentots into Christian Britain, to instruct professors in their own principles? Is it nothing to translate the Scriptures into languages which never before conveyed the word of truth to those who speak them? This, and more than this, the Society has effected.

(4.) Missionary exertions are further encouraged by the existing circumstances of the world. If we feel the curse in à more sensible degree, the more vigorous should be our exertions to disseminate that which shall destroy the curse. In this single quarter of the globe, amidst the ruin that has marked the progress of ambition, and the calamities attending a state of warfare, protracted almost beyond precedent in any age, the spirit of religion is cultivated, the worship of God is maintained, and peace finds a refuge still from the persecutions of overweening power, and of cruel oppression.

While England is spared, Europe cherishes the fond hope of future deliverance from her present chains; and, with still more animated expectation, fixes her eyes upon this country, as the storehouse of spiritual communications, whence her future supplies are to be drawn. Support missionary exertions, and realize her dream of approaching happiness! Moreover, the awful and impressive features of the present times, correspond with those which distinguished the appearance of our Lord. " For thus saith the Lord of hosts: Yet once, it is a little while, and I will shake the heavens, and the earth, and the sea, and the dry land; and I will shake all nations, and the desire of all nations shall come," Hag. ii. 6. If this prophecy was partially fulfilled at the birth of Christ, it remains to be more completely accomplished now: for he is not as yet revealed as " the Desire of all nations;" and we hope, not without reason, that these dreadful convulsions announce his approach.

APPLICATION.

1. Such are the encouragements to missionary exertions. Nor ought we to be disheartened at the narrowness of our means, when contrasted with the immensity of our design.

2. Let the disciple of the tender and compassionate Jesus, in this assembly, calmly behold the progress of moral evil, the parent of calamity, without making one effort to

arrest it in its furious and malignant course, if he can. Let him exult in his personal advantages, and see others perishing for want of them unmoved! Let him say, with benevolent John, " We know that we are of God, and the whole world lieth in wickedness;" but not in his compassionate tone, and with his bowels of tenderness—if he can. Let him, with selfish appetite, sit down to a board covered with religious plenty—to the elements, the pledges of his Master's death—without sending one morsel to the poor heathen, or affording them the crumbs which fall from this table—if he can. Let him contemplate the spirit and purpose of his Master, and withhold his hand from the work—if he can. And then will we, at the second appearance of our Lord, tell, before heaven and earth, that we pleaded a cause for which Jesus shed the last drop of his heart's-blood—and pleaded in vain!

SKETCH XXIV.

GROUNDS OF THE MISSIONARY WORK.

BY REV. C. D. GRIFFIN, D.D.,*

PRESIDENT OF WILLIAMS' COLLEGE, U. S.

"And Jesus came and spake unto them, saying, All power is given unto
me in heaven and in earth.   Go ye therefore, and teach all nations, baptizing them in the name of the Father, and of the Son, and of the Holy
Ghost: teaching them to observe all things whatsoever I have commanded
you: and, lo, I am with you alway, even unto the end of the world."
MATT. xxviii. 18—20.

I RISE to advocate the cause of missions to the heathen, and
to plead for a dying world.   My sole object is to enforce
the claims of five hundred millions of perishing men, by
some plain and simple arguments which have affected my
own mind: and I have chosen this text because it contains
some of the arguments, and suggests the rest.   Both the
authority of Christ, and his personal reward, are here distinctly brought to bear on the subject.   For his "obedience
unto death" he received the inheritance, including "the
heathen" and "the uttermost parts of the earth," Psa. ii. 8;
and the authority to manage the whole estate. This authority
he employed in sending forth missionaries to disciple all nations, and to bring to him the unnumbered millions promised
for his seed.   My argument, then, is founded,

* From a Sermon, preached September 14, 1826, before the American
Board of Missions, at Middletown, Connecticut.

I. ON THE AUTHORITY OF CHRIST.

The injunction in the text was not addressed to the eleven exclusively, but to them as depositaries of the Divine commands; and, through them, to the whole body of ministers in every age. This appears from the promise subjoined, "Lo, I am with you alway, even unto the end of the world!" Indeed, the eleven were expressly commanded to transmit to their successors all the injunctions which they themselves received, one of which was to disciple all nations. "Go ye therefore, and teach all nations,—teaching them to observe all things whatsoever I have commanded you." This command is now sounding in the ears of the ministers and churches of the nineteenth century.

II. THE EXAMPLE OF CHRIST AND HIS APOSTLES.

The Saviour of the world sent out a band of missionaries, and charged them " to preach the gospel to every creature; —and they went forth and preached everywhere" that man should repent, Mark xvi. 15, 20. No one objection can be raised against missions, at the present day, which will not equally lie against Christ and his apostles. The attempt is no more presumptuous now, than then; the prospect is no more discouraging; the difficulties are no greater; the power that is engaged to give success is the same, for the promise remains unchanged, " Lo, I am with you alway, even unto the end of the world." My argument is founded,

III. IN WHAT WE OWE TO THE HEATHEN.

Is the gospel no blessing to you? And would it not be an equal blessing to them? And are we not bound to extend to others all the happiness in our power? To say that Pagans can be as happy without the gospel as with it, is to say that the gospel is no blessing to men; and then you do not believe that it came from God? If the gospel would be no blessing to the heathen, why do you preach or support it at home?

IV. THE SACRIFICES OF THE MISSIONARIES THEMSELVES, AND THE DEBT OF GRATITUDE WHICH WE OWE THEM.

To see interesting youths, with the spirits of martyrs, offering themselves to die under an Indian or an African sun; for the love of Christ, tearing themselves from parents and brothers and sisters, to see them no more; taking an eternal leave of the scenes and companions of their youth; abandoning their native shore, and their native tongue, to bear the tidings of a precious Saviour to distant nations. To see delicate young females, who have been dandled in the lap of parental tenderness, with a heroism which nothing but Christian principles could support, tearing themselves, for the last time, from the arms of trembling mothers and speechless sisters, to encounter the dangers of the seas, and the still greater dangers of a torrid clime, in order to support their husbands by their smiles and prayers in a foreign land, among darkened Pagans. This is a scene which makes selfishness blush and hang its head; which shames all the ordinary piety which is couched in ease at home, trembling at self-denials. I beseech you to follow these precious youths with your prayers, and your tenderest concern. They have gone in the service of our Father's family—they sacrifice all for us. Shall we not follow them, with the interest of brothers and sisters, through the groves of India, and forests of America? and when we hear of their trials, their dangers, their escapes, their successes, shall we not feel as though we were receiving accounts from our near kindred? When they tell us of the triumphs of Hindoo converts; or send to our ears the young hosannahs of Syrian or Sandwich children; shall we not mingle our songs with theirs, and join in the joy, as though they were bone of our

H

bone and flesh of our flesh? Yes, dear missionaries, we will remember you, and all the sacrifices you have made, till these hearts shall cease to beat. God Almighty go with you, and keep you in the hollow of His hand, till we meet you in heaven.

V. FOREIGN MISSIONS ARE LIKELY TO PROVE THE MOST GLORIOUS MEANS OF GRACE TO US AT· HOME.

While you are feeling for pagan souls, and sending your sons to them, I firmly believe that your prayers and bounty will return into your own bosoms. Such confidence I have in God, for I have heard him say, " He that watereth shall be watered also himself," Prov. xi. 25. I believe that while you are anxious to raise heathen nations from death, you will be enabled to shake off your grave clothes yourselves; that while you are seeking to draw forth Indian children from their sepulchres, and present them alive to their rejoicing parents, your own children will start into life by your side; that while the love of distant nations glows in our hearts, it will melt us all down into love to each other, and burn up all our jealousies and strifes. Some of these effects I seem already to discern. God grant that they may increase, until the joy of America shall respond to that of Asia, and in one burst of praise rise united to heaven. May your charities return into your own bosom, and that of your children, for days and years, and an eternity to come!

VI. ALL THE WEALTH OF THE WORLD WAS GIVEN TO CHRIST AS A RECOMPENSE FOR REDEEMING OUR SOULS; AND SHALL THE INGRATITUDE OF MAN WITHHOLD FROM HIM HIS HIRE?

It will not always be thus. The time will come, when " Holiness unto the Lord" shall be written on all the possessions of men,—on the very "bells of the horses;" and when "the pots in the Lord's house," (those used for culinary purposes, in the families of the priests,) "shall," in point of holiness, "be like the bowls before the altar," which received the blood of the victims until it was sprinkled; and when "every pot in Jerusalem and in Judah shall be holiness unto the Lord of hosts," Zech. xiv. 20, 21. The common vessels used to dress our food, instead of being regarded as instruments of luxury or display, like our Bibles and psalm-books shall be all for God. Men will write "Holiness unto the Lord" on every shilling, and on every foot of ground. They will no longer labour to hoard, but to do good. That will be such a generation as has not yet appeared. A few scattered individuals have approached towards this character; but the mass of mankind, in every age, have held their property as their own, and not as a sacred deposit.

VII. These exertions are necessary to bring to Christ the seed and the kingdom, the victory and the triumph, promised him as his reward.

This world belongs to Christ. No other being has a right to erect an interest on this ground. And yet, after the lapse of eighteen centuries, two-thirds of the earth remain in Pagan, or Mohammedan darkness. Ought so great a part of a world which Christ has redeemed and owns, to continue in the hands of his enemy? If the suffrages of nations were to be collected, what would a redeemed race say? To whom would they assign a world given to Christ for redeeming them. Would they resign it to his enemy, who has despoiled it of its Eden, and covered it with briers and thorns, and turned it into a great charnel-house? or, would they give it to Him who came to rescue it from the hands of destroying devils, and died to save their souls? What is the vote of a redeemed race on this subject? If human instrumentality is wanted to drive the usurper from his seat, shall not a whole race rise up to the effort?

APPLICATION.

1. And now, my beloved brethren, I invite you to go with me, and look for a moment over the interesting scene which is opening on earth. For many years the Christian world had been sunk in a profound slumber in regard to this duty; but for the last four and thirty years they have been waking up. He who has "engraven Zion on the palms of hands," who never wants means to fulfil his promises, has sent his heavenly influence to rouse the Christian world.

2. We owe the sincerest gratitude to God for giving us our existence in such a day as this. "Many prophets and kings have desired to see those things which ye see, and have not seen them; and to hear those thing which ye hear, and have not heard them," Luke x. 24. One spirit has seized the Christian world, to send the gospel, with a great company of its publishers, to all the nations of the earth. Missionary and Bible societies, those stupendous monuments of Christian charity, have risen so rapidly, and in so great numbers throughout Europe and America, that in contemplating them, we are "like them that dream."

3. My soul is enlarged, and stands erect as I look down the declivity of years, and see the changes which these young Davids, under God, will make in all the earth. Countless millions are shortly to awake from the darkness and sleep of a hundred ages, to hail the day which will never go down. I see the darkness rolling upon itself and passing away from a thousand lands. I see a cloudless day following, and laying itself over all the earth. I see the nations coming up from the neighbourhood of the brutes, to the dignity of the sons of God,—from the stye

in which they had wallowed, to the purity of the Divine image. I see the meekness of the gospel assuaging their ferocious passions, melting down a million contending units in one, silencing the clamour of arms, and swelling into life a thousand budding charities which had died under the long winter. I hear the voice of their joy—it swells from the valleys, and echoes from the hills. I already hear, on the eastern breeze, the songs of new-born nations. I already catch, on the western gale, the praise of a thousand islands. I ascend the Alps, and see the darkness retiring from the Papal world. I ascend the Andes, and see South America, and all the islands of the Pacific, one altar. I ascend the mountains of Thibet, and hear from the plains of China, and from the jungle and pagoda of Hindoostan, the praises of the living God. I see all Asia bowing before Him, who, eighteen centuries ago, hung in the midst of them on Calvary. I traverse oceans, and hear from every floating Bethel the songs of the redeemed.

> " The dwellers in the vales, and on the rocks,
> Shout to each other ; and the mountain tops,
> From distant mountains, catch the flying joy ;
> Till, nation after nation taught the strain,
> Earth rolls the rapturous hosanna round."

Come that blessed day! Let my eyes once behold the sight, and then give this worthless body to the worms.

SKETCH XXV.

THE SACRIFICE AND TRIUMPH OF CHRIST.

BY REV. W. ATHERTON.*

" But this man, after he had offered one sacrifice for sins, for ever sat down on the right hand of God; from henceforth expecting till his enemies be made his footstool."—HEB. x. 12, 13.

THE apostle is showing, in this chapter, the superiority of the sacrifice and priesthood of Jesus Christ, when compared with those sacrifices which were offered, and those priests that gave attendance, at the Jewish altar; and on which things the Hebrew Christians had trusted for acceptance with God. He shows their great superiority by a variety of arguments. The first argument is drawn from the priesthood of the people. "Every high priest taken from among men is ordained for men in things pertaining to God, that he may offer both gifts and sacrifices for sin," Heb. v. 1; but the Christian's High Priest, is "the Lord from heaven"—"God over all, blessed for evermore." The Jewish high priests, in their official ministrations, had first to offer sacrifices for their own sins, which was a tacit confession that they were sinners. The Christian's High Priest, however, was without sin; he knew no sin, had no sin of his own to atone for, and was perfectly fitted to make atonement for the sins of others.

Another argument he draws from the sacrifices themselves : they offered the blood of bulls, and of goats, and

* From a Sermon delivered in Great Queen Street Chapel, April 28, 1833, in aid of the funds of the Wesleyan Missionary Society.

of lambs, which could not take away sin. Our High Priest offered himself a Lamb without blemish; he poured out the price of our redemption for us, which is emphatically called "the blood of Christ!"

He draws another argument from the multiplicity of their sacrifices, which were repeated, and offered year by year continually; proving that they could "never make the comers thereunto perfect." "But this man, because he continueth ever, hath an unchangeable priesthood," Heb. vii. 24. It was so full of dignity, so full of merit, so teeming with virtue; it was stamped with such an infinite desert, that such a sacrifice once offered was enough. The Jewish high priests, in humble reverence, and in readiness to serve, stood within the veil, offering the same sacrifices: "But this man, after he had offered one sacrifice for sins, for ever sat down on the right hand of God." This one sacrifice of Christ, stands opposed to the multiplicity of sacrifices that were offered under the law.

I. THIS GOD-MAN OFFERED ONE SACRIFICE FOR SIN. That was the sacrifice of himself, which we may consider as implying surrender.

1. *He offered his body.* The prophet says of him: "I gave my back to the smiters, and my cheeks to them that plucked off the hair: I hid not my face from shame and spitting," Isa. l. 6; "they gave me gall for my meat; and in my thirst they gave me vinegar to drink," Psa. lxix. 21; so that, in Isa. lii. 14, we read, "his visage was so marred more than any man, and his form more than the sons of men." These were sufferings of no common kind.

2. *But, in suffering, he offered his mind.*

The sufferings of our Redeemer's soul must be considered as the soul of his sufferings. These he anticipated at a distance, when he said, "I have a baptism to be baptized.

with; and how am I straitened till it be accomplished!"
Luke xii. 50. We must, however, go into the garden of
Gethsemane to witness this sacrifice offered. What must
have been the agony of his mind, when, in the bloom and
prime of health, supported by conscious innocence, raised
above the natural fear of death, with the prospect of an
abundant entrance into the kingdom of heaven — what
must have been the agony of his mind, when even the
vital fluid, interrupted in its natural course of circulation,
was forced through the coats of the veins, the vessels, and
integuments, and bathed his body in a sweat of blood!

3. *He offered in sacrifice his glory*—by which we understand how glory will follow up the shame. Now, our
Redeemer's feelings were not blunted and stoical; he was
alive to his reputation; his sense of indignity, and shame,
and dishonour, were exquisite—nay, they were delicately
fine; and when they called him an enemy to civil government, and a deceiver of the people; when they said, " He
is mad," " a glutton, and a wine-bibber;" when they said
he had a devil—that he was not fit to live; he must have
felt the indignity with great acuteness.

4. *He offered in sacrifice the consolations of heaven's
protection.*

This he did when he cried, " My God, my God, why
hast thou forsaken me?" Matt. xxvii. 46. Now the dogs
of hell opened their mouths on him; the strong bulls of
Bashan beset him around; now earth and hell are allowed
to do their worst; and such is that worst, as to lead him
to cry to God, Why hast thou abandoned me—why hast
thou forsaken me?

5. *He offered in sacrifice his life.* Life is dear to every
creature: " Greater love hath no man than this, that a
man lay down his life for his friend," John xv. 13; but while
we were yet enemies, Christ died for us, Rom. v. 8.

6. *He offered in sacrifice his will.*   Suffering can never be loved for its own sake; and shame and death are terrible foes.   The Redeemer prayed that the cup of suffering might pass from him, Matt. xxvi. 42; yet he gave his person into the hands of those who put it to torture: he voluntarily resigned himself to that train of overwhelming and distressing ideas, that threw his mind into an agony that bathed him in a bloody sweat: he gave up the consolation of heaven's protection.   Perhaps it may be asked,

II. For what purpose did he offer this sacrifice?

Whenever we think, or read, about the sufferings of Christ, we are immediately directed to sin:—"Christ died for our sins," 1 Cor. xv. 3.   He suffered once for sin— " the just for the unjust, that he might bring us to God." " Who his own self bare our sins in his own body on the tree." " He was wounded for our transgressions, he was bruised for our iniquities," 1 Pet. iii. 18; ii. 24; Isa. liii. 5. This Man offered himself a sacrifice for sin,

1. *To avert the consequences of it.*   Jesus Christ paid the penalty, that he might deliver the sinner from the consequences of his sins; and every sinner that accepts of the sacrifice of Christ by faith, the finger of God's mercy, dipped in the blood of his Son, writes that sinner as one over whom the second death shall never have power.

2. *He died that he might remove the presence of sin, by doing away the love of it;* by cleansing the guilty in the " Fountain opened for sin and for uncleanness,"—rendering the person " without spot, or wrinkle, or any such thing,"—that he might so renew the nature of man, so endear the principles of grace to him, that he might deny " ungodliness and worldly lusts," and live above the practises of sin.

3. *He offered himself a sacrifice to overcome the*
H 2

forfeiture of sin. Sin had forfeited the image, the love, the protection of God. Through sin, man had lost every spark of happiness in life, and comfort in death, and every title to glory; yet, by the sacrifice of Christ, we receive all that we lost in the transgression. We are now directed,

III. To the exaltation of our Redeemer.

1. *This was through the medium of his resurrection.* That Jesus Christ died on the cross, was attested by the water and the blood that flowed after the insertion of the spear, anatomically demonstrating that the heart had been pierced. And that He " rose again, according to the Scriptures," we have conclusive evidence.

2. *And he has now " sat down at the right hand of God."* God is a great and invisible Spirit, with whom literally there can be neither standing nor recumbency. We must, therefore, understand this phrase figuratively; and it is, (1.) expressive of rest. The Jewish high priest, when he entered within the veil, never sat down; his work was not done; he had to return, and to come back and " offer oftentimes the same sacrifices," if his life were spared. " But this man, after he had offered one sacrifice for sins, for ever sat down on the right hand of God." But this expression " sat down," intimates (2.) His being honoured. When we read, that Jesus Christ is at the right hand of God, we understand he is raised to the highest honour—he is raised " above all principalities and powers;" having done his work to the perfect satisfaction of his Father, it has pleased God to give " Him a name which is above every name; that at the name of Jesus every knee should bow;—and that every tongue should confess that Jesus Christ is Lord, to the glory of God the Father," Phil. ii. 10, 11.

This phrase is expressive (3.) of power, of authority, and of dominion. The right hand is employed as an emblem

of power, Exod. xv. 6; Psa. xvii. 7, etc. Now, when our Redeemer is placed at the right hand of God, we understand
him as invested with power: he is now the Ruler of all
things, the Governor of all worlds. There he shall remain,
until, according to the promise of the Father to him, " Sit
thou at my right hand, until I make thine enemies thy
footstool," Psa. cx. 1.

IV. THE PURPOSES OF HIS WILL SHALL BE FULFILLED.
Of the adversaries of Jesus Christ we observe,

1. *That Satan is the most subtle, ancient, and formidable.* But, my brethren, this adversary shall be the footstool of the woman's all-conquering Seed that was given to
" bruise his head." Another adversary of Jesus Christ is—

2. *Error.* Error may be said to be a hydra with many
heads. The first head, which presents itself in this hydra,
has the face of a beast, by which we understand the errors
of Popery—so decided an enemy to Christ, that that
system, in the New Testament, is called Anti-Christ. Another of these errors has the face of the false prophet, by
which we may understand the delusions, impurities, and
abominations of Mohammedanism.

The next has the face of a dragon, by which we understand the cruel, the impure, the licentious, the hellish
abominations of Paganism, or Heathenism. Paganism
gives to the mind the falsest idea of God; or extinguishes
the idea of the Supreme Being from the human mind.
Heathenism substitutes, in the place of the great Jehovah,
idols and devils—worships them by the impurest rites,
propitiates them by the bloodiest . sacrifices. Paganism
presents the most delusive prospect of happiness and of
safety.

Now, these are enemies to Christ, because he is light and
truth; these are false as hell, and dark as the chambers of

death. These systems degrade God's creatures, rob the Redeemer, murder the souls of men; and as such they must come down: by the general diffusion of knowledge, by the spread of the Scriptures, by the propagation of the gospel, by the piety and by the influence of God's people, these systems shall be overturned.

3. *Another enemy is to be found in wicked, unconverted men.* But these enemies shall be the footstool of the " Lion of the tribe of Judah." Upon unconverted men, Jesus Christ will employ his gospel and his word on their understandings, and his Spirit on their consciences, and his providence on their circumstances and their bodies; and these weapons shall be " mighty through God to the pulling down of strong holds." By these weapons some shall see their error—shall discover their wickedness—shall perceive their danger, and tremble at it—shall let the weapons of their rebellion drop out of their hands—shall crawl like guilty worms to the footstool of Christ's mercy— shall cordially embrace, with arms of faith, the despised Nazarene; they shall give him their hearts, and affections, and lives, in devotional obedience; and they shall joyfully suffer for his sake.

4. *Another enemy of Christ is death.* He is said to be the last enemy that shall be destroyed, 1 Cor. xv. 26.

5. All these enemies have been made by one worse than the devil himself, and that enemy is *Sin.*

To destroy sin the Son of God was manifested—for this purpose he offered himself a sacrifice for sin—for this purpose he has commanded his gospel to be preached to every creature—for this purpose he is, at this moment, seated at the right hand of God, invested with all power, with all energy, to employ whatever instrument, or agent, he thinks proper, and to give a blessing to those means that they may be effectual.

APPLICATION.

1. Here we discover, brethren, the character of sinners. They are said to be enemies to Christ.

2. We learn, again, that these enemies of Christ, these unconverted persons must be his footstool, whether at home or abroad.   Are any of you unconverted?   Are any of you in a state of hostility of mind to the blessed Jesus?   Remember, you must come down.   Will you be subdued by justice, or by mercy?   Will you be conquered by the sceptre of his grace; or will you be broken in pieces by the iron rod of his wrath?

Finally.   We see the duty of the people to extend by conquest the triumphs of the Redeemer,—the empire of the Saviour: to bring home his rebel outcasts, that they may be saved from sin and Satan's snare.

Yes; the kingdom of hell is shaking—the gates of perdition tremble.   Let us not rest, but take up a bold and manful stand in our own places, until we join in that blessed acclamation—"The kingdoms of this world are become the kingdoms of our Lord and of his Christ; and he shall reign for ever and ever.—Alleluia: for the Lord God omnipotent reigneth!" Rev. xi. 15; xix. 6.   Yes! and he will reign till he has subdued all to the obedience of faith; till death and sin are dead, and God shall be all in all!   Amen.

SKETCH XXVI.

GOSPEL HARVEST, AND CHRISTIAN'S DUTY.

BY REV. THOMAS DE WITT, D.D., NEW YORK.*

" Then saith he unto his disciples, The harvest truly is plenteous, but the labourers are few ; pray ye therefore the Lord of the harvest, that he will send forth labourers into his harvest."—MATT. ix. 37, 38.

THE words of our text were spoken by Jesus to his disciples, as he contemplated the multitudes destitute of the means of religious instruction. " He was moved with compassion on them because they fainted, and were scattered abroad as sheep having no shepherd," ver. 36. The compassion that dwelt in the heart of Jesus is not foreign to the hearts of his people, for they are of one spirit with him. The text presents, firstly, an argument for missionary efforts. " The harvest truly is plenteous, but the labourers are few." And, secondly, urges a duty in relation to them. " Pray ye therefore the Lord of the harvest," etc.

I. AN ARGUMENT FOR MISSIONARY EFFORTS. " The harvest truly is plenteous, but the labourers are few." This harvest will be gathered when the Christian religion shall universally prevail.

1. *It is great, in view of the field which it will cover.*

" The field is the world," Matt. xiii. 38. As yet Christianity has extended its influence to but a small part of the earth ; and where that influence has been found, it has been

---

* Preached at Boston, October 7, 1830, before the American Board of Foreign Missions.

partial in its character. Here and there a spot has appeared in some degree verdant, amid a surrounding wide-spread arid desert. But this desert, in all its extent, will be cultivated and rendered fruitful. All obstacles will be overcome, and the whole earth exhibit the triumphs of truth. Benighted, degraded, and oppressed Africa shall become enlightened, elevated, and disenthralled. The wall of China (like that of Jericho) shall fall at the sound of the gospel. The castes of the Hindoos shall be broken; and one bond, in the faith and service of Christ, shall unite them. The heathen shall every where " cast their idols to the moles and to the bats," and worship " the only true God, and Jesus Christ whom he hath sent." The worship of the false prophet shall cease; and the pure light and peaceful influence of Christianity shall spread over the regions where now Mohammedanism exerts its sway. The isles shall receive the law of the Lord; all the perversions of the religion of Jesus shall be removed, and the truth be received in love, and exhibit its fruits wherever professed! Then shall be realized

—— " Scenes surpassing fable,
Yet true !—scenes of accomplish'd bliss !"

2. *The harvest is great, in view of its many blessings.*

The religion of Christ blesses the life which now is, and prepares for happiness in the life to come. It exalts the intellectual character of man;—it restores that balance and harmony in the intellectual and moral powers of man, which are so important in the proper cultivation of both;—it corrects those prejudices, and subdues those corruptions, which prevent the investigation and reception of truth.

Take the map of the world, and select those countries where Paganism, Mohammedanism, and Popery bear sway, and let the following inquiries receive an answer. Are knowledge and intellectual cultivation generally diffused ?

Are civil and religious liberty enjoyed? Is the female character elevated and respected? Are the duties of domestic
life discharged, and its delights mutually participated? Do
purity and peace pervade the community? The negative
to these inquiries appears in full view. If we take the contrast, and mark the countries where the Bible has shed its
influence, we discover the blessings adverted to, all following
in the train.

But the religion of Christ sustains its distinguishing and
commanding value, as a revelation of truth and grace, and
as the great instrument of our deliverance from everlasting
death. The truths peculiar to it respect man's fallen and
ruined state; redemption through the atoning merits of the
Divine Saviour; the regenerating and sanctifying influence
of the Holy Spirit in restoring to that holiness, "without
which no man shall see the Lord," Heb. xii. 14. These
truths, and others immediately connected with them, constitute the vitality of the religion of the gospel.

3. *The harvest must appear great in view of the instrumentality it requires.*

The great result is to be accomplished by the faithful use
of those means which God has, in his wisdom and goodness,
appointed. As in the natural world, means must be used
in preparation for harvest; and as, ordinarily, the product
will correspond to the skill and diligence with which the
means are employed; so also, in the spiritual world, means
are equally necessary; and a like correspondence in the
product will exist. "It pleased God by the foolishness of
preaching to save them that believed," 1 Cor. i. 21.

As we look farther, through the heathen world, how large
and waste is the field; while, in parts remote from each
other, a solitary labourer is found. The regularly ordained
missionaries from different Christian denominations among
the six hundred millions of heathen, in different parts of the

world, as far as ascertained, amount to about six hundred and fifty. They are, in some cases, aided by assistants and native teachers. Still, how emphatically is the harvest great, and the labourers few; while some parts of the field are already white for the harvest.

4. *The harvest is great, in view of the means and prospects furnished by Providence.*

God, in advancing his kingdom on earth, prepares the way in arranging the events of his providence. He raises up instruments qualified for his work; and often opens the way before them, as they go forth crying, " Prepare ye the way of the LORD; make straight in the desert a highway for our GOD," Isa. xl. 3. The Bible Society multiplies copies of the Scriptures, in the various languages of the world, and supplies the place of the gift of tongues. It is needless to specify the various forms of Christian charity, which, commencing with infancy, lays the basis of a scriptural and religious education, and follows man in every course and state of life; and seeks to apply the best relief of sin, and want, and woe. The efforts of the present day for arresting and turning back that fell destroyer, intemperance, which has annually slain its thousands and tens of thousands, and which has interposed such formidable obstacles to the success of the gospel, are of incalculable worth.

· The spirit of missions, which characterizes the present period, commenced with the revival of religion in the churches. Domestic and foreign missions have grown and strengthened in connexion with the power of religion. The era of foreign efforts is identified with the prosperity of religion at home. The events which have recently transpired mark the present as an interesting crisis in the history of the world. The Christian will, with care, study the page of prophecy, and the movements of Providence, and mark the light which they mutually shed on each other.

II. THE TEXT URGES OUR DUTY IN RELATION TO MIS-
SIONARY EFFORTS : " Pray ye the Lord of the harvest, that
he will send forth labourers into his harvest." The discharge of the duty enjoined by our Saviour supposes,

1. *That we cherish a deep and constant sense of our
dependance upon Divine grace.*

The private Christian, in the divine life, is " clothed
with humility;" lives a life of faith in the Son of God; and
seeks continued supplies of the grace and help of the Spirit.
So the Christian church should always be found in the attitude of " leaning on her Beloved," Sol. Song viii. 5; and
should realize that all her springs are in God.

2. *This duty requires habitual and fervent remembrance
in our private devotions.*

Love to the Redeemer's cause is not a transient emotion
in the Christian's heart; but it is a fixed principle, and growing habit of soul. He " prefers Jerusalem above his chief
joy." He should then be frequent, fervent, importunate,
and persevering in his intercession.

3. *This duty requires union in Christians.*

Addressing his assembled disciples, Jesus said, " Pray
ye," Matt. vi. 9. The true disciples of Jesus are united in
spirit and service. The words of our Saviour's prayer are
memorable : " That they all may be one; as thou Father
art in me, and I in thee, that they also may be one in us:
that the world may believe that thou hast sent me,"
John xvii. 21. What Christian can be reluctant to engage
in a service so delightful and animating, as united prayer
for the coming of Christ's kingdom on earth ?

4. *This duty requires the use of all proper means for
suitably training labourers for the missionary field.*

In our favoured churches, where the Spirit's influence is
enjoyed, let the subject of foreign missions be presented in
just prominence. In our theological seminaries, let a careful

inquiry and deep interest be cultivated and cherished among their members, who shall soon go forth to preside in the churches of our own land, to give a tone to their sentiments and feelings, or else to enter themselves upon the glorious work.

5. *This duty requires that all the churches of Christ should systematically and efficiently aid in the promotion of the cause of missions.*

It cannot be necessary to argue the duty of professed Christians to give their prayers, their property, and labours to this cause. The Christian judgment needs not be convinced, but the Christian conscience needs to be awakened, and the heart affected. Christians should learn to give, not from the impulse of momentary excitement, but from the deliberate conviction of duty, in the discharge of which the heart seeks its highest joy. Systematically, I say, because it is to be regretted, that so many churches so readily relax their efforts, until some new impulse be given, which soon spends itself. These are like the mountain streams, fed by sudden showers, which soon pass away.

APPLICATION.

Let every pastor present the claims of this cause prominently before his people, and feel that its prosperity is identified with the success of his labours at home. Let information be generally extended, and every means to excite interest, and combine effort, be employed. While in opposing the march of truth, various errors and conflicting interests combine, let the church of God arise in her strength, and in unbroken columns march onward, under the banners of her great Captain, from victory to victory. While the enemy opposes and rages, we remember, " They that be with us are more than they that be with them," 2 Kings vi. 16. God's truth is great, and must finally triumph.

SKETCH XXVII.

THE FUTURE PROSPERITY OF THE CHURCH THE EFFECTS OF DIVINE INFLUENCE.

BY REV. ROBERT JACK, OF MANCHESTER.*

" He shall cause them that come of Jacob to take root: Israel shall blossom and bud, and fill the face of the world with fruit."

ISAIAH xxvii. 6.

THE text is supposed to have had its literal accomplishment when Jerusalem was delivered from the destroying army of Sennacherib.   But the grace of which it speaks did not terminate in that great temporal deliverance.   It is understood, by Christian interpreters, to extend to the times of the gospel; and to lay a foundation for our hope of nobler blessings, and of better days.   The posterity of Jacob were a highly-favoured people; and were distinguished from the other nations of the earth by the most honourable appellations, and by the most exalted privileges.   After, however, many vicissitudes, for disowning and rejecting the Messiah when he came, they were disinherited by the offended God of their fathers, deprived of all their peculiar privileges, expelled from the land of promise, and are become miserable wanderers among the nations.   What shall we say, then, to these things?   Is there no Israel now to be found, among whom God's name is great?   Yea, verily,

* Preached before the Missionary Society, at the Tabernacle, May 13, 1807.

though Israel, according to the flesh, be no more the people of God, still there is " a royal priesthood, an holy nation, a peculiar people," a true circumcision, " which worship God in the spirit, and rejoice in Christ Jesus, and have no confidence in the flesh," Phil. iii. 3. Many sinners of the Gentiles, " who sometimes were far off are made nigh by the blood of Christ," Eph. ii. 13; and have become, through faith, the spiritual children of Abraham—the true Israel of God. Such, the Scriptures assure us, are " Israelites indeed," John i. 47; though Abraham be ignorant of them, and Israel, according to the flesh, acknowledge them not, Isa. lxiii. 16; for " if ye be Christ's, then are ye Abraham's seed, and heirs according to the promise," Gal. iii. 29.

There is a period, however, announced in ancient prophecy, a happy period, when " Israel shall be a blessing in the midst of the land," Isa. xix. 24. Converted to the faith of Christ, and restored to their own land, we have ground to believe that they shall be incorporated with the Christian church in one spiritual society, of which Israel according to the flesh was a figure. No remaining distinction shall then subsist betwixt Jew and Gentile, Barbarian and Scythian, bond and free. They shall all be one in Christ Jesus, Col. iii. 11. No longer shall they regard each other as " strangers and foreigners, but fellow-citizens with the saints, and of the household of God," Eph. ii. 19.

The text may be considered as a promise of prosperity to the church; first, in respect of number; secondly, in respect of spiritual vigour; thirdly, in respect of beauty; fourthly, in respect of fruitfulness; fifthly, in respect of joy; and, lastly, in respect of stability, and in respect of extent. These particulars, in dependance upon Divine aid, we now propose to illustrate.

I. THE PROMISE RELATES TO THE PROSPERITY OF THE CHURCH IN RESPECT OF NUMBER.

Under the ancient dispensation, the spiritual Israel were comparatively few. The walls of the church then enclosed but a small portion of the earth. "Salvation," at that time, was only " of the Jews," John iv. 22; and the joyful sound was never heard beyond the precincts of the promised land. But, at the commencement of the Christian dispensation, the wall of partition was broken down, and the boundaries of the church were greatly enlarged. Even among the Jews, multitudes were made " a willing people." New creatures were hourly born in Zion, and came forth to " newness of life," numerous, or rather innumerable, as the drops of dew " from the womb of the morning." Yea, what shall we say? By the diligence of the apostles, the sound of the gospel soon went " into all the earth, and their words unto the ends of the world," Rom. x. 18. And the Gentiles received the word gladly.

II. THE PROMISE RELATES TO THE PROSPERITY OF THE CHURCH IN RESPECT OF SPIRITUAL VIGOUR.

Others remain in a state of spiritual death. They are, as the Scripture emphatically expresses it, dead while they live, 1 Tim. v. 6. But concerning them " that come of Jacob," it is here asserted, that they shall take root. They are not like the tender herb, which springeth up in a night, and withereth in a night; for " the righteous," it is promised, " shall flourish like the palm-tree: he shall grow like the cedar in Lebanon," Psa. xcii. 12. The reason is plain—the root, to which they are united by a living faith, is firm and immovable. Though the branches may be violently shaken, and their blossoms blighted by the rude blasts of corruption and temptation, yet " the root of the righteous shall not be moved," Prov. xii. 3.

And may not all this be expected to be more completely realized in the case of those who shall live in the happy period to which the promise in the text particularly refers. "He shall come down," it is promised, "like rain upon the mown-grass; as showers that water the earth," Psa. lxxii. 6. "And many people shall go and say, Come ye, and let us go up to the mountain of the Lord, to the house of the God of Jacob; and he will teach us of his ways, and we will walk in his paths: for out of Zion shall go forth the law, and the word of the Lord from Jerusalem," Isa. ii. 3. May it not be supposed, therefore, that believers shall make rapid progress amidst all this extraordinary cultivation?

III. THE PROMISE RELATES TO THE PROSPERITY OF THE CHURCH IN RESPECT OF BEAUTY.

Christ himself, "the branch of the Lord, *is* beautiful and glorious," Isa. iv. 2; and believers in Christ, are made comely through his comeliness put upon them, Ezek. xvi. 14. How beautiful are the trees of the field when adorned with the leaves of spring! Thus beautiful are the spiritual children of Jacob. We cannot contemplate but with wonder and delight, the transforming energy of the gospel in the days of the apostles. The believers not only increased in number, but flourished in grace. How beautiful must the daughters of Zion have appeared, when their knowledge was sound and spiritual, when their faith was firm, their repentance deep, their hope steadfast, their zeal fervent, their love abounding; when the gentleness of Christ spread an amiable lustre around them; when humility, as a veil, at once clothed and adorned them; "when the peace of God, which passeth all understanding," kept "their hearts and minds through Christ Jesus," Phil. iv. 7; and when patience under suffering had its perfect work in them.

The beauty of believers, evidently, is of an internal nature, for "the king's daughter is all glorious within," Psa. xlv. 13; and with this the greatest beauty of external form is not worthy to be compared. "Solomon, in all his glory," was not so elegantly arrayed as "the lilies of the field;" and yet, what is the beauty of the fairest flower, to that of a saint adorned with the robe of the Redeemer's righteousness, and decked out with the fair flowers of implanted grace? There can be no doubt that the gospel still produces the same happy effects in all by whom it is truly believed. Wherever "the incorruptible seed" of the word, is sown by the hand of the Spirit, it changes the unkindly soil of the human heart, and restores, in some degree, the moral beauty of our nature. And how much more may this be expected to take place at that happy period, when God "shall cause them that come of Jacob to take root, and when Israel shall blossom and bud." How delightful the prospect, that a time shall arrive when "pure and undefiled religion" shall universally prevail; when love to God and to man, when truth and righteousness and peace shall be generally and powerfully diffused; and when the evils shall cease with which men, by the indulgence of their guilty passions, have been grieved and tormented.

IV. THE PROMISE RELATES TO THE PROSPERITY OF THE CHURCH IN RESPECT OF FRUITFULNESS.

Believers are denominated in Scripture, "trees of righteousness," Isa. lxi. 3, to intimate that they should "bring forth fruit unto God." It is not enough that they are covered with the leaves of a holy profession; and blossom with the flowers of pious resolutions, and good endeavours. It is necessary, also, that in their season they be "filled with the fruits of righteousness, which are by Jesus Christ, unto the glory and praise of God," Phil. i. 11. Among the branches ingrafted into Christ, there is, indeed, a consider-able variety. Some are slender, and others strong; some more, and others less, productive. All, it is true, bear good fruit: but even in this respect a variety is less or more observable. They flourish not all in the same way. Some are eminent for one virtue, and some for another; neither is any of them equally fruitful at all times. Such fruits, however, as they do at any time produce, are of excellent quality. Nor are their fruits more distinguished by their perfection of excellence, than they are often by their great-ness of number. They abound " in every good word and work."

V. THE PROMISE RELATES TO THE PROSPERITY OF THE CHURCH IN RESPECT OF JOY.

It is when the dews of heaven " drop upon the pastures of the wilderness," that it is said, " the little hills rejoice on every side." It is when "the vallies also are covered over with corn, that they shout for joy, and they also sing," Psa. lxv. 12, 13. The abundant joy of New Testament times, especially of the times referred to in the passage before us, is often spoken of in Scripture. " Behold," saith the Lord, " I create Jerusalem a rejoicing, and her people a joy. And I will rejoice in Jerusalem, and joy in my people: and the voice of weeping shall be no more heard in her, nor the voice of crying,—for as the days of a tree are the days of my people, and mine elect shall long enjoy the work of their hands.—Violence shall no more be heard in thy land, wasting nor destruction within thy borders; but thou shalt call thy walls Salvation, and thy gates Praise," Isa. lxv. 18, 19, 22; lx. 18.

VI. THE PROMISE RELATES TO THE PROSPERITY OF THE CHURCH IN RESPECT OF STABILITY.

It is here promised, that the Lord " shall cause them that

I

come of Jacob to take root." The vicissitudes which take place in human affairs, teach us the vanity of the world, and the perishing nature of all that seems most durable in this region of shadows. When we read the history of nations, what do we read but the history of incessant revolution, one dominion erecting itself upon the ruins of another? Those kingdoms and empires which seemed established on the firmest foundations, have long since crumbled down, and have left not a wreck behind. Sunk beneath the weight of years, the most venerable institutions have, at length, mouldered into dust. The church of God, however, has been like Mount Zion, which cannot be moved, but abideth for ever,—built upon " the Rock of Ages," the emissaries of hell, after all their malicious attacks, have found themselves utterly unable to prevail against her. " Thine eyes shall see Jerusalem a quiet habitation, a tabernacle that shall not be taken down; not one of the stakes thereof shall ever be removed, neither shall any of the cords thereof be broken," Isa. xxxiii. 20.

VII. THE PROMISE RELATES TO THE PROSPERITY OF THE CHURCH IN RESPECT OF EXTENT.

We have already seen that the promise relates to the prosperity of the church in respect of *number*. We have, also, seen that this number shall be exceeding great. It follows, of course, that the boundaries of the visible church must be enlarged; and, indeed, the text leads us to expect that her walls shall encompass the whole habitable world. " His name shall endure for ever : his name shall be continned as long as the sun: and men shall be blessed in him : all nations shall call him blessed.—He shall have dominion also from sea to sea, and from the river unto the ends of the earth. They that dwell in the wilderness shall bow down before him,—all nations shall serve him,"

Psa. lxxii. 17, 8, 11. He " will say to the north, Give up ; and to the south, Keep not back : bring my sons from far, and my daughters from the ends of the earth; even every one that is called by my name," Isa. xliii. 6, 7.

From the manner in which it is expressed, it is evident that in all the happy events to which it refers, the agency of God shall be signally conspicuous. Mark the phraseology—" He shall *cause* them that come of Jacob to take root." In his works of providence and of grace, God frequently sees it meet to employ secondary causes as the instruments of his operation ; yet here, efficacy depends entirely on his superintending influence. It is his hand which sustains the great chain of causes and effects; and his agency which pervades and animates the worlds of nature and of grace. It is " not by might, nor by power, but by my spirit, saith the Lord of hosts," Zech. iv. 6.

APPLICATION.

1. What gratitude ought we to feel, that we have been favoured with the gospel! " Through the tender mercy of our God ; whereby the day spring from on high hath visited us, to give light to them that sat in darkness and in the shadow of death, to guide our feet into the way of peace," Luke i. 78, 79.

2. How little reason have Christians to complain that they have no prospect of seeing, in their day, the happy period to which the text refers. Have they not heaven in prospe t ? There they shall enjoy happiness, boundless as their la rgest wishes, and lasting as their immortal souls !

3. What powerful encouragement does this subject afford to missionary exertions! We have seen that the Scriptures abound with promises of great prosperity to the church in the latter days; and we know that higher security cannot,

in the nature of things, be given, than a Divine promise. " The heavens and the earth may pass away," but one word which the mouth of the Lord hath spoken, cannot fail of accomplishment.

4. How careful ought we to be, to attend to the state of our own souls in the sight of God. Have we the greatest reason to be thankful that " to us is the word of this salvation sent?" And should we not be earnestly concerned to improve it to our own salvation? How apt we are to undervalue our privileges, because we have never known what it is to be deprived of them! May God make us " wise unto salvation through faith which is in Christ Jesus;" and may we, at last, reap the fruit of this heavenly wisdom, in " receiving the end of our faith, even the salvation of our souls!" Amen and Amen.

SKETCH XXVIII.

HAPPY INFLUENCE OF FOREIGN MISSIONS ON THE CHURCH.

BY THE REV. DAVID ABEEL,
OF THE UNITED STATES, MISSIONARY TO CHINA.

" Spare not, lengthen thy cords, and strengthen thy stakes."—ISA. liv. 2.

THE text is a command given to the church,—in other words, a duty enjoined upon Christians. The only way to ascertain both its precise meaning, and the best mode of its accomplishment, is to consult the preceding and following verses. "Enlarge the place of thy tent, and let them stretch forth the curtains of thine habitations: spare not, lengthen thy cords, and strengthen thy stakes; for thou shalt break forth on the right hand and on the left; and thy seed shall inherit the Gentiles, and make the desolate cities to be inhabited."

The whole passage, then, refers to the conversion of the Gentiles, or heathen; and furnishes the following important suggestion, that THERE IS NO SYSTEM OF MEANS SO WELL CALCULATED TO GIVE EXPANSION AND STABILITY TO THE CHURCH OF CHRIST, (not merely to lengthen her cords, but also to strengthen her stakes,) AS FOREIGN MISSIONARY OPERATION.

The direct benefits of missionary exertions upon the heathen, and their reflex action upon the churches which put forth these exertions, are both to be considered in estimating the efficacy of these means. It is a question of great interest, and one which cannot be too freely discussed, nor too quickly determined, whether, for the good of the world, the main energies of the church ought to be expended upon countries nominally Christian and comparatively limited; or upon the more extensive and populous regions, now shrouded in pagan darkness and Mohammedan delusion? The decision of this question would indicate to many a mind, now vacillating and distressed; it would assure the confidence of the doubtful; it would recall his distracted attention, and concentrate his divided efforts; it would send forth streams of vital influence through those appropriate channels, which, for aught we know, are now empty and dry.

There are several reasons which are supposed by many to favour the opinion, that Christian exertion is less productive among pagan nations than at home.

1. *There are preliminary barriers which oppose the efforts of the missionary, and which do not exist in Christian lands.*

Of these, the most important are strange languages, and strong prejudices. That these are real obstacles, ignorance alone will deny. There is, perhaps, nothing more trying to a sensitive heart, than to be surrounded by crowds of deluded and dying men, between whom and yourself there is no medium of intellectual communication. An ocean rolling between could not more effectually separate you from the objects of your compassion. In some countries, the difficulties of acquiring languages yield to nothing but the most persevering labour. This, however, is not every where the case. Perhaps no two languages are equally difficult of attainment. There are places where even transient traders and travellers pick up the native tongue, and soon become eloquent in its employment. As the number of missionaries increase, the difficulties of languages are reduced, and the facilities for their acquisition multiplied. Nay, missionaries not merely abbreviate the term of pupilage to their successors; but furnish them with useful labour, even during their necessary studies. There are daily services to be performed at every station, which cannot be dispensed with, and which do not demand the employment of the tongue. And these services are generally proportioned, in number and variety, to the efficiency of men engaged.

Another preliminary obstacle mentioned to the successful efforts of the missionary, is prejudice. In a few prominent heathen countries of the world, this barrier appears almost impregnable. China, Japan, and Cochin China, have marshalled their forces on their frontiers, and bade defiance to foreign aggression. But, even to these countries, there are points of attack which they cannot guard. The gospel is gaining access to China through numerous channels; and, sooner or later, every barrier shall be undermined, and a highway through every part of this empire be prepared for the servants of the Lord.

In almost every land, where missionary efforts have been continued for any considerable time, prejudices have invariably yielded ; and, generally, when they begin to subside, they rapidly disappear, and seldom return.

(2.) Another reason for which, it is believed, Christian effort is more profitable at home than abroad, is the systematic and stubborn opposition which the gospel meets from the established forms of civil government and pagan superstition. How far such opposition will be exerted where the Romish religion has loaded the cause of Christianity with its own opprobrium, we can only conjecture. Experiment has proved, that these obstacles scarcely ever prevent the introduction of the gospel, or greatly arrest its progress in any country.

(3.) A third reason, which may be supposed to operate against the comparative advantages of foreign missionary labour, is the risk and waste of life which it involves. If there be, as there doubtless is, a difference in the mortality of ministers in pagan and Christian nations, the reasons are obvious—the number of missionaries is so limited, that they labour harder, and suffer more, than their brethren at home; and thus far, they have occupied the most unhealthful positions, often under the greatest disadvantages. When missionaries are sent forth in sufficient numbers to supply the stations now possessed, and to occupy the far more extensive and important countries of Northern India, and all the higher divisions of Asia and Europe, the scale will turn; and health and life will probably be enjoyed to as great a degree and protracted a limit in the unevangelical world, as within the present boundaries of Christendom.

This, however, is but one view of the subject. There are arguments which favour the opposite opinion. There are arguments which give a high degree of probability to the conclusion, that the direct results of gospel efforts are greater in pagan than in Christian lands. Among the reasons for such an opinion, is that one which induces almost all ministers of the sanctuary to exchange the sphere of their labour at home; and which would, if they were consistent with their principles, send great numbers of them abroad. The souls to be saved are much more numerous— much more needy. Another reason is, the means of usefulness are both more various and extensively operative.

A further reason, which shows the superior influence of foreign labour, is the activity of native converts. Notwithstanding all that has been uttered by foes, and feared by friends, of the comparative fruitlessness of foreign missions, if the number of converts, in Christian and heathen lands, were divided by the proportion of gospel-ministers allotted to each sphere of labour, it is probable Christians at home would never again put the question, Where are the fruits of foreign missions?

If, in connexion with the number of souls actually saved, we estimate the instrumentality prepared, not only for present, but for future operation, we believe but few could hesitate in ascribing the greatest influence upon the church and the world, to foreign missionary exertion. And even if it could be showed that Christian efforts among the heathen are not as productive as at home, even then the chief argument which supports the doctrine presented in the text remains untouched.

2. *We believe that foreign missions are the best means of lengthening the cords and strengthening the stakes of the church*, because they establish and promote an action and reaction between themselves and the churches, which is most powerful and advantageous to both parties. This may be demonstrated by several facts.

I. MISSIONARY LABOUR INCREASES THE PIETY AND ENERGY OF THE CHURCHES.

The missionary spirit includes among its essential endowments, faith, prayer, self-denial, deadness to the world, charity, beneficence, heavenly-mindedness, a willingness to submit to sufferings and hazards, and a supreme regard for the glory of God. If such be the spirit which disposes and prepares men to engage in the work of converting the heathen, it is not difficult to perceive how the churches are benefited by missionary labour.

1. *There is the stimulus of example*, than which nothing is more influential. Hold up to the churches those with whom they are under equal obligations, but who have far

exceeded them in the " work of faith, and labour of love," and you bring a motive to bear upon them which piety cannot resist.

2. *It operates through sympathy.* We are brethren. Our work, our aim, our strongest desires, our highest honour, our dearest interests, our eternal recompense are the same. Just so far as we are sanctified, what one feels, and attempts, and accomplishes, must powerfully interest and actuate another.

3. *There is the duty and blessedness of necessary co-operation.* We must labour together. Missionaries are " the messengers of the churches." The churches must send them forth, sustain them with their prayers and contributions, and supply the increasing demand for men, which the opening field requires. The energy of the one increases the energy of the other. The missionary prepares work for the churches, and throws the obligation of its performance upon them; and can the churches remain inactive, when urged to exertion by such a fearful responsibility?

4. Again. *It diverts the mind from those unimportant points of doctrinal difference, and metaphysical distinction, and abstruse speculation,* which squander the time, and pervert the talents, and ruin the souls of thousands.

5. *It operates, too, through the influence of its own greatness.* It expands the mind, liberalizes the soul, elevates the aim; arouses faculties and feelings which nothing else could have addressed; and produces efforts and results which no other object could command.

These are some of the invaluable effects of missions upon the churches. But where are your facts? say they who regard this doctrine as a mere splendid theory. Such facts we are capable of furnishing.

(1.) Nothing more powerfully arrests the attention of youth and children, than missionary narratives. By these means, they are taught how much they differ from the heathen; and how they ought to pray, and contribute, and labour for their salvation.

(2.) Much has been attributed to the reaction of missions, as a means of producing our revivals, and improving all our home institutions. How much the education, and tract, and Bible societies owe to the strong appeals we furnish them, let the burden of their reports, and especially the eloquence of their agents, attest.

These are some of the channels through which the richest blessings are poured into the churches from missionary stations.

II. MISSIONARY OPERATIONS NOT ONLY INCREASE THE PIETY AND ENERGY OF THE CHURCHES, BUT GREATLY ASSIST IN SUPPLYING THEIR DOMESTIC DESTITUTION.

Our former position being admitted, this is its legitimate consequence. If every Christian could be brought to employ all his talents, it would require but a small proportion of the present number—perhaps only the reduced proportion of Gideon's army—to accomplish a greater amount of good than is now effected.

(1.) We have referred to the influence of foreign missions upon the young. Many a converted youth has had his attention directed to the ministry through the reading of missionary journals.

(2.) The reaction of missions upon the domestic interests of individual denominations, is instructive.

(3.) When we speak of the vigour which missionary exertions throw into our domestic institutions, we refer to a very natural operation. That man who has courage to attempt a great enterprize, despises the difficulties of a small one. The energy produced by the one, overlooks all the appalling trifles of the other.

III. THE CHURCH, THROUGH MISSIONARY EFFORTS, PLACES HERSELF IN THE BEST, AND, INDEED, IN THE ONLY POSITION FOR RECEIVING THE MOST ABUNDANT SPIRITUAL BLESSINGS.

1. *These efforts have a direct tendency to remove the most serious obstructions to piety and efficiency.*

Where the work of evangelizing the world is carried on with energy, it indicates and produces self-denial and liberality. We need not stop to show that nothing is more repugnant to eminent holiness, or usefulness, than a selfish parsimonious spirit. It is abhorrent in the eyes of a holy God. "For the iniquity of his covetousness," said Jehovah, " was I wrath, and smote him," Isa. lvii. 17.

2. *It secures to us those promises which are connected with enlarged exertions.*

"The liberal soul shall be made fat: and he that watereth shall be watered also himself," Prov. xi. 25. "If thou draw out thy soul to the hungry, and satisfy the afflicted soul, then shall thy light rise in obscurity, and thy darkness be as the noon day: and the Lord shall guide thee continually, and satisfy thy soul in drought, and make fat thy bones: and thou shalt be like a watered garden, and like a spring of water, whose waters fail not," Isa. lviii. 10, 11.

IV. IT MUST ENCOURAGE AND ENABLE THE CHURCH STILL MORE TO EXTEND HER LIMITS, AND THUS TO RETURN TO THE HEATHEN WORLD THE FULL INFLUENCE OF HER IMPROVED CONDITION.

This consequence is certain. It would be a dictate of selfish policy, if it were only a secular interest. Missionary effort is its own reward

We have seen that it not only demands large resources, but supplies the resources it demands. There is, however, a nobler principle for this enlarged policy, than personal recompense. Confidence is gathered from success, and energy from action.   Nothing so effectually convinces the church of the impotence of her own might, and the necessity and adequacy of her Redeemer's promised aid, as the effort to restore a rebellious world to its God.   It is the most stupendous enterprize, in which mortals have an agency. It taxes the utmost strength; and then makes demands upon faith, which infinitude alone can meet.

APPLICATION.

1. This subject teaches, that lengthening the cords of the church, is strengthening her stakes.   The two are inseparable; and they who confine themselves within their own limits, and labour first and exclusively to improve their domestic interests, without obeying the injunction and following the order of the text, will probably accomplish as little at home as they attempt abroad.

2. Our only authority for preaching the gospel—the promises and predictions of the word of God—the purchase of the Saviour's death—the triumph of his oppressed church —the highest glory of his mediatorial reign,—all demand the universal diffusion and dominion of Christianity.

3. Church of the living God, awake!   Thy slumbers, O how guilty, how cruel!   Thy husband—thy Redeemer— bids thee awake : and what he says to all, he says to each —awake!

SKETCH XXIX.

THE CHRISTIAN WARFARE.

" For the weapons of our warfare are not carnal, but mighty through God to the pulling down of strong holds."—2 Cor. x. 4.

THIS world was created by Christ, and for Him.   He, there-fore, is its rightful Lord and Ruler.   He is the one blessed and glorious Potentate, unto whom all homage and tribute should be paid.   Sin introduced anarchy and rebellion into our world.   Man revolted from God, allied himself to Satan, the usurper, and placed himself in an attitude of defiance to the Most High.   God could have easily over-thrown his rebellious creatures; he could have destroyed them with " the breath of his mouth," and " the bright-ness of his presence."   But " in wrath hath he remembered mercy."   He adopted an expedient of grace by which his banished ones might not be expelled from him.   The rebel now has the offer of life—now he may return to God, and be forgiven.   The preaching of the gospel is that instru-mentality which God employs for restoring men to his favour.   "Through the ignorance that is in them," men place themselves in opposition to the gospel, Eph. iv. 18. They refuse to hear it, or do not believe it.   They cavil at its doctrines, or refuse to obey its precepts.   In one word, they dislike Christ's kingdom; and say, with the servants in the parable, " We will not have this man to reign over us," Luke xix. 14.   Now, to subdue these is the great end of the Christian ministry.   Graciously to conquer these is the design of the preaching of the cross; and the text refers to the character of our weapons and the success of our efforts. " The weapons of our warfare," etc. Notice,

I. THE WARFARE REFERRED TO.

" Our warfare." Now, our warfare is distinguished from all' other scenes of conflict:—

1. *It is Divine, and not diabolical.* War is the general result of hellish passions, and sin. See Jas. iv. 1, 2. Most wars originate from beneath. This is a divine and heavenly warfare. The Son of the ever-blessed God is the " Captain of our salvation."

2. *This is a holy, and not an unrighteous war.* Wars generally arise from avarice, or ambition, or revenge; and are generally wicked and abominable in the sight of God. This war, on the other hand, is based on righteousness. It is the cause of truth, and justice, and equity. It is the cause of holiness against sin. Of obedience against rebellion. Of the reign of God, against the usurpation of the prince of darkness.

3. *It is a benevolent, and not a carnal war.* War aims at spreading misery, devastation, and death. War is one of those insatiable monsters, that has often spread terror, and misery, and woe, through the length and breadth of our world. Peace, comfort, health, and felicity, are exiled by its terrific influence. Our war is one of compassion, of tenderest goodness, and sweetest mercy. Paradoxical as it may appear, our banners bear the symbol of a Lamb. And this is the inscription, " Glory to God in the highest, and on earth peace, good-will toward men," Luke ii. 14. It produces real and abiding blessings, and spreads comfort and felicity in its triumphal course. It offers health, and peace, and life.

4. *It is a blessed and not an accursed war.* It bears

along with it every national, domestic, and personal blessing. It strews its flowers of gladness all around. " The
wilderness and the solitary place shall be glad for them;
and the desert shall rejoice, and blossom as the rose," Isa.
xxxv. 1. Contrast those countries where it has extended
its conquests, and those where Satan the usurper still
reigns. In the one, is intelligence; in the other, ignorance.
In the one, civilization; in the other, barbarism. In the
one, domestic comfort; in the other, family despotism. In
the one, man sinks to the level of the brute; in the other,
he rises almost to an equality with angels. Notice,

II. THE STRONG HOLDS IN WHICH SINNERS ENTRENCH
THEMSELVES IN THEIR OPPOSITION TO GOD. Of these, we
notice,

1. *The strong hold of ignorance.* Satan blinds his
votaries. Ignorance is essential to the duration of his
kingdom. It is the kingdom of darkness. Error is the
main pillar on which it rests. Now, men do not know the
true state of things. They will not consider the great
question. They will not come to the light. This is
criminal ignorance—wilful closing the eyes against the light
of heaven.

2. *The strong hold of prejudice.* This is the general
result of ignorance. Hence, how readily persons seize
hold of the most trifling objections to religion. Any foolish
thing will satisfy them, if it be against God's holy word
and truth. Sometimes this prejudice is against doctrines,
or duties, or against the people of God. It is often, however, deadly and fatal.

3. *The strong hold of pride.* This is a common barrier
to the salvation of the soul. Sin commenced with it. It
is one of the last things to be given up, yet it is incom-
patible with the spirit of the gospel. " God resisteth the

proud, and giveth grace to the humble," 1 Pet. v. 5. Sinners must be abased. Men must confess their iniquity. They must repent, and receive the kingdom of God as a little child, Mark x. 15. They must become nothing, and "Christ be all in all." Thus the gospel was foolishness to the Greeks.

4. *The strong hold of Mammon.* Love of this present world. A desire to gain the riches of time. Setting the affections on things on the earth. This was the strong-hold of Balaam, the false prophet—he preferred gain to godliness, Numb. xxii., etc. This was the stronghold of Gehazi, the servant of Elisha, 2 Kings v. 20, etc. Of the young man who came to Christ, Matt. xix. 22. Of Judas, Matt. xxvi. 15. Of Demas, 2 Tim. iv. 10. Of Simon Magus, Acts xviii. 18. Of Ananias and Sapphira, v. 1—10.

5. *The strong hold of unbelief.* The rejection of the truth. Not crediting the gospel. Men do not believe their state so evil and dangerous. They will not believe "that all have sinned," Rom. ii. 23; and that "the wicked shall be turned into hell," Psa. ix. 17. They will not believe in the requirements of the gospel, "repentance toward God, and faith in our Lord Jesus Christ," Acts xx. 21. Neither do they believe the threatenings of the word of God. Unbelief is a gross attack upon the truth of God, and continually throws back the offer of grace and salvation. These are some of the strong holds. Observe,

III. THE WEAPONS BY WHICH THEY ARE TO BE OVERTHROWN. Now, the weapons are described, negatively, as "not carnal;" and then, positively, in their efficiency, "mighty through God." Observe, carnal weapons are disowned. Among these we notice,

1. *The sword.* This was the weapon by which Mohammedanism was extended. This was the weapon Peter drew

forth to defend the Saviour in the garden. This has too often been employed by the intolerant, and the dominant sects of the professed churches of Christ. This may make slaves, hypocrites, and formalists.

2. *Temporal reward is a carnal weapon.* The multitude followed Christ because of the loaves and fishes. Men have been known to purchase proselytes in this way. Is not this calculated to extend cupidity and deceit.

3. *Sophistry and specious reasonings are carnal weapons.* This was one of the chief weapons of the ancient schools of philosophers. They reasoned, and philosophized, and had their profound mysteries, etc. But " my speech and my preaching was not with enticing words of man's wisdom, but in demonstration of the Spirit and of power: that your faith should not stand in the wisdom of men, but in the power of God. Howbeit we speak wisdom among them that are perfect: yet not the wisdom of this world, nor of the princes of this world, that come to nought: but we speak the wisdom of God in a mystery, even the hidden wisdom, which God ordained before the world unto our glory," 1 Cor. ii. 4—7.

Now, carnal weapons we totally disown and reprobate, in all matters of conscience and religion. Observe, our weapons are the truths of the gospel. The " sword of the Spirit, which is the word of God;" and this used plainly, simply, yet earnestly, is effective to the overthrow and " pulling down of the strong holds" of sin and Satan. The strong hold of ignorance is overthrown by the gospel of truth. The strong hold of prejudice, is to be met by the simple facts and statements of the gospel. The strong hold of pride, is to be overthrown by the revealed and exalted glories of another world. The strong hold of Mammon, by offering the riches of eternity. The strong hold of unbelief, by the persuasive statements of the evideuces of Christianity. The gospel can do all this. It is mighty to produce all these momentous and glorious effects. It is God's own instrument. It is full of the wisdom and power of God. It is that by which the Spirit carries on and perpetuates the kingdom of Christ. Numerous are the evidences of its blissful triumphs. They have existed in all ages, in all countries, and in all ranks and classes of mankind. Many of you are evidences of it—"ye are our epistles written in our hearts, known and read of all men," 2 Cor. iii. 2.

APPLICATION.

Learn,

1. The only means we are to employ for the extension of Christianity. We repudiate all carnal weapons—the sword and bayonet instrumentality, etc. We must avoid intolerance, bigotry, and coercion. The truth is to convert the world, and lift it up to a holy state of divine exaltation and bliss. And the truth must be preached in love.

2. These means must be faithfully and perseveringly employed. We are responsible to God, and to our dying fellow-men, for an earnest devotedness to the eternal interests of our perishing race.

3. The means we employ are Divine, and must ultimately and universally prevail.

SKETCH XXX.

THE GLORY AND PROSPERITY OF THE CHURCH.

BY REV. W. HANNAH, D.D.*

"I will be as the dew unto Israel: he shall grow as the lily, and cast forth his roots as Lebanon.—They that dwell under his shadow shall return; they shall revive as the corn, and grow as the vine: the scent thereof shall be as the wine of Lebanon."—HOSEA xiv. 5, 7.

OUR text represents three things : first, the influence which God promises to his church; secondly, the prosperity which his church shall enjoy in consequence of that influence; and, thirdly, the subsequent extension of the church in the world around it.   Let us observe,

I. THAT SPIRITUAL INFLUENCE WHICH ALMIGHTY GOD HERE PROMISES TO HIS CHURCH.

" I will be as the dew unto Israel,"—a metaphor drawn from the oriental dews, which, in many respects, were remarkable; and which presented to the minds of the people in that country a very forcible view of that influence which was thus suggested.   It is,

1. *A copious influence.*   Oriental dews abound during the dry season, often supplying the place of rain, penetrating the sources of vegetable life, and being pre-eminently

* From a Sermon in aid of the funds of the Wesleyan Methodist So-ciety, preached in Lambeth Chapel, London, April 26, 1833.

remarkable for copiousness and plenteousness—a circumstance of the utmost importance to the prosperity of those
countries ; and exceedingly adapted, therefore, for the
expression of this promise.   It is,

2. *A refreshing and renovating influence which is promised here.*   The dews descending abundantly on those
eastern countries, reached the very sources of vegetable
life, spread a new balm and beauty over the whole scene,
caused all things to revive, and flourish in new vigour.   We
are reminded of " times of refreshing from the presence of
the Lord," Acts iii. 19 : an expression which, in our own
day, particularly suggests this as something which shall
refresh, strengthen, and invigorate that which is thirsty and
faint.   There you look for the influences which God has
promised to bestow.   They are not only copious enough
to fill all your capacities; but are so refreshing as to change
your own spiritual state, and give beauty, and glow, and
glory to that which before was desert.   It is, also,

3. *A fertilizing influence which God promises here.*
The design of all dew is to promote a greater measure of
fertility.   It is encouraging to know, that all the influence
which God bestows, leads to the production of a spiritual
and practical effort more eminently to advance the diffusion
of his glory.   If the Spirit descend copiously from on high,
it is that converts may " spring up as among the grass, as
willows by the water courses," Isa. xliv. 4.   If the Spirit
descend, then will " the wilderness be a fruitful field,
and the fruitful field be counted for a forest," Isa. xxxii.
15.   All things flourish in new life, and in new fruitfulness.

4. *It is silent and instantaneous, yet most mighty in
its operations.*   Silence is the energy of God.   Look around
you at this season of the year.   A short time since, all was
the dreariness and desolation of winter : a mighty change

is now transpiring all around us; every thing begins to wear the hue of beauty, thus proving a mighty change in the vegetable world. What has accomplished it? Has there been aught very noisy? aught very instantaneous? aught to strike men's senses, or to attract especial observation? Nothing of the kind—God has sent forth his own silent and pervading influence; he has penetrated the veil; he has changed the whole scene by his own silent energy; and he has given new life, and new beauty, and new glory. And may we not justly expect, that he will proceed in the same way to pour out his influence on his church?

II. Our text has reference to the prosperity which the church shall enjoy in consequence of this influence.

And here the prophet, alluding to a tree, has drawn a beautiful representation of that sort of prosperity which we ought most earnestly to covet.

1. *There is the fair promise of future fruit.* " I will be as the dew unto Israel,"—more literally, " I will be as' blossom on the lily,"—as a tree refreshed by the influence of spring; he shall put forth new blossoms, like the lily, so fair, so lovely: he shall yield promise of most encouraging and renovated life, and more abundant fertility.

2. *But a growing stability in the life of God is a second part of this prosperity.* " He shall cast forth"—he shall strike—" his roots like Lebanon." The allusion is to the cedars of Lebanon, remarkable for striking their roots deep, rising to an eminent height, becoming a monument of permanence and strength. If the prophet had mentioned the blossom merely, it might be thought he had mentioned what was very pleasing and very fair; but he passes to the growing stability of it. That church, thus flourishing in its new blossoms, shall, at the same time, strike deep its

roots—take fi rther hold of the soul—shall be more entirely rooted in " the truth as it is in Jesus."

3. *An enlargement of existing members of the church in Divine grace,* is a thorough proof of this prosperity. "His branches shall spread,"—his branches shall go forward, increasing in size—becoming more capable of leaf, and of fruit too. I cannot think that this applies to the accession of new members, so much as to the enlargement of members already existing—their growth in the spiritual life. We sometimes love to select for contemplation, seasons when Christians have attained, by the power of God, a more eminent degree of Divine grace; when we may see them rising into their proper magnitude, conveying to us the lovely representation of what Christian men ought to be.

4. *This prosperity discovers itself in the church's spirituality.* " His beauty shall be as the olive tree, and his smell as Lebanon." When we speak of the fruits of Christian piety, we may not improperly distribute them into three classes : fruits of special devotedness to God; fruits of personal purity and circumspection ; and fruits of practical charity, fruits of doing good to others. These fruits abound amidst the influence of God, when he pours forth the dew of his blessing. Another mark of this prosperity is,

5. *The healing influence which a prosperous church diffuses ;* thus blooming, and taking new root, and enlarging her branches, and sustaining new fruit. The description closes with saying, " His smell shall be as Lebanon ;"—the fragrant influence shall spread itself from him as from the odoriferous plants and shrubs on Mount Lebanon. There shall be something inviting and healing in that influence which this prosperous church possesses. How fragrant is the influence of holy tempers, when all the man's dispositions are involved with the influence he has received from

on high! How fragrant are holy words, when a person's conversation is with grace, and abundantly filled with that holy unction which descended from heaven! How fragrant are holy actions! It follows,

III. THAT THERE SHALL BE AN EXTENSION OF THE CHURCH.

1. *By an accession of new members.* "They that dwell under his shadow shall return," an expression somewhat ambiguous of meaning. The fact, doubtless, is, that many shall turn from their manifold wanderings, to dwell under the shadow of this prosperous church. The prophet may have had three classes of persons on his mind; at least, we may apply the expression to three classes.

The *first* constitutes the apostates from the truth.

The *second* class may comprehend those who are indifferent and careless. While the church is neglected, these persons lay disregarded.

The *third* class embraces the distant pagans, whom the prophet seems more especially to have had in view. These neglect the church of the living God, when it is destitute of his blessing; but when it flourishes, then they, of every class and of every name, are ready to return to "dwell under its shadow," and the blessing of its protection. You have reason to expect this will be the case, if God shall prosper us by his own presence.

2. *There shall be an increase of life in these new members of the church :*—"They shall revive as the corn." New life is given to them. At first, they appear naked and unpromising as the corn; they decayed and died like that corn; but, by the blessing of the God of grace, as well as of the God of providence, they revive; they live again as that corn; and, in connexion with the living church, they possess its living influence. "They shall grow as the

vine," another Scripture emblem of fertility, reviving in
newness of life; they shall yield divine fruit, fruit corres-
pondent to that of the true church of God; they shall
flourish yet more and more, in all that shall bring glory to
God and benefit to man.

3. *They shall present an acceptable memorial to the
God whom they have chosen.* "And the scent thereof
shall be as Lebanon;" or rather, "The memorial thereof
shall be as the wine of Lebanon," used in libation, poured
forth as an acceptable offering upon the altar of God.
These converts to the flourishing churches, growing in
number and abounding in spiritual life, shall bring their
offering as a memorial, and pour it forth on the altar.   It
shall be a memorial of themselves, presented as a libation
to God; it shall be a memorial of their service, yielded
without reserve, to Him who has called them to glory and
to virtue; it shall be the memorial of their gifts—they yield
to him what they have, as well as what they are : and each
new memorial, poured forth on the altar of God, shall come
up with acceptance in his sight.   His dew gave the prosperity, which, spreading itself into this extension of blessings and hopes, shall be presented again back to God, holy
and acceptable in his sight!

APPLICATION.

1. We learn, from this subject, to repose our entire trust
in God for the prosperity of the church.   It is only when
he becomes " as the dew unto Israel," that Israel prospers.
Paul may plant, and Apollos may water; but God alone
can give the increase, 1 Cor. iii. 6.

3. The usual order of God's proceedings, when he pours
forth his blessings, is to give increased grace to his church.
What does the revival of religion properly mean?   Unquestionably, it properly and strictly means, something

K

which re-lives in the church : the parched and withered
field revives, lives again, when it is visited with the plentiful
shower; long languishing and decaying, it lives again when
the right appliances are used.

In conclusion. Let us learn to cherish the confident hope
that God, even our God, will not forsake us. We may
look east and west, and north and south, no human effort
is able to withstand him who is God. Let a Christian man
go forth, not in his own weakness, but relying on God's
power; let him go forth, filled with the spirit of prayer,
and faith, and zeal; let him go forth, testifying his Lord
and Saviour with the Holy Ghost sent down from heaven,
and we care not what class of people he may visit : be they
ever so degraded, they shall be raised; be they ever so
barbarous, they shall be renewed; be they ever so prejudiced, they shall be conquered; be they ever so alienated,
they shall be restored. Let us go forward, trusting in God;
let us trust in His blessing, and we shall find that barbarian, Scythian, bond, and free—every country, and people,
and tongue—shall be ready to yield to an influence so especially proceeding from God—shall turn to a flourishing
church; and present the Christian memorial on their altar.
And the cross of our Lord Jesus Christ shall bring salvation to all!

SKETCH XXXI.

DIFFUSION OF CHRISTIANITY DEPENDENT ON THE EXERTIONS OF CHRISTIANS.

BY REV. HENRY GREY, A.M., EDINBURGH.*

" And a vision appeared to Paul in the night ; There stood a man of Macedonia, and prayed him, saying, Come over into Macedonia, and help us."
ACTS xvi. 9.

THE request presented to the apostle, in this striking vision, conveys in it an expressive indication of the dependance of man on the assistance of his fellows, and of the obligation under which we are consequently laid to help one another. This dependence, and this obligation, may be traced through human life, in all the variety of its circumstances ; but is particularly deserving of our consideration, in reference to our spiritual and eternal interests. God has appointed, that the knowledge of religion, and the blessings of salvation, should be communicated to others, through the instrumentality of those who have previously been blessed with them ; and He has thus imposed on those who know him, a duty peculiarly honourable and important. We may add, that their success, in discharging this high duty, usually bears some proportion to their fidelity ; and that the actual extension of the knowledge and blessings of salvation seems, in a great degree, to correspond with the activity, zeal, and perseverance exerted in the propagation of them.

* Preached in Lady Glenorchv's Chapel, before the Edinburgh Missionary Society, April 2, 1818.

I. WE BEGIN WITH SOME GENERAL OBSERVATIONS.

1. *It cannot be doubted, that those grand arrangements of providence, which determine the general condition and circumstances of the human race, were designed, by infinite wisdom, to call into exercise the moral principles and feelings of man.* God has assigned to each class of beings its appropriate character and relations; and that dependence of man on his fellows, which requires the exercise of mutual sympathy, and reciprocal kind offices, forms a grand law of human nature, and gives rise to many important duties, and many peculiar enjoyments. The neglect of the obligations imposed by this law, is the source of a large portion of human wretchedness; a cordial compliance with its demands would go far to restore man to his proper rank as a moral agent; and adorn his character with some graces of singular excellence, which, we think, are unknown to those higher intelligences who are exempt from suffering and sin.

2. *This grand law of mutual dependence may be traced in operation, through all the different orders of society and departments of life.* And in proportion as any state advances in civilization—in proportion as labour is divided, and art perfected, and human life replenished with accommodations and comforts—the dependence of man on his fellows becomes more and more conspicuous. The blessings of religion are the gifts of sovereign mercy, flowing from the bosom of infinite love; but, in dispensing them, God is pleased to make use of human agency. We remark,

3. *That true religion is neither the invention of human genius, nor the deduction of human reason; but is founded on the actual circumstances of mankind, and on those positive discoveries which God has made of his character and will.* God has appointed that the great facts on which it rests, should be made known, from generation to generation, by an unbroken succession of living witnesses.

4. *The obligation under which we lie to help one another in our spiritual concerns, extends through all the various circumstances of life, and is particularly interwoven with its most interesting relations.* This is the highest department of a parent's duty. But to look beyond the family circle. Is it not the duty of every one to help his neighbour in this important concern? Consider,

II. The dependence of man on man, and the consequent obligation of mutual assistance, with a more particular reference to those nations destitute of the Gospel.

1. I ask, *Whether the necessities of the nations destitute of the Gospel, do not furnish a powerful claim on all the help we can possibly afford them?* Of their melancholy condition, in a moral view, little need be said to convince those who acknowledge the justness of the representations which the word of God gives us, of the present circumstances of the human race. Those characters of ignorance, guilt, and sin, which it attributes universally to fallen man, are most distinctly traced in those portions of mankind whom God has left most entirely to themselves.

2. I ask, *Whether the means with which you are furnished of supplying the necessities of the nations, do not impose peculiar obligations?* The God of love has made a provision for the recovery of fallen man, and you are acquainted with it. He has declared, that he "is in Christ reconciling the world unto himself, not imputing their trespasses unto them," 2 Cor. v. 19 ; and to you has this word of reconciliation been committed. A remedy is prepared of sovereign efficacy to cure the moral maladies of man, and raise his soul to eternal life ; and you are entrusted with this remedy. Can you suppose it lawful to withhold it from the millions who are incessantly dying for want of it?

3. I ask, *Whether the declared will and purpose of God, do not place beyond all doubt, our obligation to impart the Gospel to the heathen?* Look into the Bible, and say, Was it for you only the Saviour died? for you only the Holy Ghost was promised? for you only the gates of heaven were opened? No; He "gave himself a ransom for all, to be testified in due time," 1 Tim. ii. 6. The world is the ample theatre on which His grace is to be displayed.

The character of the gospel corresponds with its design. It is simple and spiritual, having nothing in it of a local or limited nature : its blessings are such as all may enjoy ; its services all may perform ; its precepts all may obey.

APPLICATION.

1. Would that I may have conveyed any due sense of the necessities of the nations, or of your obligations to help them !

2. These nations might have been our benefactors, had God willed it ; and, more faithful to their privileges and to the claims of brotherhood than we have been, might have sent us their apostles, their ministers of reconciliation, their ambassadors of peace.

3. It was not a seraph from the throne, but a man of Macedonia, who stood before Paul, and prayed him, "Come over, and help us." Many men, the men of many lands, approach you with this prayer. Christ asks of those who love him, obedience to his commands, the fulfilment of his declarations. He pleads by his cross and intercession; by the consolations of a throne of grace ; by all your peaceful joys, and happy privileges ; by the blessed hope of immortality,—he entreats you to be fellow workers with him in fulfilling the purposes of his love, and in communicating to " the Gentiles the unsearchable riches of Christ!"

SKETCH XXXII.

THE INFLUENCE OF CHRISTIAN TRUTH.

BY REV. JOSHUA BATES, D.D.,*

PRESIDENT OF MIDDLEBURG COLLEGE, U. S.

" The truth shall make you free."—JOHN viii. 32.

THAT Christianity, believed and regarded, has a tendency to exalt the character and increase the happiness of mankind, is a doctrine clearly implied in our text. " Then said Jesus to those Jews which believed in him, If ye continue in my word, then are ye my disciples indeed; and ye shall know the truth, and the truth shall make you free." Without repeating the whole context, or giving a disquisition on the metaphorical language which runs through it, I shall be justified in calling your attention, at once, to the doctrine already stated; and leading you to consider at large, the *influence of Christianity on the character and happiness of mankind.*

I. LET US CONSIDER THE INFLUENCE OF CHRISTIANITY ON THE CHARACTER AND HAPPINESS OF MAN, VIEWED SIMPLY AS AN INTELLECTUAL BEING.

If we can prove, that Christianity encourages a spirit of

* From a Sermon, preached in Northampton, Massachusetts, September 21, 1825, at the Sixteenth Annual Meeting of the American Board of Commissioners for Foreign Missions.

free inquiry and philosophical investigation—that it tends to enlarge the sphere of human knowledge, and promote intellectual improvement—the inference will follow, that it elevates the character, and adds to the happiness of man-kind.　This must be admitted, or stupidity is a blessing; and unrestrained indulgence of passion, a duty.　I know much has been said in praise of ignorance; and even genius, with all her inventions and acquisitions, has been charged with the crime of entailing mischief and misery on the world. But experience satisfactorily confutes the presumptuous charge.　The happiness of ignorance and stupidity is only negative; it is the appropriate happiness of the brute, not of man—not of beings endowed with intellectual foresight, and capable of anticipation.

Whatever, therefore, tends to promote intellectual im-provement, and advance the cause of science, must elevate the character and increase the felicity of man; must give to the individuals, who are brought under its influence, increased susceptibility of enjoyment, and additional power of rendering others happy.　Now such, we contend, is the natural tendency of Christianity.　Its very spirit is liberty—not only liberty of action, but liberty of thought, liberty of inquiry.　It challenges investigation—it awakens curiosity —it dignifies truth.

For further proof and illustration of our position, let us appeal to facts.　Where has science prevailed?　By whom has literature been refined?　In what ages and countries has philosophy—sound, salutary philosophy—been most suc-cessfully cultivated?　A reference to history, and a view of the civilized world, will furnish an answer to these inquiries, at once proving and illustrating our doctrine.

Talents, sanctified by Divine grace, and moved by Chris-tian motives, constitutes a mind like Newton's—consistent, splendid, happy; and leads to such investigations as he made, which, like the orbs of heaven, whose tracks he followed and whose laws he revealed, will continue to enlighten and guide all future generations.   Let us consider,

II. THE INFLUENCE OF CHRISTIANITY ON THE CHARACTER AND HAPPINESS OF MAN, VIEWED MORE PARTICULARLY AS A MORAL BEING.

The discussion of this topic we commence with the broad position, that in proportion as man feels and regards his moral relations, other circumstances being equal, will be his power of enjoying and communicating happiness.

I point you, with confidence in the result, to those Christian countries, where no arbitrary restraints are imposed on free inquiry; and to those individuals who receive the Bible as the word of God, yield a willing submission to its authority, and abide by its decisions, without gainsaying; who have imbibed the spirit of the gospel, and received its peculiar truths in love; who, in the very language of inspiration, have been " born again, not of corruptible seed, but of incorruptible, by the word of God," 1 Pet. i. 23; and are, therefore, sincere, experimental, practical Christians.   Let the appeal be made here; and let facts decide the question, if in the minds of any it remains a question, What is the moral tendency of Christianity?   Let us consider,

III. THE INFLUENCE OF CHRISTIANITY ON THE CHARACTER AND HAPPINESS OF MAN, VIEWED AS A MEMBER OF CIVIL SOCIETY, AND A SUBJECT OF CIVIL GOVERNMENT.

Christianity exalts the character and promotes the happiness of mankind, by giving at once the blessings of social order and civil liberty.   Standing on the history of the world, I can establish this position.   Nothing like civil liberty, united with social order and security, now exists in any country beyond the limits of Christian influence. And within these limits, the degree of settled liberty may be pretty accurately measured by the purity and extent of this influence.

It has gradually modified and improved the law of nations, leading them to admit in theory, and begin to feel in practice, that they are moral persons, bound by moral obligation, to observe, in their intercourse with each other, the great Christian law of love. Especially, has it improved that portion of international law, which relates to war—softening its rigour, mitigating its horrors, and thus preparing the way for that mighty and glorious change, which it is destined to effect, when " they shall beat their swords into ploughshares, and their spears into pruning hooks,"—when " nation shall not lift up sword against nation, neither shall learn war any more," Isa. ii. 4.

APPLICATION.

1. In making an application of the subject of this discourse, I have little to say: for the lessons of gratitude, and consolation, and duty, which it suggests, are exceedingly obvious ; and they must already have been presented to every reflecting mind, and impressed on every pious and benevolent heart. How obvious, my Christian brethren, is the inference, that we are under peculiar obligations of gratitude, to our God and Redeemer, for our distinguished Christian privileges. We live in Immanuel's land! To us Christianity has come, in all her simplicity and splendour, in all her beauty and glory. We have the Bible in our hands; we may learn its truths, and obey its injunctions without fear or restraint.

2. Again. How obvious is the lesson of consolation and joy, which flows from our subject, in connexion with the prophetic assurance of the future triumphs of the gospel.

If Christianity, in its limited operations, has done so much to meliorate the condition of mankind, what must be its effects, when its influence shall have become universal and unrestrained; reaching all lands, purifying all hearts, and controlling the counsels of all nations!

3. Finally. How obvious is the inference from our doctrine, that it is the duty of every Christian to aid the cause of Christian missions. The wretched state of the heathen, of Jews, of Mohammedans, and even of multitudes nominally Christian, must awaken the tenderest sympathies, excite the most ardent and importunate prayers, and rouse all the energies of the renewed soul.

My brethren, we have placed before us the strongest motives to induce us vigorously to engage in this cause of love. The sublimity of the enterprize, the certainty of ultimate success, the signs of the times, and, what is paramount to all other considerations, the command, the last command, of our blessed Redeemer, urges to active exertion and persevering effort in this cause!

SKETCH XXXIII.

THE UNSEARCHABLE RICHES OF CHRIST.

BY REV. MELVILLE HORNE.*

" Unto me, who am less than the least of all saints, is this grace given, that
I should preach among the Gentiles the unsearchable riches of Christ."
EPHESIANS iii. 8.

IN pleading the cause of missions, it occurs to me, that I
cannot do better than call your attention to the animated
words I have read to you.

I. " THE UNSEARCHABLE RICHES OF CHRIST."
(1.) They are riches of heavenly knowledge.
(2.) Riches of redeeming love.
(3.) Riches of pardoning mercy.
(4.) Riches of sanctifying grace.
(5.) Riches of consolation and hope.
(6.) Riches of immortality and glory.
(7.) All of them " riches of Christ;" and all of them
" unsearchable."

II. AMONG WHOM ARE THEY TO BE PREACHED?
1. Paul's commission, and that of the other apostles, was
to " preach the gospel to every creature," Mark xvi. 15;
and *to bring all nations to the obedience of the faith.*

* Preached before the London Missionary Society, at St. Saviour's Church,
Southwark, May 12, 1797.

. 2. *St. Paul thoroughly understood that the gospel he preached was emphatically the gospel of the Gentiles.*

As such the angels announced it to the shepherds—" Behold, I bring you good tidings of great joy, which shall be to *all* people," Luke ii. 10.   Agreeably to this idea, at the birth of Jesus, they proclaimed, not peace in Judea, but " peace on earth."

3. *The manner in which St. Paul speaks of the calling of the Gentiles is highly worthy of observation.*

He calls it a mystery—" the mystery of Christ—revealed unto the holy apostles and prophets by the Spirit; that the Gentiles should be fellow-heirs, and of the same body: —to the intent that now unto the principalities and powers in heavenly places might be known by the Church the manifold wisdom of God, according to the eternal purpose which he purposed in Christ Jesus our Lord," Eph. iii. 4, 6, 10, 11.

III. I PROCEED TO OBSERVE ON THE DIGNIFIED IDEA ST. PAUL HAD OF THE APOSTOLIC MISSION.—" Unto me is this grace given."   Let us cast our eye,

1. *On the labours and sufferings of the mission:* " I think that God hath set forth us the apostles last as those appointed unto death: for we are made a spectacle to the world, and to angels, and to men," 1 Cor. iv. 9.   Again, " We are troubled on every side, yet not distressed; we are perplexed, but not in despair; persecuted, but not forsaken; cast down, but not destroyed; always bearing about in the body the dying of the Lord Jesus."   " In all things approving ourselves as the ministers of God, in much patience, in afflictions, in necessities, in distresses, in stripes, in imprisonments, in tumults, in labours, in watchings, in fastings," 2 Cor. iv. 8—10; vi. 4, 5.   All his crosses and losses he accounted as nothing, so that he might

communicate to miserable men "the unsearchable riches of Christ."

2. *But let us not dismiss this part of the subject without further inquiry into the grounds of St. Paul's triumph.*—"Unto me is this grace given, that I should preach among the Gentiles the unsearchable riches of Christ." And is it not a high honour to be made a "steward of the mysteries of God," a dispenser of "the unsearchable riches of Christ?" If dignity be derived from the greatness of the power we serve, what more can be wished than to be the ambassador of God, the servant of the King of righteousness and peace? If the royal David deemed it an honour to be a door-keeper in the house of his God, (Psa. lxxxiv. 10;) well might St. Paul glory in the honourable dispensation of life and peace to mankind.

IV. The forcible admonition given to ministers and missionaries, to think humbly and soberly of themselves as they ought to think.

"Unto me, who am less than the least of all saints." What! Paul, the miraculous convert of Jesus Christ! Paul, the teacher of the Gentiles, and "not a whit behind the very chiefest apostles," 2 Cor. xi. 5. Paul, who had been caught up into the third heavens, seen the visions of the Almighty, and heard unspeakable words, 2 Cor. xii. 2, 4; who had "suffered the loss of all things," and accounted the loss of all as nothing—who had laboured, and suffered, and done more good than all the apostles—who had founded more churches, than many ministers have converted souls—is this man the least! yea "less than the least of all saints!" Wonderful humility! Blessed gospel, which is capable of producing this lovely temper in the proud heart of Saul the persecutor!

Mark, brethren, upon what point St. Paul makes this

comparison of himself to turn. It is not riches, learning, power; nor does it turn upon ministerial talent, labour, or success. No; whatever distinctions, real or artificial, prevail among men, they all vanish in the presence of that grand and everlasting distinction which God makes between the man that feareth him, and the man that feareth him not, Mal. iii. 18. The point of honour is true holiness. It is not to preach Christ, but to love him; it is not to convert others, but to be converted ourselves to the image of His holiness, which constitutes our honour and felicity in time, and in eternity.

1. *When the Lord will make a man a chosen vessel, eminently serviceable in the church, it is the method of his grace to humble that man in the dust, and to remove from him every ground of vain glory.* This is necessary to secure all the glory to the Lord, to whom alone it is justly due. It is, also, necessary to bring the souls of his saints to an absolute dependence on the Lord's wisdom, grace, and power, for all good to themselves and others. And, in the last place, it is of the utmost importance to our own safety and comfort, lest we should be lifted up with pride even by the graces bestowed upon us, and the important services we are enabled to perform.

2. *That it is impossible a missionary should engage in his work in a better spirit than of that humility of which St. Paul is the example.* The man who is brought to see himself as "the chief of sinners," and "the least of all saints," is happily freed from all confidence in the flesh. His talents, labours, sufferings, and success are with him of no account. He goes out of himself to live in Christ— for Christ, and upon Christ. He receives, from the Redeemer, "grace to help in every time of need." Feeling with he is nothing, he also feels that "Christ is all, and in all."

APPLICATION.

1. Let us, then, every day place our dear missionaries under the shadow of the Rock of Israel. The Lord requires it; and the missionaries claim it at our hands. We subscribe money; they give their lives. We preach missionary sermons to polite congregations; they compass sea and land, and feel the extremities of hunger, thirst, cold, and weariness, in preaching to stupid heathen, who, it may be, will some day reward their love with a shower of stones, or a volley of spears.

2. " The harvest truly is plenteous, but the labourers are few : pray ye therefore the Lord of the harvest, that he would send forth labourers into his harvest," Luke x. 2. And may we, who are ministers of the word, who have it in charge to dispense " the unsearchable riches of Christ," and who glory to call ourselves God's ambassadors—may we be made to feel the attractions of this calling! " Now unto the King eternal, immortal, invisible, the only wise God, be honour and glory for ever and ever! Amen." 1 Tim. i. 17.

SKETCH XXXIV.

JESUS CHRIST'S INSTRUCTIONS TO THE SEVENTY DISCIPLES.

BY THE REV. H. HUNTER, D.D.*

"After these things the Lord appointed other seventy also, and sent them two and two before his face into every city and place, whither he himself would come. Therefore said he unto them, The harvest truly is great, but the labourers are few: pray ye therefore the Lord of the harvest, that he would send forth labourers into his harvest. Go your ways: behold, I send you forth as lambs among wolves. Carry neither purse, nor scrip, nor shoes: and salute no man by the way," etc.—LUKE x. 1—20.

AT the time when our blessed Lord sent out the seventy, by two and two, he was preparing to follow them in the last circuit which he made through Galilee, being within the last six months of his abode upon earth. What he addressed to them on that memorable occasion, may, with the change of a few circumstances, serve to admonish, warn, and instruct us all; and especially those whom we are sending out in His name, on a progress much more extensive, but precisely with the same view. I trust all will listen to them, therefore, with that attention, deference, and humility, which are due, not to the words of a mere man like themselves, but of Him who spake as never man spake.

I. CHRIST SENT OUT THE SEVENTY BY PAIRS, seeming to say, with Joseph to his brethren, "See that ye fall not out by the way," Gen. xlv. 24.

* Delivered at Zion Chapel, on the designation of the first missionaries to the Islands of the South Sea, July 29, 1796.

The little district of Galilee was thus parcelled out into thirty-five subdivisions; and thereby the labour and danger were diminished, by being equalized. Besides, each missionary was thus provided with a known and tried friend, embarked in the same cause with himself, whose conversation would relieve the tediousness of the way, mutual confidence would be inspired to the discharge of their important trust, and credit would be secured to a message delivered under the concurring testimony of two witnesses.

II. OUR BLESSED LORD FAIRLY AND FAITHFULLY WARNED THE SEVENTY OF THE DIFFICULTY AND DANGER OF THE CHARGE WHICH THEY WERE UNDERTAKING.

The labour and difficulty he represents under the idea of an ample harvest, to be reaped by the hands of a few' labourers. The harvest-field is a scene of more than ordinary exertion, toil, and fatigue, even when labourers are abundant: it calls for unremitting application through the whole day, and frequently through the night—it demands emulous yet friendly energy.

The danger of the enterprise is represented in the character here given of human nature: "Behold, I send you forth as lambs among wolves." "Beware of men," Matt. x. 17. Mortifying view of human nature! and, alas! it is not the exaggerated account of a discontented, irritable cynic, inflamed with hatred against mankind; but a true representation of the case from one who knew it well, and who bitterly deplored that depravity which he was constrained to expose. Man a wolf to man!—to his brother—his benefactor! Man a victim to the fury of him whom he sought to save!

III. OUR LORD CAUTIONS HIS MISSIONARIES AGAINST AN OVER CURIOUS AND MINUTE REGARD TO ACCOMMODATION, PREPARATORY TO THEIR ENTERING ON THEIR MISSION, AND WHILE EMPLOYED IN EXECUTING THE BUSINESS OF IT.

Observe, he would inculcate on them an unbounded confidence in the care of Providence, and perfect contentment with such provision as the hospitality of those whom they visited might, from time to time, supply. They are enjoined to disregard some particulars which most men would deem essentially necessary to a journey: " Carry neither purse, nor scrip, nor shoes." An anxious solicitude about conveniences, much more about fantastical gratification and indulgence, betrays a mind unsubdued to the authority, and uninfluenced by the example, of the Lord Jesus. It betrays the sickly appetite of a spoiled child, which must be tempted and pampered with delicacies; not the manly spirit of the intrepid youth, who cares not how hard he lies, and how coarsely he fares, provided he gets forward. " I have learned: in whatsoever state I am, therewith to be content. I know both how to be abased, and I know how to abound ; every where and in all things I am instructed both to be full and to be hungry, both to abound and to suffer need," Phil. iv. 11, 12.

IV. OUR LORD RECOMMENDS TO THE DISCIPLES UNDIVIDED, UNDEVIATING ATTENTION TO WHAT WAS SPECIALLY COMMITTED TO THEM.

This is plainly implied in the injunction, "Salute no man by the way." And this is by no means an encouragement to practise rudeness and incivility; for the gospel inculcates not only the weightier matters—" Whatsoever things are true, whatsoever things are honest, whatsoever things are just, and whatsoever things are pure," but those also which " are lovely and of good report," Phil. iv. 8 ; and ordains that " all things be done decently and in order," 1 Cor. xiv. 40. But the salutations of the east were and are formal, tedious, and ceremonious; and custom sanctioned them so far, as to suspend and interrupt the most serious and necessary business. It became needful, there-fore, on urgent occasions, to dispense with the customary laws of decorum.

"The King's business requireth haste." When a dark world is to be enlightened; when the "dead in trespasses and sins" are to be quickened into "newness of life," let the servant of Jesus Christ give his whole heart to it. "Let the dead bury their dead," Matt. viii. 22.

V. Our Lord's instructions to the seventy re-specting their work, and the manner in which they were to perform it.

This consists of three articles: they were to proclaim peace wherever they went; they were to " heal the sick;" and to announce the immediate approach of the kingdom of God. What a copious return for the lodging and re-freshments of a day! And it is thus that the great God acknowledges and remunerates the little services which men render him in the person of his ministers. " Say, Peace be to this house," verse 5.

" Heal the sick." The seventy were endowed with mi-raculous powers of healing. They had this supernatural seal affixed to their commission; and thus an effectual door was opened for them to the hearts of those to whom their message was addressed. We pretend not to send you forth armed with such power as this,

But " say unto them, The kingdom of God is come nigh unto you." This prepared the inhabitants of Galilee for the personal visit of the Saviour of the world; thus was his approach announced in " every city and place, whither he himself would come;" and thus are these, our mission-ary brethren, to " go forth," I trust, in the spirit and power of Elias, in the spirit and power of John Baptist; as " a voice crying in the wilderness, Prepare ye the way of the Lord, make straight in the desert a highway for our God," Isa. xl. 3. A finger pointing out—a tongue proclaiming, " Behold the Lamb of God, which taketh away the sin of the world," John i. 29.

VI. CHRIST ENCOURAGES HIS DISCIPLES WITH THE ASSURANCE, THAT HE SHOULD CONSIDER THE RECEPTION WHICH THEY MET WITH, AS GIVEN TO HIMSELF.

Every instance of neglect or insult which should be offered to them, as disrespectful to him, and consequently to God; and every expression of kindness and benevolence to them, as a personal favour. " He that heareth you heareth me; and he that despiseth you despiseth me; and he that despiseth me despiseth him that sent me," Luke x.16.

VII. OUR LORD INSTRUCTS HIS DISCIPLES TO KEEP THEIR HEARTS WITH ALL DILIGENCE, FROM THE EMOTIONS OF SELF-GRATULATION AND COMPLACENCY IN THE HOUR OF SUCCESS.

To the full extent of his promise, and beyond it, his presence and power had accompanied them. This they joyfully acknowledged on their return, " saying, Lord, even the devils are subject unto us, through thy name," ver. 17. But even this was surpassed by a still dearer, and more deeply interesting consideration : " Notwithstanding, in this rejoice not, that the spirits are subject unto you ; but rather rejoice, because your names are written in heaven," ver. 20. Hereby their great, their eternal all was effectually secured.

To conclude. Let every professed Christian consider himself specially commissioned to declare and to live " the truth as it is in Jesus," in the ears, and before the eyes of a careless and unbelieving world!

SKETCH XXXV.

INSUFFICIENCY OF MERE HUMAN EFFORTS TO EVANGELIZE THE HEATHEN WORLD.

BY REV. T. S. CRISP.*

"Not by might, nor by power, but by my Spirit, saith the Lord of hosts. Who art thou, O great mountain? before Zerubbabel thou shalt become a plain."—ZECH. iv. 6, 7.

WE are endeavouring to rear a temple for God, by spreading the gospel, and building up the church of Christ in the heathen world. Our cause is great, our difficulties many; but God is all-sufficient. We notice,

I. THE CONVERSION OF THE HEATHEN WORLD IS A VAST AND DIFFICULT UNDERTAKING.

Many considerations may be adduced in proof of this positiou. Let us select a few, which are obvious to every one.

1. *Reflect on the object aimed at.* It is no other, than the conversion of souls to God. This object is so momentons, that, under any circumstances, it is worthy of every effort by which it can be rendered attainable. Compare it with any thing else : with the conquests of ambition, or the nobler triumphs of liberty; the splendour of great achievements, or the benefit of useful discoveries; the treasures which art and labour amass, and the luxuries which these treasures purchase; the blessings of peace,

---

* From a Sermon preached in the Wesleyan Chapel, Great Queen Street, Lincoln's Inn Fields, at the Annual Meeting of the Baptist Missionary Society, June 20, 1821.

the sweets of friendship, and the most refined endearments of social life: great and alluring as these objects are, the conversion of souls is still greater. Nay, the conversion of one single soul outweighs them all.

2. *Look at the dimensions of the field on which we have entered, in seeking the conversion of the heathen.* " The field," said the Saviour, " is the world," Matt. xiii. 38. The whole world was before the apostles when they commenced their labours: not a spot could they visit, beyond the borders of the promised land, which the tidings of mercy, and the Spirit of life accompanying these tidings, had ever entered.

3. *Think on the obstacles arising to this undertaking, from the degraded state of the heathen world.* Various are the forms which idolatry assumes; but each presents some peculiar character of evil. It is difficult to say, which proves the greatest barrier to the reception of the truth—the grossness of some, or the refined sensuality of others. We know not on which to look with the greatest pain: the mind of an idolater, sunk to the lowest point of intellectual debasement, his ideas few, confined within a narrow space, and as grovelling as they are few; or the faculties, acute and polished, capable of taking a large and lofty range, while the mind thus elevated, is only rendered the more enslaved, in proportion to the force with which it embraces the delusions and abominations of heathenism.

Idolatry, thus produced and nourished, becomes like an enemy intrenched within an impregnable fortress. All the strong, evil passions are on its side; from them it receives its character and complexion. Corruption is on its side; for it is the source from which it sprang. A guilty conscience is on its side; for, while the principles of idolatry are such as palliate the guilt of sin, its rites are calculated to soften down whatever yet remains of misgiving and uneasiness in the conscience. And though mere frivolous ceremonies can never impart solid peace, yet they lull and stupify; and, in this deadly repose, the soul is unwilling to be roused and disturbed. The senses and appetites are on its side; for pomp and parade, rioting and mirth festivals and shows, licentious indulgence, and secret abominations, suit the depravity of the fleshly mind. "Wherein they think it strange that ye run not with them to the same excess of riot," 1 Pet. iv. 4. This is the element in which the carnal mind delights to live and to revel. Oh! with what force, and to what a depth, must that religion strike its roots, on which forbidden fruits is seen to grow so luxuriantly. How, then, shall the overthrow of this mighty evil be brought about? This leads to the second general remark, that

II. IT IS VAIN TO ATTEMPT IT BY HUMAN POWER AND MIGHT. "Not by might, nor by power," said the Lord to Zerubbabel. Let it, then, be observed,

1. *That human power, in itself, is quite insufficient to effect this object.* Whatever the skill and energy of man may produce, they can never bring about a great moral renovation in the world. The force of human authority has made men hypocrites, but not believers. The power of the sword has been effectual in destroying the faithful; but this weapon of death has never become the instrument of life, by raising up others in their place. Human laws have exerted their energy, and have produced abject, hollow, constrained submission, not the voluntary homage of the heart. Armies have gone forth to demolish the works of man; but armies cannot "build the temple of the Lord of hosts." Great is the power of persuasion: nothing greater than the force of mind over mind. But what was the effect of this before the gospel came? "The world by wisdom knew not God," 1 Cor. i. 21. Among

the celebrated nations of antiquity, the human intellect had reached its highest elevation, and was enlarged to the greatest dimensions. Yet all that was effected by the majesty of eloquence, and the charms of poetic fiction, by the researches of philosophy, and the strength of moral reasoning, was an exchange of the barbarism of rude idolatry, for a system of theology as licentious as it was complicated.

Has any system of morals, invented and propagated by the power of man, been attended with efficacy, in subduing the corruptions of the heart? Where has such a spectacle ever presented itself? One system, indeed, there was, which did operate with mighty force. Mohammed tried what could be effected by might and by power. And did he succeed? He succeeded to the utmost in leaving to posterity a lasting, awful monument of what human power alone can do. It could give an air of sanctity to gross sensuality. It could stupify and intoxicate the mind, laying prostrate its intellectual faculties, and brutalizing all the feelings of the heart. It could reduce man to the most odious vassalage by which the mind has ever been fettered; while it exalted a mortal to a dreadful eminence, from which he looked down on whole regions, overspread with blasphemous and infernal delusions, more deadly in their effects than the ravages of the locust, the horrors of war, or the desolations of the plague. But where is the spot, however contracted, over which the same kind of power has spread spiritual life and moral liberty, peace of conscience, and purity of heart? No where: nor can these blessings ever be seen, where no higher power is at work than that of man.

2. *In effecting this object, God will not make a display of human power and might.* In establishing his spiritual kingdom among mankind, how frequently has God chosen

L

" the weak things of the world to confound the things
which are mighty!" 1 Cor. i. 27.   A nation is selected
for the purpose of stripping Satan of his glory, and tram-
pling him in the dust.   And what is this nation?   Their
progenitor was a wanderer in a strange land.   They themselves were oppressed by tyrants, and hated by surrounding
nations: they passed through a long and bitter captivity:
they were sometimes brought so low, that their state became almost hopeless.   Yet, while the greatest monarchies
rise and fall, this people are preserved, that from them may
spring " the Desire of all nations."   He comes!—but He is
clothed in all the feebleness of a mortal body.   He is the
subject of want and sorrow, of opposition and cruelty, to
which he voluntarily yields.   He is betrayed and deserted,
derided and crucified.   And, in his crucifixion, he passes
through that overwhelming desolation of mind, which even
exceeds the sufferings of the body.   Yet, in the midst of all
this, what is He doing?   He is contending, single-handed,
against all the powers of darkness—bringing glory to God—
spreading peace through the earth—raising the guilty from
hell to heaven—and reconciling Divine justice and mercy,
in the pardon of the rebellious.

Survey the history of the church, from that period down
to the times in which we live, and the truth of the language
of the text will receive abundant confirmation.   I refer to
the Reformation from Popery.   This was brought about
by the instrumentality of one agent principally—the immortal Luther.   It is, indeed, true, that the way was, in
some measure, prepared for that emancipation of the mind,
which then took place.   The writings of such men as
Wycliffe had diffused some light through the regions of
popish darkness.   But where was the man to be found to put
a finish to the great enterprise of chasing away the shades
of night?   How, then, is the great object we are aiming

at, to be effected? We can cheerfully answer this question by observing, that though it is " not by might, nor by power," yet,

III. It is by the Spirit of the Lord of hosts.

This is a part of the subject on which it is pleasant to expatiate. If there be anything which is as delightful as it is certain, it is that the things which are impossible with men, are possible with God, Matt. xix. 26; and where men must confess the inadequacy of their efforts, the power of the Spirit is there seen to shine and triumph.

The following considerations will show that all the good now going forward among the heathen, must be traced to the influence of the Spirit of God.

1. *The great work of converting and purifying souls belongs peculiarly to Him.* He exerts an influence, which, in the Old Testament, is brought forward under the image of pouring " water upon him that is thirsty, and floods upon the dry ground," Isa. xliv. 3. For all the holy animation and vigour, all the activity and fruitfulness, which belong to the renewed soul, proceed from him. In the gospel economy, his office is distinctly stated. To him is ascribed the first awakening of the soul—for we are " born of the Spirit," John iii. 4.

2. *The instrument employed for thus converting the heathen world, is peculiarly His own.* The closed eye admits not the light—the callous heart receives not the truth; yet it is the " word of God" only, which works effectually in the soul. It is by " the Truth" alone, that we are sanctified. " For our gospel came not unto you in word only, but also in power, and in the Holy Ghost," I Thess. i. 5.

3. *It is the peculiar office of the Spirit to honour the Lord Jesus Christ.* It is the office of the Spirit to reveal

the Saviour effectually to the heart; for " He shall receive of mine," said Christ, " and shall show it unto you," John xvi. 14.   And why does He thus employ his influence, to show forth the power and love, the glories and grace, of the Redeemer?   Why does he give the Cross such mighty attractions, rendering this the object around which all the affections and hopes of redeemed sinners rally as their centre?   Because it is thus that Christ is honoured; for, says the Saviour, " He shall glorify me."   In attempting an improvement of the subject on which we are now dwelling, observe,

(1.) That it shows the principle which ought to pervade the exertions of missionary societies: a principle of dependence and humility, a willingness to ascribe all the glory to Him, to whom alone it belongs.

(2.) This subject affords encouragement under difficulties.   Let us silence every objection which carnal reason would suggest; and excite ourselves to fresh, unwearied ardour, by continually looking up to the strong for strength. " Our sufficiency is of God," 2 Cor. iii. 5.

(3.) This subject is calculated to give elevation to our hopes.   Whatever God's purposes may be, it is as certain that they will be accomplished, as that they have been formed.   " The residue of the Spirit" is with Him, who is "the head over all things to the Church;" and that which remains to be given is equal to that which remains to be done.

(4.) This subject teaches us in what way every one may effectually promote the interests of missionary societies. The question which Saul addressed to Christ on the road to Damascus, is one which every genuine friend to the cause of the Redeemer will seriously and honestly ask— " Lord, what wilt thou have me to do?" Acts ix. 6.   If the mind be devoted to God, there will be no difficulty in finding an answer to such an inquiry

SKETCH XXXVI.

THE UNIVERSAL GREATNESS AND GLORY OF GOD'S NAME.

BY REV. B. W. MATTHIAS, M.A.,*
OF TRINITY COLLEGE, DUBLIN.

" For from the rising of the sun even unto the going down of the same my name shall be great among the Gentiles; and in every place incense shall be offered unto my name, and a pure offering : for my name shall be great among the heathen, saith the Lord of hosts."—MAL. i. 11.

THE prophet Malachi lived at a period when the Jewish nation had sunk into a deplorable state of immorality and impiety. The people had forgotten the lesson which their captivity seems to have taught them for a time; as they had previously forgotten that which was intended for them by the dispersion of the ten tribes belonging to their original family. Acknowledging God in their profession, they appear, at this particular period, to have in every other respect denied him.

The eternal God expostulates with the people by his prophet, and reminds them of the special kindness which he had bestowed on Jacob their ancestor, and the privileges which he had granted to him beyond those bestowed on Esau; and, marking the little effect which these things had on them, He declares that He had no pleasure in them, and would receive no offering at their hands, ver. 10.

* From a Sermon, preached at St. Bride's Church, Fleet Street, May 1, 1820, before the Church Missionary Society.

But " from the rising of the sun even unto the going down of the same," Jehovah declares, " my name shall be great among the Gentiles; and in every place incense shall be offered unto my name, and a pure offering." As though He had said, " You refuse to bring me offerings? Know, that pure offerings shall be presented to me, and in abundance—not from one solitary nation, consisting of comparatively but few individuals, but from all people on the face of the earth—from the rising of the sun even unto the going down of the same! In all the vast extent of my lower creation, I shall be celebrated and honoured; my name shall be great; and my creatures, influenced by my Spirit, shall be found willing to present, not the maimed, the blind, and the lame,—but the incense of prayer and thanksgiving; and the pure offering of a heart cleansed by my Spirit, and washed from its stains in the blood of my Son." In this prediction, we shall consider,

I. THE SUBJECT BROUGHT BEFORE US.

It is, that the name of the Lord shall be great among the heathen; and that, in every place, incense shall be offered to His name, and a pure offering. The first stated here is, that,

1. *The name of Jehovah shall be great.* " My name shall be great among the Gentiles." Melancholy, in every respect, is the view of the heathen world! Whether we consider its present corruptions, or its future prospects, its state is most awful! And all arises from this—that they know not God. But they *shall* know Him!—and so know him, that his " name shall be great."

(1.) They shall know Him as the only " living and true God," 1 Thes. i. 9; and that all the idols which they have worshipped, are but vanities and lies, and things that cannot profit, Jer. ii. 11.

(2.) Jehovah shall be further known among the heathen, not only as " the living and true God," but as a *Holy God*, a God of rectitude and purity—the very reverse of their present deities! What are the characteristics of these gods? Abomination! What, frequently, is their worship? Abomination! How miserably, then, is the human mind degraded, when its god and its worship are both abominable! Into what a wretched state of degradation, I say, must a human being be plunged, when the god whom he worships, and the worship which he offers, are all defilement and all impurity!

(3.) They shall likewise know him to be a gracious God, as well as holy, (Psa. lxxxvi. 16; cxi. 4, etc.) What must be the state of mind of that creature, who approaches his god in the morning, trembling and agitated, with an earnest cry, " Do not kill me!" To such a man, can we not make known " the Father of mercies, and the God of all comfort?" 2 Cor. i. 3. And even, on the common feelings of humanity alone, can we stand by unmoved, while the goodness of our God is thus unknown to three-fourths of his intelligent creatures? Can you remain inactive, when you may, by his blessing, rescue them from the thraldom of such a bondage, and make them acquainted with Him, whose nature and whose name are Love? 1 John iv. 8, 10, etc.

(4.) Jehovah shall be known among the heathen, in the only character in which man can know him with safety and comfort—He shall be known as God the Saviour, 2 Cor. v. 19. Towards the close of the forty-fifth chapter of the prophecies of Isaiah, the inspired writer, when speaking of the idolatry of mankind, and the character under which God shall be known among them, "a just God and a Saviour;" adds, " Look unto me, and be ye saved, all the ends of the earth: for I am God, and there is none else."

When we speak of his being known under the character of " God the Saviour," how many delightful reflections burst on the mind !   He shall be known, to use the words of Him who knew him best, and, therefore, could best describe him—his beloved Son—He shall be known as that God, who of his own mere mercy " so loved the world, that he gave his only-begotten Son, that whosoever believeth in him should not perish, but have everlasting life," John iii. 16. When He is thus known among them, his name shall be great and honoured.

2. *And what shall be this honour?*   " In every place incense shall be offered unto my name, and a pure offering."

(1.) Incense shall be offered, in every place, to the name of the Lord.   The import of the expression in the text, that incense shall be offered to His name, is—that prayer shall be made.   But, in considering this point, let us advert to the connexion.   The sacrifices preceded ; and the prayer, externally exhibited by the incense, was afterwards offered. This is calculated to teach us a most important lesson.   It is this : that *that* prayer only is efficacious in the sight of heaven—that *that* prayer only comes up before God as incense, which is connected with and dependent on the merits of the Great Atonement.   In the view of this atonement it is that David says, " Let my prayer be set forth before thee as incense; and the lifting up of my hands as the evening sacrifice," Psa. cxli. 2.

(2.) It is added—" and a pure offering; for my name shall be great among the heathen, saith the Lord of hosts." The apostle Peter describes Christians as a " holy priesthood, to offer up spiritual sacrifices, acceptable to God by Jesus Christ," 1 Pet. ii. 5.   Such a holy priesthood shall the heathen become, under the powerful influences of the grace of the Holy Spirit; and such sacrifices shall they offer !

But what are these offerings? David says, "The sacrifices of God are a broken spirit: a broken and a contrite heart, O God, thou wilt not despise," Psa. li. 17. Through the knowledge of the gospel, the heathen shall be broken down under a sense of their guilt, corruption, and misery. They shall come to God, not to plead their own merits; but, smiting on their breasts, like the publican in the temple, (Luke xviii. 13,) they shall offer the acceptable sacrifice of "a broken heart," and "a contrite spirit!" St. Paul speaks of another offering—"I beseech you therefore, brethren, by the mercies of God, that ye present your bodies"—yourselves, not the bodies of animals—"a living sacrifice, holy, acceptable unto God, which is your reasonable service," (Rom. xii. 1.) This sacrifice also shall the heathen present: they shall offer unto the Lord, themselves, their souls and bodies, to be a reasonable, holy, and lively sacrifice unto Him. Believing in Christ, as the Saviour who redeemed them to God by his blood, Rev. v. 9, and knowing themselves to be part of his "purchased possession," Eph. i. 14, they shall feel that "they are not their own, but are bought with a price;" and shall therefore glorify God in their bodies, and in their spirits, which are God's, 1 Cor. vi. 19, 20.

Finally. Praise and thanksgiving to God, and every exercise of Christian benevolence toward man, are parts of that pure offering, which shall be presented to the eternal God. In the last chapter of St. Paul's Epistle to the Hebrews, the apostle dwells on this subject. Speaking of Jesus, he says, "By him let us offer the sacrifice of praise to God continually, that is, the fruit of our lips giving thanks to his name. But," he adds, "to do good and to communicate forget not: for with such sacrifices God is well pleased." The sacrifice of a devoted heart, the sacrifice of a grateful tongue, expressing itself in praise and thanksgiving, and the sacrifice of a benevolent soul consecrated to the service of God and of human kind—these are well-pleasing sacrifices; these are the blessed offerings, which the now perishing heathen shall be enabled to present to the Most High God.   Let us now consider, .

II. What ground we have to conclude that this prediction shall be accomplished.

He makes the assertion at the beginning, and he repeats it at the end of the verse to assure us of its certainty:—" For from the rising of the sun even unto the going down of the same my name shall be great among the Gentiles; and in every place incense shall be offered unto my name, and a pure offering: for my name shall be great among the heathen, saith the Lord of hosts."   We may argue the accomplishment of this promise,

I. *From the truth of the eternal God.*   " God is not a man, that he should lie; neither the son of man, that he should repent: hath he said, and shall he not do it? or hath he spoken, and shall he not make it good?" Numb. xxiii. 19. " Ask of me," Jehovah says to the Saviour, " and I will give thee the heathen for thine inheritance, and the uttermost parts of the earth for thy possession," Psa. ii. 8. Has not the Redeemer claimed this inheritance?   We may infer the accomplishment of this promise,

2. *From the power as well as the truth of God.*   It has be said, that there are insuperable difficulties in the way of converting the heathen—that it is an idle thing to look forward to such an event—that you must first civilize them; and, till you have conferred that benefit on them, you cannot make them Christians.   But what says matter of fact? Preach the gospel to them, as they can be brought to comprehend it: that will be the most powerful of all instruments in civilizing them.   Let the great work in the South

Sea Islands bear witness! Let the rapid improvement of the liberated negroes in Sierra Leone testify! Let the elevation to social enjoyments of even Hottentots, and Greenlanders, and Esquimaux, point out the path to civilization! The grace of the gospel tempers the soul of even savage man, and fits it to seek after whatever may exalt human nature.

3. *The zeal which God has for his own glory*, presents another and a most forcible argument in proof that this promise shall be accomplished.

Having now offered such evidence as naturally presents itself, in proof that this glorious prediction shall be accomplished, it becomes us to bring the subject home to ourselves, and to consider,

III. THE LINE OF CONDUCT THESE TRUTHS DEVOLVE UPON US.

It pleases God to work by second causes; and, if this great prediction is to be accomplished, means must be used for that end. It is, therefore, one of the first duties incumbent on Christians, in order that this prediction may be accomplished,

1. *That those of them, who are qualified for the work, should proclaim the truth as it is in Jesus, to the perishing heathen.*

2. *You should advance the cause of missions by your influence.* Your time and talents will be most nobly employed, in exciting in others a feeling and interest in the cause of the heathen.

3. *You should advance the cause of missions, by the pecuniary means which God has given you.* The silver and the gold are his, Hag. ii. 8: a portion of them has, through his Providence, fallen to you; and it is but right, therefore, that you should use them for his glory and the good of his creatures.

4. But prayer and supplication are still more important than the silver and the gold. Oh, bear ever in mind, what it is that supports the hands of missionaries in the important and difficult work in which they are engaged—it is that grace and influence which God has promised to bestow on them.

APPLICATION.

1. Christian friends,—ere we part, permit me to ask you, or, rather, let each one ask himself, What am I doing? or, How am I affected in this cause?

2. Much, undoubtedly, has been done, of late years, by the Christian world; much has been done by Great Britain; and much has been done by the Society, on behalf of which I am now pleading! But look to the world, and let me ask you, Has enough been done?—No! not one thousandth part of what should have been done!

3. In this labour of love, Christians, we must abound more and more. If ever, then, you prayed for the cause of Christ among the heathen before, pray more earnestly now: if ever you have used influence for the advancement of His glory before, use more now: if ever you have contributed before, contribute more now—that you may hasten the accomplishment of this Divine prediction, "For from the rising of the sun even unto the going down of the same my name shall be great among the Gentiles; and in every place incense shall be offered unto my name, and a pure offering: for my name shall be great among the heathen, saith the Lord of hosts!"

SKETCH XXXVII.

THE WILDERNESS MADE GLAD.

BY REV. JAMES FOOTE, M. A.*

"The wilderness and the solitary place shall be glad for them; and the desert shall rejoice and blossom as the rose."—ISA. xxxv. 1.

IN prosecuting the idea suggested in the text, we shall, in dependance on Divine aid, take a view of some of the features of a desert, in which it resembles those of the heathen world; endeavouring, as we proceed, to show how, in the latter case, these features would be changed, or improved, by the introduction of the gospel.

I. A DESERT MAY BE CONSIDERED AS BARREN AND UN-CIVILIZED

So, in general, are heathen countries. But, instead of unfruitfulness and barbarism, Christianity would introduce culture, civilization, and every thing which, in connexion with these, tends to promote the substantial comforts of life. The Bible and the plough go together,—they are gradually penetrating into the inmost recesses of its deserts, where already the eye is occasionally refreshed by cultivated spots, like so many fruitful islands rising from the bosom of the ocean. A wilderness may be considered,

II. AS A PLACE OF DREARY SOLITUDE.

It is here called, "the solitary place." But the gospel

* Preached before the London Missionary Society, at the Tabernacle, May 12, 1819.

would introduce the endearments of society; or, at all events, sweeten solitude itself. When we take a view of many parts of the heathen world, the want of human beings, the awful solitariness, is most obvious. How numerous, how vast, and how beautiful the tracts of country, both in the old and new world, where not even one rational creature exists to rejoice in the bounty, or to celebrate the praises of the Creator! And where there are some inhabitants, they are often so thinly scattered, that the solitude is thereby only rendered the more sensible. Can this be a desirable state of existence? It is also worthy of notice, that among even the more numerous tribes of savages, social enjoyment is but small. They are strangers to the more delicate pleasures of domestic life, and to the enlivening flow of sentiment. They have, indeed, their feasts: but these are seasons of diabolical, rather than of human mirth. Then their extravagant madness often ends in scenes of rioting and blood; and it is always preceded by corresponding depression of spirits. Their habitual character, undoubtedly, is retiredness, melancholy and taciturnity. On the other hand, true religion gives birth to those feelings which prompt man with confidence to seek man; while, at the same time, it enlarges the mind, and furnishes many rational and enlivening topics on which men delight to speak out of the abundance of the heart. I observe,

III. THAT A WILDERNESS MAY BE CONSIDERED AS A PLACE OF INHUMANITY AND CRUELTY.

And that such are heathen countries, Scripture declares in these words—" The dark places of the earth are full of the habitations of cruelty," Psa. lxxiv. 20. How common in heathen lands has been, and still is, the exposure of female infants! A missionary, in South America, once reproved a married woman of good character, according to the standard of character prevalent there, for following this custom. The defence she made proved at least, in the most convincing manner, the cruelty under which her whole sex there groaned. " I wish to God, father," said she with tears, " I wish to God, that my mother had by my death prevented the distresses I endure, and have yet to endure as long as I live. Can human nature endure such tyranny? What kindness can we show our female children equal to that of relieving them from such oppression, more bitter a thousand times than death? I say again, Would to God, that my mother had put *me* under ground the moment I was born!"

An excellent author, speaking of the Jaina, in Mysore, says, that " in a quarrel among the Brahmins, on account of some difference of religious sentiment, the party which obtained the victory, caused the priests of Jaina to be ground to death in oil-mills." He further observes, that at Tonoru, where this cruelty took place, though certain animals are very numerous and very hurtful, it is reckoned a very grievous sin to destroy any of them. Thus the very persons who shudder at the thought of a mischievous animal being killed, applaud the Brahmins for having ground the Jainas to death in oil-mills !

IV. WHEN WE HEAR OF A WILDERNESS, WE THINK OF A PLACE OF COMFORTLESS SORROW.

The promise that the wilderness shall be gladdened and made to rejoice, implies that it is previously the seat of sorrow and mourning. Assuredly the heathen world is a wilderness of comfortless sorrow, as it contains not within itself the means of soothing the sad distress with which it is filled. But such a wilderness would be gladdened by the gospel, which would bring home to the afflicted and

the dying "the peace of God, which passeth all understanding," to "keep their hearts and minds, through Christ
Jesus;" and through him, also, the powerful consolations of
the Holy Spirit, the Comforter. Thus the promise would
be fulfilled, "When the poor and needy seek water, and
there is none, and their tongue faileth for thirst, I the
Lord will hear them, I the God of Israel will not forsake
them," Isa. xli. 17.

Lastly. LIKE A WILDERNESS, THE HEATHEN WORLD IS
A PLACE OF AWFUL DANGER.

"I was in perils," said the apostle Paul, "in the wilderness," 2 Cor. xi. 26. "Where there is no vision the
people perish," Prov. xxix. 18. We may hope that there
are a few exceptions, in some way which we cannot comprehend; but most certainly, the general rule is, "Where
there is no vision the people perish!" Those who have
the gospel offered to them, and yet reject it, perish with a
more aggravated condemnation than those who never had
any such offer; but this does not render the state of the
heathen safer than it would otherwise have been; for, in
the words of the apostle Paul—"As many as have sinned
without law shall also perish without law," Rom. ii. 12. A
perilous wilderness, then, well represents the spiritual
danger of the heathen world.

IMPROVEMENT.

The subject may be applied in reference both to those
in Christian, and to those in heathen countries.

1. *Let us improve it as furnishing ourselves with ground
of gratitude and admonition.* How thankful ought we to
be, when we contrast our own happy situation with the
state of those who "sit in darkness, and in the region and
shadow of death!" How thankful should we be, when we

compare our present state with that of our heathen forefathers; for, in superstition and cruelty, the ancient Britons
seem to have been equal to any savage tribe now on the
face of the earth. Many are the advantages of a civil,
political, and local nature which we enjoy; but it is the
light of revelation which either gives them birth, or enables
us fully to avail ourselves of them. " Blessed is the
people that know the joyful sound," Psa. lxxxix. 15.
" Blessed are your eyes, for they see: and your ears, for
they hear," Matt. xiii. 16. But while we make this general acknowledgment of the goodness of the Lord, in
thus visiting our land with the gospel of his grace,

2. *It becomes us to consider whether we have personally*
embraced it. It is an observation peculiarly worthy of the
wise man, that God " hath set the world in the heart,"
Eccl. iii. 11. Now, what is that world in the heart originally, but a moral " wilderness"—" a solitary place"—" a
desert." It bears no fruit to the glory of God; it knows
not communion with its Maker; it is a stranger to every
pure and substantial joy. But whenever the truth is received in the love of it, the result is " righteousness, peace,
and joy, in the Holy Ghost." Let us ask ourselves, If the
gospel be to us the chief source of gladness and rejoicing?

3. *Let us improve the subject in reference to the heathen,*
whose sad state we are now assembled to commiserate.
We have been often told, but we are not yet sufficiently
impressed by the consideration, that not one-fifth part of
the human race have yet been made acquainted with the
gospel. Endeavour then, if you can, to form some conception of the aggregate of misery which exists among the
destitute multitude. Think, oh think! of the unmitigated
woe, and awful danger of " the waste, howling wilderness."

While, however, the glory of this work is the Lord's, he
condescends to employ human instruments; nay, according

to his wise détermination, such instruments are necessary. The ministry of reconciliation is committed to ambassadors, who are to beseech sinners to be reconciled to God, 2 Cor. v. 20. "How shall" heathen "believe in Him of whom they have not heard? and how shall they hear without a preacher? and how shall they preach, except they be sent?" Rom. x. 14, 15. Hence the necessity for missionaries.

5. *But it is necessary for the Christian public to remember that the means of support must be furnished.* I am not disputing with those who are opposers of this work, but am taking it for granted that your appearance here declares you to be its friends. We are not entitled to dictate. Only be it remembered by us all, " He which soweth sparingly shall reap also sparingly; and he which soweth bountifully shall reap also bountifully," 2 Cor. ix. 6.

6. *Already, He who is to be crowned Lord of all has gained some of his most signal triumphs, in modern times, through this instrumentality.* Consider these triumphs as pledging thee to similar exertions; and then, at last, it shall be seen that thou wast honoured to bear a conspicuous part in the full accomplishment of this delightful prophecy—" The wilderness and the solitary place shall be glad for them, and the desert shall rejoice and blossom as the rose!" Amen.

SKETCH XXXVIII.

MEANS OF THE WORLD'S CONVERSION.

BY REV. CHARLES HALL,

ONE OF THE SECRETARIES OF THE AMERICAN HOME MISSIONARY SOCIETY, NEW YORK.

"After those days, saith the Lord, I will put my law in their inward parts, and write it in their hearts; and will be their God, and they shall be my people. And they shall teach no more every man his neighbour and every man his brother, saying, Know the Lord: for they shall all know me, from the least of them unto the greatest of them, saith the Lord."

JER. xxxi. 33, 34.

THE happy period predicted in this passage has been the desire and the expectation of the church in every age. It has been the burden of prophecy and of prayer. Thousands of the noblest spirits that ever walked the earth, as they beheld this consummation in distant prospect, have kindled into rapture; and, to hasten its approach, have tasked their utmost energies. The delay of this wished-for redemption of the world, has ever been a subject of the church's lamentation. As we look backward over her history, we see her, in every period, prostrate before God, and crying, "Thy kingdom come!" while a long line of patriarchs, prophets, and saints moving in sad procession, lift their tearful eyes, and stretch out their supplicating hands, saying, Why do thy chariot wheels so long delay?

Who is there among us, having any sympathy with Christ, that has not shared in this feeling, and uttered this cry? How is it possible for a Christian to look out upon the world—to contemplate our race grovelling in sensuality, and ravening with malevolence, until earth groans with

suffering, and heavens weep in pity—and not pray that
the days of darkness may be shortened? Who has not
often inquired, with inexpressible desire, for some more ex-
peditious mode of evangelizing the earth? Who has not
asked, If there be not, in the resources of Omnipotence,
some more potent means that have ever yet been employed,
to bring men back to God?

Such passages of inspiration as our text, are adapted to
quiet our impatient solicitude, not only by furnishing an
assurance of the ultimate accomplishment of our highest
hopes; but also by intimating the *mode* in which God's
wisdom will operate to produce the glorious result.

I. LET US INQUIRE WHAT INSTRUMENT WILL BE EM-
PLOYED TO BRING ABOUT THE BLESSED CONDITION OF THE
HUMAN FAMILY PREDICTED IN THE TEXT.

*This instrument is Divine truth, most expressively called
in the text, Knowledge of the Lord:* that is, the exhibition
of the Divine character, more than any other truth, before
all consciences, is to be the mighty engine, by which heaven
will work out the moral revolution of the world. Do any,
at first view, imagine that this is a means too simple to
accomplish so vast a result? But what is it to " know the
Lord?" or, rather, what is it not? All moral truth, every
conceivable motive to goodness, is involved in knowing
Him—in a *true* idea of the holy Lord God. To know the
Lord—to have the true conception of the REAL GOD,—is
the most perfect law which a man can have before his conscience. What is the moral law itself, but God's character
—a catalogue of his perfection, written out in the form of
precepts? The soul that knows what God is, sees in-
tuitively what itself ought to be. He has only to present
Himself, as he is, for ever before the mental view, in order to
keep men under perpetual admonition of right and wrong.

You see, at once, why Paganism is a system of wretchedness, even for the life that now is; and why Christianity
restrains and blesses even those whom it does not convert,
by continually holding up before them at least some dim
portraiture of the true God. The power of the Divine
character and example, as a persuasive to virtue, and pre-
ventive of sin, is immeasurably great. Such a conception
as that of a perfect, almighty Being—the Upholder and
Governor of all things, is the grandest of which the mind
is capable. The idea of a present God, a real, living, all-
knowing, all-pervading Spirit, having an infinite aversion
to sin, and love of goodness, is a thought that bows down
the soul in utter abasement, and sways over it an infinite
authority. In proportion to the clearness with which this
idea is apprehended by men, are they brought under the
control of moral motives. It is, therefore, with a most
beautiful propriety, that the Scriptures use the phrase,
" knowledge of the Lord," as a comprehensive term for all
truth and goodness. To know him, is to know his character, his government, his rights, his claims on us, and our
duties to him. It is to know his plan of mercy,—his Son,
and his Spirit—his pardoning and sanctifying grace. Let
us now ask,

II. By what methods and agency is this grand
instrument to be applied to the renovation of the
world? How is this knowledge of the Lord to be spread
all over the earth, and to be brought in contact with every
human heart?

In reply to this deeply-interesting inquiry, we remark,
that the holy Scriptures, all along, throughout the whole
line of promise and prophecy, speak in such a way as to
imply two different and distinct eras under the new dispensation; and they very plainly teach, that the truth will be

spread in a different manner in each of these eras. One of these is spoken of as coming after a certain state of things. Thus, in the text, "After those days, saith the Lord, I will put my law in their inward parts," etc. When the period thus indicated shall arrive, we are taught to expect a larger measure of the Divine influence—a measure quite above and beyond that which now accompanies the preaching of the gospel. This special influence will probably differ in degree, rather than in kind, from that which is ordinarily enjoyed. It will act more directly and more efficiently on the hearts of men. It will not be independent of all use of means; but there will be in it so much of God—the effects will be so speedy and so great, that means will be comparatively unobservable. Thus, in the text, this great moral revolution, is ascribed to an immediate agency of God himself. The Lord saith, " I will PUT MY LAW in their inward parts, and WRITE IT in their hearts."

Other expressions, denoting sovereign acts of the Deity, are also employed: such as "pouring out my spirit upon all flesh," Joel ii. 8. " He shall come down like rain on the mown grass: as showers that water the earth."—" Truth shall spring out of the earth; and righteousness shall look down from heaven," Psa. lxxii. 6; lxxxv. 11. Such, then, is the way in which the knowledge of the Lord will be diffused in the latter day. God will, by his providence and Spirit, with amazing rapidity and grandeur, accomplish the renovation of the world. We know not how soon this happy period shall arrive, but come it surely will. The day is on the wing, when the empire of sin in this world shall be overthrown, and the crash of its fall shall reverberate afar through the dominions of God.

But ere that time arrive, there is another era—an era in which the truth is to be spread mainly through the instrumentality of the church. It is in *this* period that we are placed. The time has not yet come, in which God will specially interpose for the immediate triumph of holiness. He observes, and requires his people to observe, an established connexion between means and ends. For all the good he will bestow, " Thus saith the Lord God ; I will yet for this be inquired of by the house of Israel, to do it for them," Ezek. xxxvi. 37. They shall reap only as they sow. If they desire his kingdom to come, they must deny themselves, and labour for that object. If they wish men to be saved, they must place truth before them, and press its claims upon the conscience. The language of the text teaches this—In that day, saith the Lord, " they shall teach no more every man his neighbour and every man his brother," etc. Observe, it shall *then* be no longer needful— implying, that *till* then it *is* needful to *teach* men, individually, to know the Lord. Here, then, we have the mode in which God wills that the great instrumentality for converting the world shall now be applied : it is by the direct efforts of his people to spread the truth. For the present, the command of God leaves this great work in the hands of his people. " Go ye therefore, and teach all nations," etc., Matt. xxviii. 19, 20. " Go ye into all the world, and preach the gospel to every creature," Mark xvi. 15. " How shall they believe in him of whom they have not heard ? and how shall they hear without a preacher ? and how shall they preach, except they be sent ?" Rom. x. 14.

In this stage of the church's history at least, it is evidently the Divine arrangement that men shall be themselves the instruments of saving their own race. That this is the way to do a great work, we learn from the analogies of the natural world. How are the coral isles of the ocean made ? Not by being upheaved, by some great convulsion, from the bosom of the deep ; but by the ceaseless labours of little insects, each of which works in its own place, and adds its

mite to the accumulated mass. It stops not to form com-
binations and lay plans, but labours in its sphere. How is
the huge globe watered, and made productive? Not by
great seas, but by little streams, or, rather, by single drops
of rain and dew, each refreshing a single leaf, or blade of
grass. How is bread produced for the millions of mankind?
Each stalk of corn becomes responsible for a limited number of grains. And, in the moral world, we see the same
results produced in the same way. How is it that vice is
propagated? How are drunkards, gamblers, and infidels
made? Not by wholesale, but by individual contract.
One corrupt heart infects some other heart: one polluted
soul taints some other soul with the infection of its own depravity; and thus recruits are ever multiplied for the host
of Satan. Let it be so in the work of salvation. Let each
Christian labour to rescue his neighbour and his brother,
and how soon will the world " be filled with the knowledge
of the Lord !" Nor will such benevolence be restricted to
its own immediate circle. A genuine concern for the salvation of *one* soul, is of the nature of the most enlarged phi-
lanthrophy. Thus it has ever been. The men who have
done the greatest good in the world, and most command
our veneration for the sublimity of their benevolence, have
begun their career of well doing by blessing their own immediate circle. Some of our most devoted missionaries,
were first missionaries in their own families and in their own
villages. Thus it was with Martyn, and Brainerd, and
Gordon Hall—this was the spirit of Harlan Page. Thus
it has been with some beloved living examples. Ere they
went abroad to foreign fields, they were living epistles among
us, known and read of all with whom they came in contact.
This is what must abound, ere the world will be converted—
personal holiness, as the vital principle; personal labour, as
the mode of effort; and individual persons, as the subjects.

APPLICATION.

From this subject we learn,

1. The true remedy for all our social and political evils. It is, by spreading the knowledge of the Lord. We must " teach every man his neighbour and every man his brother." Every Christian must bring the power of the character and law of God to bear upon some one or more consciences. Then, private friendship, truth, and righteousness, and public faith, and the majesty of law, will reign in our land; the sabbath will be honoured; the Holy Spirit will dwell among us; God will be our God, and we shall be his people.

2. We also learn the excellence of those methods of doing good, which exercise the conscience on questions of personal duty. Hence the excellence of all those forms of effort in which teaching is employed: the mother amid her children—the teacher of a sabbath-school, or Bible class—the faithful distributer of tracts—and, pre-eminently, the pastor and the missionary.

3. Finally. This subject illustrates the mode in which revivals of religion may be promoted. A revival that shall penetrate the *mass* of the community, must be carried into it by the *living agents*, who are accustomed to mingle *with* the mass; and who will go" hither and thither, attaching themselves to individuals.

Henceforth, let our course be the simple plan, not to wait for others, but each one do the *first good thing that offers*, and then the next—and the next; and thus proceed, filling up our lives with a succession of individual acts of usefulness.

SKETCH XXXIX

THE ONLY REMEDY FOR A WORLD'S GUILT AND MISERY.

"The cross of our Lord Jesus Christ."—GAL. vi. 14.

IN all systems there are greater and lesser principles—truths vital, or essential; and truths minor, or of less importance.　So it is in religion.

Natural religion has, as its essential principles, the existence, the wisdom, and power of God.　Revealed religion is based on the Divine authenticity of the Scriptures.　Evangelical religion holds forth, as its leading truth, the doctrine of the cross of the Lord Jesus Christ.　It is to this subject our text calls our attention; and which is identified with the avowal of the apostle, "God forbid that I should glory, save in the cross of ourLord Jesus Christ," Gal. vi. 14. Let us look at the cross of Christ in several lights

I. AS CONNECTED WITH CERTAIN FACTS.

These facts have to do with the death of the Lord Jesus. Observe, the hatred of the Jews towards him.　See the tide of persecution rising until the waves go over his head; and, at length, he is arrested—tried—falsely accused—and deemed worthy of death.　But the Jews cannot execute the sentence on him, inasmuch as they are now tributary to the Romans, for the sceptre has departed from Judah, and the law-giver from between his feet, Gen. xlix. 10. Christ is, therefore, delivered to the Romans; and at their tribunal he is pronounced innocent: thus his righteousness is vindicated by the Pagan ruler.   At length, they prevail with Pilate to put him to death; and by this means the death of Christ is attested to mankind.   Thus one of the main facts of the gospel is established, so as to set at defiance the cavillings of sceptics to the end of the world.

Then follows, too, the manner of his death—crucifixion, a Roman punishment of the most barbarous and debasing character.   Thus Christ's humiliation was the deeper; and hence the exclamation, " Who humbled himself, and became obedient unto death," etc., Phil. ii. 8.   To this cross, Christ was nailed—on it he was suspended for several hours —and from it He gave his Spirit into the hands of his Father. Such are the facts : solemn—affecting—important !

II. IN THE CROSS OF THE LORD JESUS CHRIST WE SEE THE VIVID ILLUSTRATION OF OLD TESTAMENT SCRIPTURES.

Here the ancient ordinance of the passover, having answered the end of a commemorative institution of the delivery of the Israelites, meets with its antitype—Jesus " the Lamb of God," stretched on the ignominious cross !   Here prophecies which referred to the abasement of the Messiah, the violence of his enemies, his being " numbered with transgressors ;" his meekness under the grossest provocations, are all fulfilled.   Had Isaiah been a spectator, instead of a prophet, living 700 years before the event, could he have been more clear and explicit?   See Isa. lii. 14; liii. 7, etc.   It is equally true as striking, that priests, Levites, and prophets all contributed, by type and sacrifice and mediation, to the interest which attaches to the cross.

III. IN CONNECTION WITH THE CROSS OF THE LORD JESUS CHRIST THE MOST ASTOUNDING PHENOMENA IS PRESENTED FOR CONTEMPLATION.   On no other occasion did events of so marvellous a character occur.

(1.) There was the supernatural darkness. " Now from the sixth hour there was darkness over all the land unto the ninth hour," Matt. xxvii. 45. A darkness so palpable, that it is said, the stars appeared; and this was for three hours, from the sixth to the ninth hour—from twelve till three o'clock. At a time when an eclipse of the sun was impossible; for it was at the time of the passover, when the moon was full, and opposite to the sun. Then,

(2.) As the high priest ministered in the holy place, "the veil of the temple," which divided the holy from the holy of holies, "was rent in twain, from the top to the bottom."

(3.) " The earth did quake, and rocks rent; and the graves were opened." Now, here was the finger of Deity pointing to the sublimity of the event which was to affect the destination of myriads, and universal nature bowed and did homage to the mandate of Jehovah.

IV. IN THE CROSS OF THE LORD JESUS CHRIST THE DOCTRINE OF THE ATONEMENT IS EXHIBITED TO THE WORLD.

(1.) Either the Sufferer was innocent or guilty. Even Pilate attests his innocency, and washes his hands, as far as may be, from the guilt of his death, Matt. xxvii. 24.

(2.) His life was either taken from him, or he delivered it up. He had declared that he had power to lay it down, and he had power to take it again, John x. 18. He laid it down. "And Jesus cried with a loud voice, and gave up the ghost." He could have left the cross and saved himself.

(3.) He died for himself, or for others. He had done nothing worthy of death, Luke xxiii. 22. " He came to seek and to save that which was lost," xix. 10. As the good Shepherd, he laid down his life for the sheep. As the " Lamb of God," he was offered for the sin of the world.

(4.) He died either merely as an example, or substitute! It is evident it was both. In his own spirit, meekness—

patience—clemency—devotion. But in his sorrows, Divine desertion—horror of soul—intense agony of spirit. " My God, my God, why hast thou forsaken me?" If a martyr only, thousands have had more joy, more ecstasy, etc., than the Prince of martyrs. How shall we solve the enigma? It is here, " He was wounded for our transgressions, he was bruised for our iniquities," Isa. liii. 5. It is here, " For thus it is written, and thus it behoved Christ to suffer," Luke xxiv. 46. It is here, " When we were yet without strength, in due time Christ died for the ungodly," Rom. v. 6. It is here, " Christ also hath once suffered for sins, the just for the unjust, that he might bring us to God," 1 Pet. iii. 18. It is here, "He is the propitiation for our sins, and not for our's only, but also for the sins of the whole world," 1 John ii. 2. It is here, " For ye are not redeemed with corruptible things,—but with the precious blood of Christ, as of a lamb without blemish, and without spot," 1 Pet. i. 18, 19. Finally, " Having made peace through the blood of his cross," etc., Col. i. 19, etc.

> "See there, my Lord upon the tree !
> I hear—I feel, He died for me ! "

V. In the cross we see the awful nature of sin, and the infinite tenderness of Divine compassion.

God determined to punish sin, as it deserved; and to save the sinner, as he desired. He did both in the cross of Christ. He called to a guilty world to behold the infinite evil of iniquity. To see his hatred, his utter abhorrence of it. Its essential, irreconcilable contrariety to his nature, perfections, and laws, so that his own Son—his coequal self—his fellow—if he interposed for the guilty, this well-beloved Son must bear the falling shower of descending wrath. The sword must fall, and either the sinner or the Saviour must receive it. The flood—the destruction of Sodom, etc., had exhibited the evil of sin. But on the cross it is written in characters of blood: and that blood the blood of Christ, and that finger the finger of his Father.

What love to the guilty! "Herein is love, not that we loved God, but that he loved us, and sent his Son to be the propitiation for our sins," 1 John iv. 10. "God so loved the world, that he gave his only begotten Son, that whosoever believeth in him should not perish, but have everlasting life," John iii. 16. We mistake the subject, if we conceive Christ appeasing and overcoming the dislike of the Father to us; for Jesus was the gift of God, and the evidence of his love to our world. "God so loved the world," etc.

VI. THE CROSS OF THE LORD JESUS CHRIST IS THAT WHICH IS TO AFFECT THE MORAL DESTINIES OF OUR WORLD.

(1.) Placed on the summit of Calvary, that it might not be concealed. Without the gate of Jerusalem, to signify the whole wide world's interest in it.

(2.) It is to be the spiritual magnet by which men are to be brought to Christ. "And I, if I be lifted up from the earth, will draw all men unto me," John xii. 32.

(3.) It is to be borne by the Christian missionary not in the form of a crucifix, but as the grand element of the gospel; and wherever it goes it saves or it destroys—it kills or makes alive. It elevates to the Divine favour and heirship to glory; or it writes, on the brow of the unbeliever, his condemnation and everlasting woe.

(4.) Look at the church of God—the spiritual, universal, catholic church, including all saints, etc., they are distinct and separate from the world. They are saved, holy, etc. In each instance the change has been effected by the power of the cross. There is not an exception. Whether the convert be an idolatrous Brahmin—a savage New Zealander—a debased Hottentot—or an intellectual European, —the power of the change, was the power of the cross.

(5.) Contemplate the ranks of the beatified. An innumerable company of every nation, " From the east, and from the west, from the north, and from the south,"— and every one justified, sanctified, and glorified, by the influence of the cross. These have all " washed their robes, and made them white in the blood of the Lamb: therefore are they before the throne of God," Rev. vii. 14.

I. In conclusion. Let me say to the sinner, the cross is your only hope. And the radiance of the cross is sufficient to light and lead any, and every sinner to God. Oh! despise it not, reject it not; fly to the shelter of the cross.

2. To the Christian—the cross is your only boast. " Thanks be to God, which always causes us to triumph in Christ," 2 Cor. ii. 14. Self is abased—services disowned, as the basis of acceptance—righteousness disclaimed—an arm of flesh rejected. Say, with St. Paul, " Yea, doubtless, and I count all things but loss for the excellency of the knowledge of Christ Jesus my Lord," Phil. iii. 8. " God forbid that I should glory save in the cross of our Lord Jesus Christ, by whom the world is crucified unto me, and I unto the world," Gal. vi. 14.

Finally. The cross is the great theme of ministerial discourse. There are other doctrines to be taught; but, then, they are in connexion with the cross. There are promises to be declared, but they are the promises of the cross. There are blessings to be offered, but they are the blessings of the cross. There are duties, but such only can be performed in the strength and grace of the cross. There are privileges, but they are the purchase of the cross. There is holiness, but it is the washing of the blood of the cross. There is heaven, but it is a heaven in the centre of which is elevated the cross. " The Lamb which is in the midst of the throne" will be celebrated in the songs of the redeemed for ever and ever!

SKETCH XL.

THE GUILT OF NEGLECTING THE SOULS OF OUR BRETHREN.

BY REV. JOHN SUMMERFIELD, A.M.,
OF THE METHODIST EPISCOPAL CHURCH, UNITED STATES.

"We are verily guilty concerning our brother, in that we saw the anguish of his soul, when he besought us, and we would not hear; therefore is this distress come upon us."—GEN. xlii. 21.

THIS subject affords a fine opportunity to discourse on the nature and power of conscience—the candle of the Lord. It is not necessary to inquire whether it be ever altogether silenced. *Sleep* and death, however, are two things. See the frozen snake—bring it to the fire! "There is no peace, saith my God, to the wicked," Isa. lvii. 21; they are always subject to bondage through fear of death.

Johnson said, Infidels are of two classes—fools and wretches : if they refuse to think, it is madness; if they do think, it is misery! Why did Felix tremble? Why were the joints of Belshazzar's loins loosed, and why smote his knees one against the other? Dan. v. 6. Why not interpret the handwriting favourably—as the record of his greatness? etc. Herod, though a Sadducee, thought that John the Baptist was risen again : his conscience was too much for his creed. The light will break in through some chink or other. M. de Staël said, " It was in the power of adversity to make every man superstitious in spite of himself;" rather say, Revive the conviction of a Deity.

See the text—comment on it. What similarity of circumstances was there in the situation of these men that

brought Joseph to mind?—famine!—strange land!—
governor treated them roughly!—put three days in hold!—
they feel they need pity! *Conscience* says, "*You* cannot
look for it, for you showed none."

"Blessed are the merciful: for they shall obtain mercy,"
Matt. v. 7. We only knew the *fact* before, but now we
hear of the entreaties which Joseph made—his tears!—his
cry, O Judah, O Reuben, waxed fainter and fainter, till
it died on the ear—and they sat down to eat and drink.—
Wretches!

You, my friends, are now indulging vengeance on them,
in their situation—but expend it not *all* on them! Some
nearer you—I mean not your neighbours, but *you.* Have
you never enjoyed yourselves, when the cry of distress has
been heard? Yet I mean something higher than this!
While you sit down to eat and drink in spiritual privileges,
what millions are in more pitiable circumstances? "We
are verily guilty concerning our brother;" and I hope to
bring this matter home, and convict every one of you!

(Thank God, "The Jews have no dealings with the Samaritans," is not a text often preached on in modern times.
Bunyan said, "Master Prejudice fell down and broke his
leg; I would," said he, "that he had broken his neck too.")

Mr. Ward said, "I have attended many missionary meetings in England, yet in all you indulge too much in congratulation; if you had seen the wide-spread fields of heathenism as I have seen, etc. *Nothing* comparatively is done;
not enough to wipe off the reproach for long neglect."
"We are verily guilty concerning our brother." We proceed, then, to notice,

I. THE SOURCES FROM WHENCE THESE CONVICTIONS ARE
TO BE DERIVED.

II. WHAT INFLUENCE THIS OUGHT TO HAVE ON US.

I. The sources from whence these convictions are to be derived.

We cannot condemn a criminal till we convict him. I arraign this whole audience! I charge them with guilt. Consider, then,

1. *The relation of the sufferers—our brethren!* This was the sting in the text—our *brother:* not a stranger, though then our conduct was merciless! Nabal. I hope there are none of his descendants here this morning; you cannot use *his* words in reference to any of the human race. God "hath made of one blood all nations of men for to dwell on all the face of the earth," Acts xvii. 26; all are *your* brethren. See the Hindoo, African, Esquimaux: each says, "Am not I thy brother?" I catechise thee, "Art not thou his brother by infirmities?" His follies and his crimes have stamped him man!

2. *The wretchedness of their state.* Joseph's state was nothing compared with those who address us. You say, however, "Joseph besought them; but the heathen do not beseech us; they are satisfied with their condition." The more pitiable! See the maniac: in his wild ravings he fancies himself a king: is he therefore to be less compassionated? I have seen the infant play with the ensigns of its mother's death. "Precious babe!" said I, "ignorant of thy loss!" So here: their "lack of knowledge" prevents them from being sensible to their condition.

But you say, "Joseph's brethren saw the anguish of his soul." True: and here I feel the disadvantage of my position. If you could but see what a missionary sees! Could I but lead you, not to heathen sensualities—to name which would be a shame—but to their cruelties! Could I show you the devotee lying on sharp spikes, or casting himself under the ponderous car of Juggernaut; could I fix your eyes on children leaving their aged parents to expire on the damp banks of their idol river, or parents casting their children to the crocodiles of the Ganges, or sons lighting the funeral pile of their mothers, you would not keep from me even a ring on your finger.

Philosophers sneer when we talk of the dreadful state of the East; and many Christians concede too much to them. I do not say, God cannot save a heathen; the *influence* of the *fact* of the gospel extends farther than the *Revelation*. In reference to infants, this is certain, and Scripture itself assures us that " in every nation he that feareth God, and worketh righteousness, is accepted with him," Acts x. 35. Yet, after all, without a preparedness there can be no heaven; and Mr. Ward said he had not found anything resembling real holiness among all the heathen with whom he had been conversant. Idolatry is not merely a weakness, as some say; it is a regular system of sensuality and crime. It originates in the vices men love, and hates the virtues which God approves. Do the Scriptures talk lightly of it? It not only tolerates vices, but hallows them; cruelties and crimes are sanctified. It is iniquity personified; yea, the devil deified, and hell incarnated! You inquire, " May there not be with God a secret method of saving the heathen?" I answer, if secret, we know nothing about it, and have nothing to do with it. If revealed, where? The Scriptures say, " Neither is there salvation in any other: for there is none other name under heaven given among men, whereby we must be saved," but the name of Jesus, Acts iv. 12. The heathen feel their guilt; yet they know nothing of the " fountain opened to the house of David and to the inhabitants of Jerusalem for sin and for uncleanness," Zech. xiii. 1. But we shall discover still farther evidences of our guilt by considering,

3. *Our orders to succour them.* This succour is not optional with us. It is commanded in every injunction to

benevolence and beneficence; and this must, of course, include the highest kinds of them. " Freely ye have received, freely give," is the Divine requisition, Matt. x. 8.

The goodness of the Master is often impugned, because of the wickedness of those servants who neglect or violate the command. (The brute on the seventh day.) One is rich and the other poor. Does God love the rich more? No; but only makes him his almoner: but if the rich hoard it up, shall the Master be condemned? Now, our Saviour said, " Go ye into all the world, and preach the gospel to every creature," Mark xvi. 15. Had the command been acted upon ever since it was given, the earth would now be " full of the knowledge of the Lord, as the waters cover the sea." " But if the gospel be so valuable," say some, " why has it spread so little?" I reply by another interrogatory, Has God no attribute but his *power?* We know that God will be able to justify himself, but we never shall be able to justify ourselves. " We are verily guilty concerning our brother." Another evidence of our guilt will appear when we consider,

4. *The possibility of affording them succour.* " Withhold not good from them to whom it is due, when *it is in the power of thine hand to do it,*" Prov. iii. 27. Our duty to the heathen is based on no impossibilities. Our inability is moral, yea, wilful. We make a difference between the means and the end; the end is his, the means are ours. There is a difference, also, between means and miracles. Miracles have ceased, because they are no longer necessary. Without them the Indian castes have been broken. Without them the Hottentot has been elevated and Christianized, though some said, the swine would receive the gospel as soon. Look, too, at the South Sea islands: long we endured sneers; but now behold language and laws, schools and churches, virtue and piety rising on the ruins of barbarism. If miracles

were necessary, we should not have been so guilty; for we could not have furnished the gift of tongues. Yet we could teach them their native language. I repeat, then, that means are our's, and results are God's. If you knew a village perishing by a disease, and you had an infallible remedy, and yet should withhold it, would you not be verily guilty concerning your brethren? If you see the unsuspecting traveller crossing a rotten bridge, and you warn him not, can you be innocent?

5. *Consider the facilities we have in this cause of compassion.* "If the prophet had bid thee do some great thing, wouldest thou not have done it? how much rather then, when he saith to thee, Wash, and be clean?" 2 Kings v. 13. Our duty is to commence missionary exertions, whatever may be the peril. But have you gone forth at a peradventure *if* the heathen were salvable! No; you knew God's word; you knew "God so loved the world, that he gave his only begotten Son, that whosoever believeth in him should not perish, but have everlasting life," John iii. 16. You knew his intention was that *all* should know him, "from the least of them to the greatest of them," Jer. xxxi. 34. Have we, then, ever done anything magnificent enough to do justice to the declarations of his word? No!

(1.) *Providence* has favoured us also. Governments have been favourable to civil liberty. Thus missionaries have not met with the sufferings we might have reckoned on. Not one out of the whole has been put to death!

(2.) The *grace* of God has been with us also. If no result had taken place, still our duty would have been to go. But God has blessed our labours. See the number of converts; your missions, though once feeble, have become strong, which leads me to observe,

6. *That even the efforts we have made in this work*

furnish evidence of our guilt. What is our zeal? what the number of missionary societies? what think you of *one* preacher for a whole county? But see:

All missionary societies furnish but six hundred,* and there are six hundred millions perishing.

Are you now convicted? Is there no heart here that says, " I ought to have gone out in this work." Does not another exclaim, " I have not preached often enough on the subject;" and is not the language of a third, " I have prayed too little." And methinks I hear from a fourth, " I have given nothing as I ought! so little." And a fifth confesses, " I could have influenced others, though I could not do much myself." Ah! my brethren, we are all guilty —verily guilty concerning our brother.

II. WHAT INFLUENCE SHOULD THESE CONVICTIONS PRODUCE? If sincere, they will produce four results:

1. *The depravity of human nature will be acknowledged.* This is denied by many, but there is no need *now* to go to Newgate to prove it. If man were not alienated from the life of God, he could not be thus alienated from his brother. You are proof of this degeneracy—the royal law has been broken.

2. *Deep and godly sorrow will be felt.* As in the valley of Hadadrimmon, you will retire in secret and mourn apart, Zech. xii. 11. Ah! brethren, we cannot mourn too deeply over this fatal negligence.

3. *It will lead us to apply to the mercy of God.* "Deliver me from bloodguiltiness, O God, thou God of my salvation; and my tongue shall sing aloud of thy righteousness," Psa. i. 14. The encouragement is, "With the Lord there is mercy, and with him is plenteous redemption," Psa. cxxx. 7.

* In the year 1821.

" If we confess our sins, he is faithful and just to forgive us our sins, and to cleanse us from all unrighteousness."

4. *It will awaken zeal.* A sense of Divine forgiveness will not make you forgive yourselves; you will be up and doing. It will operate, not as an opiate, but as a cordial. The inquiry will be, " Lord, what wouldest thou have me to do?"

But if this effect be not produced, I say, as Mordecai to Esther, " If thou altogether holdest thy peace at this time, then shall there enlargement and deliverance arise from another quarter; but thou and thy father's house shall be destroyed," Esth. iv. 14. So here—if you will not labour, the work will go on still, but you will be cursed!

Saurin would finish every sermon with reference to death; and Jesus said, " I must work the works of him that sent me, while it is day: the night cometh, when no man can work," John ix. 4. Life, then, is the only season in which you can serve your generation. Wesley would be willing to come down again, be despised again, and persecuted again, for the opportunities you now possess for making known the Saviour!

This may be the *last* collection—a dying grant.

What says your own welfare? I am ashamed to call on selfishness, yet God himself meets our weakness. The ark with Obed—Edom. Contrast this with the conduct of the Jews when they returned from Babylon, and neglected to build the house of the Lord. The penury they dreaded came on like an armed man. Hear the reproving language of the prophet to these idle professors: " Ye have sown much, and bring in little; ye eat, but ye have not enough; ye drink, but ye are not filled with drink; ye clothe you, but there is none warm; and he that earneth wages earneth wages to put it into a bag with holes.—Ye looked for much, and, lo, it came to little; and when ye brought it home, I did blow upon it. Why? saith the Lord of hosts. Because of mine house that is waste, and ye run every man unto his own house. Therefore the heaven over you is stayed from dew, and the earth is stayed from her fruit. And I called for a drought upon the land, and upon the mountains, and upon the corn, and upon the new wine, and upon the oil, and upon that which the ground bringeth forth, and upon men, and upon cattle, and upon all the labour of the hands," Hag. i. 6, 9—11.

Public-spirited men, though not the richest, are generally the most successful. At least, when the ear hears them, then it blesses them; and when the eye sees them, it gives witness to them, Job. xxix. 11. Yea, and devout men carry them, like Stephen, to their burial, and make great lamentation over them, Acts viii. 2.

What says your own experience? Have you lost by anything done for God?

It has been said there are three principles in religion: fear, hope, love, and love the strongest! True; and no love like that a sinner feels to a redeeming God!

What encouragement more than from past success! even *one sinner!*

I am not sorry that these applications are so frequent—these godly vexations. Do you wish exemption from them? Are you now complaining that God is answering the prayer you have so often offered, " Thy kingdom come?"

Determine what to give, with reference to a conscience near you; eternal judgment before you; and the grace of Him who, " though he was rich, yet for your sakes became poor, that ye through his poverty might be rich!"

SKETCH XLI.

THE DUTY OF PECUNIARY CONTRIBUTIONS TO RELIGIOUS PURPOSES.

BY THE REV. JOHN BROWN,*
OF BIGGAR, NORTH BRITAIN.

" Who is willing to consecrate his service this day unto the Lord?"
1 CHRON. xxix. 5.

WE are met to promote an object, the magnitude of which cannot be exaggerated; and in comparison of which, the erection of the temple itself shrinks into insignificance. At the command of Messiah our Prince, we are assembled to unite our deliberations, and contributions, and prayers, for the erection of a spiritual temple, in which not one favoured people only, but " every kindred, and tongue, and people, and nation," may present spiritual sacrifices to " the God and Father of our Lord and Saviour Jesus Christ;" and it is He who now, by the voice of one of the humblest of his ministers, proclaims, " Who is willing to consecrate his service this day unto the Lord?" The voice is on earth, the Speaker is in heaven. " The Lord is in his holy temple: let all the earth keep silence before him," Hab. ii. 20.

My object, in the following discourse, is to illustrate and recommend the duty of pecuniary contributions to religious purposes. But, instead of discussing this subject in a general way, I wish to show that " whatsoever things

* Preached before the London Missionary Society, at Tottenham Court Chapel, May 10, 1821.

were written aforetime" (of the liberality of David and his people) " were written for our learning," Rom. xv. 4; and from the passage of Scripture connected with our text, to collect some instructions respecting the manner in which this duty ought to be performed, and some arguments calculated to enforce it.   Consider,

I. THE INSTRUCTIONS IN REFERENCE TO THE MANNER IN WHICH THE DUTY OF PECUNIARY CONTRIBUTIONS TO RELIGIOUS PURPOSES SHOULD BE PERFORMED, suggested by this portion of sacred writ. We are taught by this passage of Scripture,

1. *That in contributing of our substance to the service of God, we should consider ourselves as performing a religious duty.*

It is a service—an act of duty; and as a service consecrated to God, it is an act of religious duty.   There are too many, even among those who bear the Christian name, who look on pecuniary contribution to pious purposes as a matter not of obligation, but of convenience.   They consider it as discretionary to give, or not to give.   To withhold they scarcely account a fault; to contribute they view as a kind of supererogatory virtue. This mode of thinking is utterly unreasonable and unscriptural.   Reason plainly teaches us that we are bound to devote our property, and every thing else, to the great purposes of our being—the honour of God, and the happiness of mankind.   Christianity connects every thing with Divinity—Whether we eat, or drink, or whatsoever we do, we are to do all to the glory of God: " giving thanks always for all things unto God and the Father in the name of our Lord Jesus Christ," 1 Cor. x. 31; Eph. v. 20.   The whole of the moral as well as of the strictly religious duties is described, as presenting our " bodies a living sacrifice, holy, acceptable unto God,"

Rom. xii. 1; 1 Pet. ii. 5; and acts of beneficence, and almsgiving are, in particular, represented as " *sacrifices*"— religious services. This passage teaches us,

2. *That in pecuniary oblations to religious purposes, we should give only what is really our own property.*

" Moreover," said the Israelitish monarch, " because I have set my affection to the house of my God, I have of mine own proper good, of gold and silver, which I have given to the house of my God," 1 Chron. xxix. 3. The claims of generosity, even of the noblest kind of generosity, must never be allowed to encroach on the inviolable rights of justice. " For I the Lord love judgment, I hate robbery for burnt offering," Isa. lxi. 8. However much we may deny ourselves, in order to increase our pious donations, (it is scarcely possible for us to exceed in this way,) let us never, in the slightest degree, trench on the property of another. A third lesson respecting the duty of pecuniary contribution, suggested by this passage, is,

3. *That our donations should be liberal.*

The donations of David and his people astonish us by their magnitude. In addition to the immense sums which he had amassed during his reign for the building of the temple, he, on the occasion referred to in the text, devoted to this pious purpose what is equivalent to about eighteen millions of our money, and his peoples' joint contributions considerably exceeded thirty millions.

(1.) From the circumstance of the tenth of the income of the Israelites being appropriated, by express Divine law, to pious purposes, it is surely a fair conclusion, that among the middle and higher classes, in all ordinary cases, Christians should not devote a less proportion of their worldly substance to the service of God. The liberal genius of the dispensation under which we live, manifested in rather fixing general principles, than in laying down particular rules, has certainly not produced in us its appropriate and intended effect, if it be used as a cloak for our avarice, pleaded as an apology for our parsimony; instead of being felt as an appeal to Christian honour—a stimulus to Christian liberality.

(2.) Another means of arriving at something like a general principle for determining what constitutes a liberal donation, in particular circumstances, is, reflection on the portion of our substance which we expend on what may be termed the comforts, the luxuries, the superfluities of life.

(3.) A circumstance which must be taken into consideration, in forming a judgment of what is a liberal donation in common cases, (and this is the question we are chiefly interested in,) is the degree in which God has prospered us. This is proposed by the apostle to the Corinthians as the measure of their alms-giving, " Let every one of you lay by him in store, as God hath prospered him," 1 Cor. xvi. 2. This passage further teaches us that we should,

4. *Present our pecuniary oblations from proper motives.*

In consequence of the decidedly spiritual character of the religion of the Bible, mere external action is accounted of but little value. It is only as it embodies right principle, that it assumes the form of acceptable duty. Donations for religious purposes, however liberal, if they spring from unworthy motives, cannot be pleasing to God. It is no uncommon thing to give to a religious institution from the mere force of custom—from an easiness of temper, which cannot resist solicitation—from the fear of censure— from the love of praise—from a dim, indistinct expectation that such an employment of property may have a favourable influence on the final destiny. In every such case, I need scarcely say, the donation, as a piece of religious service, cannot be acceptable to God; and as a piece of moral discipline, must be not only useless, but hurtful. They who give from such motives, can have no reward of our Father which is in heaven. The motives by which we ought to be actuated, in making pecuniary donations, are chiefly—submission to the Divine authority, regard for the Divine honour, and sympathy for the worst miseries of our fellow-men. We are taught by this passage,

5. *That our pecuniary contributions to religious purposes should be yielded in the exercise of proper dispositions.*

In performing religious and moral duties we must pay attention to the manner, as well as the motive of action, though the shortest and surest way of securing the former property, is to secure the purity of the latter. Every duty has a set of appropriate tempers, in which it ought to be performed. Cheerfulness, humility, and gratitude, are those which should peculiarly characterize our donations for religious purposes. All these tempers were admirably exemplified by David, and his pious nobles. They gave cheerfully. " Then the people rejoiced, for that they offered willingly, because with perfect heart, they offered willingly to the Lord.—As for me," says David, "in the uprightness of mine heart I have willingly offered all these things," 1 Chron. xxix. 9, 17. "God loveth a cheerful giver," 2 Cor. ix. 7. David and his people gave also in the spirit of humility. " Who am I, and what is my people, that we should be able to offer so willingly after this sort," ver. 14. Closely allied with humility is gratitude. "Now therefore, our God," says David, " we thank thee, and praise thy glorious name," ver. 13.

6. *A sixth lesson, in reference to the duty of pecuniary contribution, taught by this passage, is, that we ought to connect prayer with our donations.*

. The great object to which our donations are devoted, is one which no donations of themselves, however munificent, can accomplish. David added prayer to the liberal donations of himself and people, knowing that " except the Lord build the house, they labour in vain that build it," Psa. cxxvii. 1. " O Lord God of Abraham, of Isaac, and of Israel our fathers," said he, " give unto Solomon my son, a perfect heart, to keep thy commandments, thy testimonies, and thy statutes, and to do all these things, and to build the palace, for the which I have made provision," verses 18, 19. While we lay our humble offerings on his altar, let our ardent supplications rise before his throne. " Ye that make mention of the Lord, keep not silence, and give him no rest, till he establish, and till he make Jerusalem a praise in the earth," Isa. lxii. 6, 7. The last lesson, in reference to the duty of pecuniary contribution, taught us by this passage, is,

7. *That we should not only give ourselves, but use all our influence to induce others to give.*

We are to " consider one another to provoke unto love and to good works," Heb. x. 24. David did so; he not only presented a most princely offering himself, but he urged all his nobles to follow his example. " Who then is willing to consecrate his service this day unto the Lord?" Influence is a talent of prodigious value, it multiplies a man's power of doing good indefinitely.

II. THE ARGUMENTS CALCULATED TO URGE US TO THE PERFORMANCE OF THE DUTY OF PECUNIARY CONTRIBUTION, IN THE MANNER NOW EXPLAINED, SUGGESTED BY THE PASSAGE UNDER CONSIDERATION.

These are chiefly derived from the magnitude, the design, and the Divine appointment of the work to which our offerings are devoted, the inadequacy of the immediate agents, the pleasantness of the duty, the religious relations of property, and the short and uncertain duration of human life.

1. *The magnitude of the work to which our pecuniary contributions are devoted, furnishes a powerful argument for liberality.*

" The work is great," said David to the congregation of Israel. To erect an edifice so costly and magnificent as the temple of Jerusalem, was, no doubt, a great enterprise for such people as the Israelites, and called for the co-operation of all. But the work to which we are called on to contribute is immeasurably greater; it is nothing short of the Christianization of the whole world. A second argument for liberality in our pecuniary contributions, suggested by the passage, is to be found in,

2. *The design of the work to which they are devoted.*

The temple of Jerusalem was intended to promote the honour of Jehovah, and the welfare of the Israelitish people; and we find David urging its object as a motive to stimulate the liberality of the nobles. " The palace is not for man, but for the Lord God." The design of that great work to which we are this day called on to yield our support, may be viewed in a twofold aspect—in reference to God, and in reference to mankind; and in both, it furnishes us with invincible arguments for cheerful and liberal donations.

3. *The Divine appointment of the work, to which our pecuniary contributions are devoted, should operate as a motive to cheerful liberality.*

The building of the temple was expressly commanded by God. Jehovah said to David, " Thou shalt not build a house to my name,—but Solomon thy son, he shall build my house and my courts," 1 Chron. xxviii. 3, 6. This command, when connected with the circumstance that the donations of the Israelites were necessary to its being obeyed, was certainly a powerful motive to liberality. The diffusion of Christianity throughout the world, is plainly the will of heaven. This is intimated in the very nature of that religion. In " the Scriptures of the prophets," we have " the commandment of the everlasting God," that " the mystery, which was kept secret since the world began, but which is now made manifest,—should be made known to all nations for the obedience of faith," Rom. xvi. 25, 26. " I will declare the decree: Ask of me, and I shall give thee the heathen for thine inheritance, and the uttermost parts of the earth for thy possession." " All the ends of the world shall remember and turn unto the Lord; and all the kindreds of the nations shall worship before thee," Psa. ii. 8; xxii. 27. " All power," said the Saviour, " is given unto me in heaven and in earth. Go ye therefore, and teach all nations, baptizing them in the name of the Father, and of the Son, and of the Holy Ghost," Matt. xxviii. 18, 19.

4. *The inadequacy of the direct agents to the accomplishment of the work to which our contributions are devoted, is another argument to liberality suggested by the passage.*

" Solomon my son," says David, " is tender, and the work is great." I insist that without the support, the liberal support of the Christian public, all the admirably adapted agency will be utterly inadequate. The machinery is complete, but there must be the power to put it and to keep it in motion. Another consideration suggested by the passage, calculated to enforce the duty of pecuniary contribution, is,

5. *Its pleasantness, as exemplified in the experience of David and his people.*

" The people rejoiced for that they offered willingly, and David the king also rejoiced with great joy." Wherever the duty is performed from right principles, and with right dispositions, it is productive of pleasure. In this case the maxim holds true: " In keeping of God's commandments there is great reward;" and the words of the Lord Jesus are verified, " It is more blessed to give than to receive."

6. *The religious relations of property, as stated in the context, furnish another argument for liberality in our contributions to religious purposes.*

It is God who gives us whatever property we possess. It is " a good gift," which, like every other, " is from above, and cometh down from the Father of lights," Jas. i. 17. If we have inherited a fortune, it is by the arrangement of his providence that it has come into our possession. But this is not all. God is not only the Giver of wealth, but, in strict correctness of speech, he is its Proprietor. He can never cease to be the Proprietor of the universe, for it can never cease to be true, that he is the Creator of the universe. He gives us wealth, not in property, but in trust. Our wealth, if honestly acquired, is our own, in reference to other men; but in reference to God, it is not our own. " The silver is mine and the gold is mine, saith the Lord of hosts," Hag. ii. 8.

7. *Finally. The short and uncertain duration of human life is suggested in the context as a motive to liberality in our contributions to religious purposes.*

" We are strangers before thee," says David, " and sojourners, as were all our fathers: our days on the earth are as a shadow, and there is no abiding." The period for exertion is extremely limited. Yet a little while, and our property shall have passed to others, and over its destination we shall have no longer any control. " Your fathers, where are they? and the prophets, do they live for ever?" Zech. i. 5. Many of those, who, at the earlier celebration of this our British annual festival of Christian benevolence, took a part in the solemn, joyful services, are gathered to the congregation of the dead. Let us

N

cheerfully give a portion, a liberal portion, of that wealth to our God, the whole of which, ere long, we must surrender into the hands of his dread messenger. Solomon says, "Whatsoever thy hand findeth to do, do it with thy might; for there is no work, nor device, nor knowledge, nor wisdom, in the grave, whither thou goest," Eccl. ix. 10.

It is our consolation and joy that the progress of the work does not depend on the inferior agents—whose days are as a shadow, and have no abiding; but on the supreme Agent, who "is the same yesterday, and to-day, and for ever," Heb. xiii. 8. "Thou art the same, and thy years shall have no end," Psa. cii. 27. And he will raise successive generations to carry forward his glorious designs. "A seed shall serve him." "One generation shall praise thy works to another, and shall declare thy mighty acts," Psa. xxii. 30; cxlv. 4. The magnificent structure shall continue to extend and advance, till it reach its destined dimensions; and then "He shall bring forth the headstone thereof," amid the plaudits of all the innocent and restored intelligences in the universe of God; and it shall stand through eternity, the fairest monument of the power, and wisdom, and holiness, and love of the Divine Author. As it rises, and extends under our hands, let us raise the first notes of that anthem, which, on its completion shall peal through the universe, loud as the thunder of heaven, sweet as the music of angels, crying, "GRACE, GRACE unto it!" Zech. iv. 7.

SKETCH XLII.

HOLY GRIEF FOR GOD'S VIOLATED LAW.

BY REV. THOMAS ADKINS, OF SOUTHAMPTON.*

"Rivers of waters run down mine eyes, because they keep not thy law."

PSA. cxix. 136.

THERE is an eloquence in tears. They speak the language of nature, and they find their way to the heart. They tell us of human suffering; and in terms which, though silent, are most forcible.

There is scarcely, in nature, a more touching spectacle than to see a man weep; especially one of exalted intellect, of tried fortitude, and of enlarged benevolence. We readily believe that this natural expression of sorrow, proceeding from such a source, must be produced by causes at least proportioned to the effect, and we sympathise with both the one and the other. Such a spectacle is now presented to our view. It is a man in tears; and that man a saint, a hero, and a king. A man whose intellect, naturally of the highest order, had been carried to the utmost limits of human capacity, by sedulous culture and by Divine inspiration; whose undaunted courage had been tried, in a single-handed contest, with the monsters of the woods, and with the gigantic defyer of the armies of Israel; whose regal authority could levy a contribution on the resources of an empire, to minister to his enjoyments and to enhance

* From a Sermon, preached on behalf of the London Missionary Society.

his splendour.   But he weeps; and the deep-seated spring
of his grief pours forth torrents of tears.   He weeps, not
for himself, but for others; and they are the wicked, that
" keep not the law."   Observe,

I. The affecting subject by which the sorrow of
a holy man is excited.   It is the transgression of the
Divine law.   And hence it will be necessary,

1. *To inquire into the nature and extent of the law, the
violation of which is deplored.*

" Of law, then," to use the language of the judicious
Hooker, " there can be no less acknowledged, than that
her seat is the bosom of God, her voice the harmony of the
world; all things in heaven and earth do her homage, the
very least as feeling her care, and the greatest as not
exempt from her power; both angels and men, and creatures of what condition soever, though each in a different
sort and name, yet all, with one uniform consent, admiring
her as the mother of their peace and joy."

The law of the sacred Scriptures is only those principles
on which the Deity proceeds in legislating over the moral
universe, receiving that peculiar modification by which they
are adapted to the nature of incarnate intelligences placed
in a state of trial.   It is a moral law, as it proceeds from
the moral Governor of the world; as it is suited to the nature of moral agents; and as those sanctions are moral
by which the observance of its precepts is enforced.

This law, however, from its very character, is capable of
being violated.   As a moral law, obedience to it must be
the result of motives, and consequently voluntary; and the
power to obey, involves the possibility to transgress.

Such is the law which was impressed on the conscience
of man in a state of primeval perfection; and by the violation of which he offended his God, and lost his paradise.

Such is the law which subsequently was republished, by the audible voice of the Deity, from the bleak and barren Mount Sinai; and which, amplified to a fuller extent, and animated with more evangelical motives, appears in all its excellence in the completed canon of inspiration. The heathen, it is admitted, do not enjoy the noontide clearness of Divine revelation: night—moral night—spreads her sable canopy over them, under which storms and darkness lower. But the reflected beams of a traditional religion flicker around their path; the operations of nature and of conscience, as the constellations in the starry heavens, shed upon them a dim religious light; and all combine to reveal to man his prescribed path of duty, and to the transgressor his criminality and danger. Such is the law which the heathen possess; the transgression of which we shall now proceed to contemplate and to deplore.

(1.) This violation is deep-seated in its origin. They are *haters of God*. "The carnal mind is enmity against God," Rom. viii. 7. "What!" says the pious and learned Howe, "to be haters of God—the most excellent and all-comprehending Good! Be astonished, oh ye heavens at this, and be horribly afraid!—be ye very desolate!"

(2.) This transgression is no less flagrant in its modes, than it is deep-seated in its origin. At once, for an illustration and a proof of this fact, transport yourselves in imagination to the fields of Hindoostan. See the thirty millions of her deities personified in one, the Moloch of India, the horrible Juggernaut, whose throne is the bleached bones of his victims; whose worshippers are like demons; whose libations are human blood; and whose music is the fiendish laugh of disgusting obscenity, mingled with the din of confusion, and the groan of despair. Well might the unearthly Henry Martyn exclaim, when he beheld this spectacle, "I shuddered, as standing in the neighbourhood of hell."

(3.) This violation is, likewise, universal in its extent. The universality of human transgression is a fact as true as it is appalling. The excellent Mr. Ward, whose sphere of observation was as extensive as his power of discrimination was acute, said, " I never found one that appeared to fear God, and to work righteousness."

II. Consider the particular sources from whence this sorrow takes its rise.

1. *This sorrow arises, primarily, from the recognised relationship of one common nature, existing between ourselves and the subjects of this defection.*

The poorest savage, that either toils in chains, or roams through his native woods, may say to us in the unsophisticated language of nature, by his hopes and fears, his joys and sorrows, the beaming of his intelligence, and the aspirations of his desire—Am not I thy brother?

> * * * * " Pierce his vein,
> Take of the crimson stream meandering there,
> And catechise it well; apply the glass,
> Search it, and prove now if it be not blood
> Congenial with thine own; and, if it be,
> What edge of subtlety canst thou suppose
> Keen enough, wise and skilful as thou art,
> To cut the link of brotherhood, by which
> One common Maker bound him to mankind."

2. *This sorrow proceeds, still further, from a due estimate of the importance of man, considered as an intellectual and immortal agent.*

" The redemption of their soul is precious, and it ceases for ever," Psa. xlix. 8. Viewed in this light, the missionary cause loses the character of insignificance, which would seem to attach to a combination of a few feeble mortals and the collection of a few scattered sums, and arises to a majesty which, whilst it catches and reflects the rays of the Divine glory and throws the shadow of its protection over distant lands, buries the remote effects of its operations in the profoundest depths of eternity.

3. *This sorrow is still further increased by contemplating the imminent danger to which the subjects of this transgression are exposed.*

In considering the future probable condition of the heathen, it may be premised, that, in the equitable administration of the government of the universe, all beings will be dealt with according to their moral and natural capacities, and the circumstances in which they are placed; that punishment, if awarded, will be in proportion to crime —crime to violated responsibility—and responsibility to possessed or attainable means of knowledge.

Were we, therefore, to take the lowest ground of concession—the mere *possibility.* of the final perdition of the heathen—it would be easy to construct upon it an argument for strenuous exertion on their behalf; but when the evidence of their danger accumulates to a fearful magnitude, should not our zeal keep pace with our fears? As they pass along, they lift to us an imploring eye, to transmit to them the only revealed remedy to mitigate their present misery, and avert their future doom.

4. *This sorrow is augmented to the greatest degree by the dishonour which is cast by transgressors upon the perfections of the Most High.*

A prevailing desire for the advancement of the Divine glory, in all the possible forms of its manifestation, is the distinguishing characteristic of a holy soul. Hence, the Psalmist breathed out the fervour of his soul in that memorable prayer, a prayer which comprehends all that even he could desire—" Let the whole earth be filled with his glory! Amen, and Amen," Psa. lxxii. 19. Who can forbear to weep, when he beholds this globe, built by the hand of the Deity, and hung round with the mementoes of His goodness, designed to be a vast temple, resounding with awful voices, and filled with holy inspirations, now desecrated to purposes equally pernicious and vile; replete with foul images and filthy rites of idolatry; with daring acts of rebellion, and with sights and sounds of woe? Consider,

III. THE EXALTED CHARACTER BY WHICH THIS SORROW IS DISTINGUISHED.

1. *It is the fruit of Divine influence, and a collateral evidence of real religion in the heart.*

When the Spirit of God enters into the heart, he provides the elements of a benevolence the most exalted and refined.

2. *It assimilates to the temper displayed by the holiest of men.*

Thus, the sweet singer of Israel, amidst the cares of government and the splendours of royalty, found time and inclination to pour rivers of waters from his eyes over the wicked that kept not the law. Thus, the pathetic Jeremiah could exclaim, (ix. 1,) "Oh that my head were waters, and mine eyes a fountain of tears, that I might weep day and night for the slain of the daughter of my people!" And thus the apostle to the Gentiles, possessing as he did the most heroic resolution, the most lofty superiority to all the modes of intimidation and danger, a spirit that rose with its difficulties, and exulted in the midst of the most dismaying objects, yet combined the deepest sensibility with the sternest purpose, and melted into more than feminine tenderness, when he reflected on the moral condition of his fellow men: "Of whom," says he, "I have told you often, and now tell you even weeping, that they are the enemies of the cross of Christ," Phil. iii. 18.

3. *It accords with the spirit evinced by the higher intelligences of the universe.*

The man who identifies himself with the best interests of human nature; who, overstepping the limits of country and of clime, embraces in his affections the whole family of man, acquires an angelic character; and is only inferior to an angel, as his capacities are more limited and his nature less pure.

4. *It is in harmony with the principles embodied in the glorious work of redemption.*

That work, in all parts, from its commencement to its close, proceeds on the principle of the most exalted benevolence. There we see the eternal Father sparing not his own Son, that he might spare us. There we see the benign Spirit, to whom every form of moral contamination is essentially abhorrent, taking up his abode in the desolate dwelling of the human breast, to enlighten what is ignorant, to elevate what is low; and though often grieved and insulted, yet neither deserting his residence, nor transferring his love, till he places the selected object of his compassion, with all his foes vanquished and his stains washed away, in the cloudless lustre of the eternal throne. But " oh for a pencil dipped in living light," to trace the lineaments of the Son of God. In him all the elements of goodness were found, yet so blended as to form one perfect and translucent whole. If, however, there was one attribute of his character which prevailed over the rest, it was compassion to the souls of men. Compassion breathed in his spirit, beat in his heart, beamed in his eyes, and lived in his life. He became the weeping Babe in the manger of Bethlehem, the weary Traveller in the journey of life, the agonizing Sufferer in the garden of Gethsemane; and when the last scene of terror and of death arrived, he bared his bosom to the stroke. Nor did he stop till, by the mysterious oblation on the cross, he had harmonised all the attributes of the Divine nature in one triumphant display of mercy; and had opened a medium by which compassion, without measure and without restraint, might descend to the vilest of the vile.

IV. THE APPROPRIATE MODES IN WHICH THIS SORROW SHOULD BE EXPRESSED.

1. *One of the first and most effectual means by which this feeling is to be indicated, is by fervent and persevering prayer on behalf of the heathen.*

2. *Another mode in which this spirit is to evince itself is by contributing pecuniary support to the missionary cause.*

There are some considerations arising from the nature of this subject that may serve yet further to enforce its claims. Remember that you possess that gospel which is an effectual remedy for the violation of the law. You possess that which alone can mitigate the present misery of the heathen, and avert their future doom; which takes the burden from conscience, the bitterness from sorrow, and the sting from death—transforming that eternity, which they now contemplate with trembling horror or vain hope, into a boundless prospect of glory and of joy.   Remember—that you can communicate these blessings to them without impoverishing yourselves; for such is the plenitude of the gospel, that there may be universal participation without individual diminution—each may have all.

I would remind you that the stability of your expectations is equal to the goodness of your cause; and that the same voice that commands your activity guarantees its success. This world, that was the scene of the Saviour's sufferings, shall be no less the theatre of his triumph and his joy. " His name shall endure for ever : his name shall be continued as long as the sun: and men shall be blessed in him : all nations shall called him blessed !" Psa. lxxii. 17.

SKETCH XLIII.

THE KINGDOM OF CHRIST.

"Thou sawest till that a stone was cut out without hands, which smote the image upon its feet that were of iron and clay, and brake them to pieces," etc.—DAN. ii. 34, 35.

SOME of the most striking and magnificent revelations God ever gave in dreams and visions of the night, were those of king Nebuchadnezzar. It pleased God to select this distinguished and wonderful individual, by causing the most remarkable and striking scenes to pass before his mind during the hours of sleep. The signification of the dream referred to in our text, put the power of the soothsayers, at the time, to utter defiance; but unto Daniel, the beloved of God, was given the spirit of interpretation.

The king saw a splendid image of a human being, mighty and great; and which was particularly distinguished by the materials of which it was composed. The head was of gold, the breast and arms of silver, the other parts of the image were of brass, and the feet were partly of iron, and partly of clay. During the time the mind of Nebuchadnezzar was occupied by this imposing scene, he beheld rising up, a small stone cut out of the mountain without hands; that is, the agency by which it was brought out seemed to be invisible. He observed until this stone came in contact with the image, and smote it to powder, and scattered it before the winds of heaven; and the stone grew until it became a large mountain, and filled the whole earth.

It may be requisite for us, first, to refer to this image, and its literal signification; and then to see what this stone was intended to represent. By the head of gold was meant the Chaldean empire then existing; an empire which extended its influence through Egypt, Phenicia, Palestine, etc., and on account of its immense wealth and opulence was compared to a head of gold. You perceive the breast and arms of this image were of silver—these had reference to the Mede and Persian kingdom. The two arms represented the two kingdoms of the Medes and Persians which were united under Cyrus. Though these were very opulent and splendid, yet they were but as silver when compared to the Chaldean head of gold. The thighs of this image were represented as brass—this referred to the Grecian empire, founded by Alexander the Great, an empire which extended its influence through the greater part of the then known world. The feet are described as of iron and clay— here is a reference to the Roman empire, an empire as regards luxury, magnificence and splendour, vastly inferior to the preceding empires; but as superior in strength, physical power, and endurance, as iron is of greater utility and of more essential worth than gold. The Roman empire is described as having two legs. It has been supposed, by some persons, that the two legs were intended to represent the eastern and western divisions of the Roman empire; while others have thought, it pointed to its secular and ecclesiastical power. And, then, observe this image as it regards the legs and feet: it is described as consisting partly of iron, and partly of clay, to show the great inequality of the various parts of the empire. Some parts should be strong, so strong as to appear to be impregnable as iron; while others should be powerless, and seem to possess internal weakness, like clay. Bishop Newton has shown, in his interesting work on the Prophecies, that every sen-

tence of God, in reference to this prediction, was entirely
fulfilled to the very letter; and that the ten kingdoms into
which the Roman empire was ultimately divided, were
represented by the ten toes of the two feet of this image:
so particularly and minutely were the predictions of God
verified, in reference to this distinguished empire. As it respects the " stone cut out of the mountain without hands,"
and which smote the image and filled the whole earth,
there is no difficulty of interpretation, this is clearly the
kingdom of Jesus Christ. The spiritual empire of the Son
of God—that empire of truth and righteousness which will
extend its influence until the Saviour will overturn, overturn, and overturn, by which He shall possess universal
dominion, whose right it is to reign, Ezek. xxi. 27. We
invite your attention to several particulars connected with
this kingdom, as presented to us in the striking and symbolical language of the text.

I. IT IS EVIDENT FROM THIS REPRESENTATION THAT THE
KINGDOM OF JESUS CHRIST IS SPIRITUAL IN ITS NATURE.
There is something very graphic and important in the
words, " a stone cut out of the mountain without hands."
That is, the empire of God's Son is not an empire arising
from the ruins of preceding empires; not an empire to be
founded and supported by martial power or conquests. It
is not to be a worldly establishment, or to have secular
dominion. When Pilate asked the Saviour, he confessed
that he was a King, but said, " My kingdom is not of this
world," John xviii. 36. The throne which Christ erects,
is a throne within the heart—the kingdom of God is within
you. The laws of this kingdom are spiritual—the requirements of this kingdom are spiritual—all the arrangements,
blessings, and ordinances of this kingdom are spiritual;
they are especially adapted to the soul, and are intended

to bring human beings into a state of loyal affection to Jesus Christ, and to a state of holy obedience and spiritual adherence to Him.

II. THAT THE KINGDOM OF CHRIST IS UNIMPOSING IN ITS NATURE.

" A stone cut out of the mountain,"—mark, a stone, a simple stone, doubtless a small stone. We marvel not that Nebuchadnezzar should wish to know what that little stone signified. In this stone we see how strikingly is predicted to us the origin of the kingdom of Christ in the world. We find even the Monarch in one of the lowest conditions of life—born in a stable, and laid in a manger. When Christ came on his holy and divine mission, he had no illustrious individuals associated with him, or following in his train. His ministers were plain men, mostly fishermen —men without any temporal distinction whatever. He had nothing in his own person to attract the gaze of the human eye. A stranger to external pomp,—the reputed son of a carpenter. He wrought miracles, blessed the people, and delivered his doctrines to the world; and, contrary to all the opinions then existing, he pronounced the poor to be rich, the sorrowful to be blessed, and the persecuted happy, Matt. v. 3, etc. In Christ, and his cause, all was unimposing; and not one element of worldly grandeur existed to meet the carnal desires of the Jewish nation.

III. THE KINGDOM OF CHRIST IS REPRESENTED AS BEING PROGRESSIVE IN ITS CHARACTER.

The " stone cut out of the mountain without hands," while observed by the king, increased; and it became greater and greater, and higher and higher, until it rose to a mighty mountain, every thing else being insignificant when compared with it; and, at length, it filled the whole earth.

But in its progress to this consummation it came in contact with the image, and smote it, and ground it to powder. What a splendid representation of the progress of the Saviour's empire! It was originally a small stone cut out of the mountain without hands; but it grew mightily, and greatly prevailed. "And the stone that smote the image became a great mountain, and filled the whole earth."

IV. THIS KINGDOM IS TO BE TRIUMPHANT IN ITS ACHIEVEMENTS.

It was predicted that the stone should smite the image, and the image was smitten. What victory more triumphant, what conquest more absolute, and what prediction more verified! Something might be gathered from the facts of past times, what shall be the result of everything which sets itself up against God's anointed Son! Surely, as it is written, they shall be broken in pieces; this stone shall break in pieces every such image and power, that shall be arrayed against the progress and triumph of the empire of truth in the world. This stone shall come in contact with every established form of false religion in the world,—with Paganism, and its thousand rites; with Judaism, which the gospel has superseded. This stone shall come in contact with idolatry, that hydra-headed monster; and with another splendid image, Mohammedanism, which Providence has allowed to be set up and exist for centuries, and which has yet scarcely felt the power of Christian influence. Yet that foul image is doomed to fall; in connexion with the Papal superstitions, and all the multifarious rites of heathenism; whether they may resemble the head of gold, the breast of silver, the thighs of brass, or the feet and toes of iron and clay. Christianity refuses to coalesce with any of the systems and forms of religion men have invented, or set up in our world.

V. That this kingdom will be universal in its extent.

This stone must fill the whole earth. Not be as Judaism was, the religion of one land; but the religion of the world. All obstacles are to be removed, and universal power and dominion are to be given into the Saviour's hands, so that

" Jesus shall reign where'er the sun
    Does his successive journeys run;
    His kingdom stretch from shore to shore,
    Till suns shall rise and set no more."

VI. This kingdom is to be everlasting in its duration.

In the 44th verse of this chapter it is stated, that this kingdom shall be for ever; that is, it will be the last and closing dispensation connected with our world's duration. This kingdom is not like the Chaldean, to be succeeded by the Mede and Persian; the Mede and Persian by the Grecian; or the Grecian by the Roman. When this kingdom shall have attained all its achievements, the Saviour shall reign over all nations and people and tongues. Then shall all proclaim his praise, and rejoice in his dominion, which shall be an everlasting dominion, Psa. cxlv. 13.

In conclusion, observe,

1. The kingdom of Christ is associated with human agency. It is to be promulgated by means and instrumentality. He calls us to spread that gospel which we have received; and he will hold all his people responsible in this matter.

2. To extend this empire is the duty of every individual Christian. I should be satisfied to make this the test of a man's religion; because, if the love of Christ dwell in his heart and soul, he will ardently desire Christ's cause to be

extended. "There remaineth yet very much land to be possessed," Josh. xiii. 1.

3. Personal effort, in our respective spheres, is also necessary. The increase of godliness in our own land. The salvation of our families, and perishing neighbours at home. How much is yet to be done!

4. The enemies of the gospel will be crushed to pieces by the triumphant Saviour. The precious chief corner-stone, which will be a sure and stable foundation to the believer, will grind to powder the proud rejecter of God's Anointed. To all will the gospel be the savour of life unto life, or of death unto death, 2 Cor. ii. 16.

Finally. How glorious will be the day when this stone shall become a mountain, and fill the whole earth! When all the splendid visions of prophecy shall be realized! When peace and concord, righteousness and truth, love and mercy, holiness and knowledge, shall beautify our world! When the tabernacle of God shall be with men; and when one song shall resound from shore to shore, and from the rising to the setting of the sun. Hallelujah! Hallelujah! for "the kingdoms of this world are become the kingdoms of our Lord, and of his Christ; and he shall reign for ever and ever," Rev. xi. 15. Amen. Even so, come Lord Jesus, come quickly!

SKETCH XLIV.

THE SPIRIT OF THE LORD, THE BUILDER OF HIS SPIRITUAL TEMPLE.

BY JUSTIN EDWARDS, D.D.,

PRESIDENT OF THE THEOLOGICAL SEMINARY, ANDOVER, MASSACHUSETTS, U.S.

"Not by might, nor by power, but by my Spirit, saith the Lord of hosts."
ZECH. iv. 6.

THIS was spoken by the angel of the Lord, concerning the building of the second temple. It is the explanation of a vision, which was seen by the prophet Zechariah, the object of which was to show him, and through him, to make known to the people, a truth which it was of great importance that they should clearly understand, and deeply feel: viz., that while they must, themselves, make strenuous and persevering exertions to build the temple, their dependance for success must be placed, not upon themselves, or upon creatures, but upon the Spirit of the Lord. This is a truth of universal application, with regard to every good work; and of fundamental importance to all people. For this reason God takes a variety of ways to make it known, and to impress it upon the hearts of men. And for this same reason, I invite your attention to it at this time. This temple is the church; that holy, spiritual building, which is "built upon the foundation of the apostles and prophets, Jesus Christ himself being the chief corner stone," Eph. ii. 20. It is to be composed of all true be-

lievers who shall ever have lived, from the first moment of
creation, to the last moment of time. They may not belong to the same denomination; or spend life on the same
side of the wall which they have set up; but if they believe
on the Son of God, and are so joined to him as to be
" one spirit," they shall form a part of his spiritual temple.
Europeans, Asiatics, Africans, Indians—all, of every age
and colour, and out of " every kindred, and tongue, and
people, and nation," who believe on the Lord Jesus Christ,
shall thus be " builded together for an habitation of God
through the Spirit," Eph. ii. 22.

I. FROM THE GREATNESS OF THE WORK WHICH IT WAS
NECESSARY TO PERFORM, IN ORDER TO LAY THE FOUNDA-
TION, IT APPEARS THAT THE SPIRIT OF THE LORD MUST
BE THE BUILDER OF THIS SPIRITUAL TEMPLE.

It was a work which none but God himself could perform. Nor could He even do it, in the wisest and best
way, though he was almighty, and had all creation at his
disposal, in less than four thousand years.

The physical creation He could complete, and in the
wisest and best way, in a single week. " He spake, and it
was done; he commanded, and it stood fast," Psa. xxxiii. 9.
But to prepare the way, even to lay the foundation, of this
eternal habitation for himself, he must operate throughout
the kingdoms of nature, providence, and grace, for thousands and thousands of years.—Nor is this all. He, who
" was in the beginning with God," " and was God," must
himself leave the glory which he had before the creation;
take upon him " the form of a servant;" and labour, and
" become obedient unto death, even the death of the cross,"
Phil. ii. 8. And as under its awful, crushing weight, " he
bowed his head, and gave up the ghost," the sun turned
away, the rocks broke asunder, and the dead started from

their graves, to adore him that liveth, but *was* dead, that *they* might live for evermore, Rev. i. 18.

II. FROM THE FOUNDATION ITSELF.

This foundation is the Son of God—"the brightness of his Father's glory, and the express image of his person," Heb. i. 3; in whom "dwelleth all the fulness of the Godhead bodily," Col. ii. 9. "By him were all things created, that are in heaven, and that are in earth, visible and invisible, whether they be thrones, or dominions, or principalities, or powers: all things were created by him, and for him: and he is before all things, and by him all things consist;"— and he "is over all, God blessed for ever," Col. i. 16; Rom. ix. 5. To him the Father saith, and he knows, "Thy throne, O God, is for ever and ever: a sceptre of righteousness is the sceptre of thy kingdom," Psa. xlv. 6; Heb. i. 8. Such is the foundation of this temple—"God manifest in the flesh," 1 Tim. iii. 16. "Behold I lay in Zion for a foundation, a stone, a tried stone, a precious corner stone, a sure foundation," Isa. xxviii. 16. "For other foundation can no man lay than that is laid, which is Jesus Christ,—the true God, and eternal life," I Cor. iii. 11; 1 John v. 20.

III. FROM THE MATERIALS OUT OF WHICH THE TEMPLE IS TO BE MADE.

These, as they are in their natural state, universally; and as they would be, without the Spirit and grace of God, eternally, are described by him, as walking "according to the course of this world, according to the prince of the power of the air, the spirit that now worketh in the children of disobedience: among whom also we all had our conversation in times past in the lusts of our flesh, fulfilling the desires of the flesh and of the mind; and were by nature the

children of wrath, even as others," Eph. ii. 22, 23.   And
who can take these materials and make them alive, and fill
them with " love, joy, peace, long-suffering, gentleness,
goodness, meekness, faith, and temperance," (Gal. v.
22, 23,) but he who " spake, and it was done ;" who
" commanded, and it stood fast ?"   Can you do it?   Can
any man do it?   Let him make the experiment.   And to
make it under the most favourable circumstances, let him
be a parent, and try it upon his own child.   Let him re-
nounce all dependence on God, and the influences of his
Spirit, and then take that child, who is now an enemy to
his Maker, and, if he can, create him " anew in Christ
Jesus unto good works," and cause him to glow like a seraph
in the Divine service.   No; not an infidel parent on earth
can do this; and not a Christian parent will dare to attempt
it.   All the dedications of children to God in baptism; all
the prayers and tears of pious parents while wrestling with
God for their salvation, are a standing testimony that the
work must be done, not by might, nor by power, but by the
Spirit of God.   Even children, to be alive unto God, "must
be born again;" "not of blood, nor of the will of the flesh,
nor of the will of man, but of God," John iii. 7; i. 13.
Does any one still doubt?   Let him try the experiment
upon *himself*.

   Has any one ever done this, of himself merely—by his
own unaided wisdom, righteousness, and strength, without
the Spirit and grace of God?   Who is he?   When, or
where?   Go through creation, and ask every soul, that has
" passed from death unto life," Who made you to differ?
How were you saved?   And they will all answer, " By grace
were we saved through faith ; and that not of ourselves,
it was the gift of God," Eph. ii. 8.   That God must be
the Builder of this glorious edifice, is, if possible, still
more plain

IV. FROM THE OBJECT FOR WHICH IT IS TO BE CREATED.

The object for which this spiritual temple is to be erected, is, to show angels, "principalities, and powers, in heavenly places,—*the manifold wisdom of God*," Eph. iii. 10. Oh the exceeding riches of his grace in *his kindness towards men, through Jesus Christ:* an object which is infinite; and which, as it unfolds with ever-increasing brightness, will call forth, from multitudes which no man can number, in louder and louder strains, Allelulias to God and the Lamb, for ever and ever. Who can accomplish this but God himself? Can an angel do it? Can a superangelic creature? Can any creature, however exalted, show, by his productions, the manifold wisdom of God? No man, or angel, or superangelic creature, can conceive a thousandth part of the riches of that grace, which, at such a sacrifice, has opened an eternity of bliss to a world infinitely undeserving.

But suppose he could conceive, and could display all the riches of that grace, he could not be the builder of this temple; for Jehovah will not give his glory to another, Isa. xlii. 8. And the object of this temple, is, not that any creature may display; but that GOD may display the exceeding riches of his grace, and his manifold wisdom. Of course, no creature can build it: for no creature can display wisdom which he does not possess; and no building can display more wisdom than is possessed by the builder. But this building is to display more, infinitely more, than is possessed by all creatures in the universe.

(1.) In conclusion. If the Spirit of the Lord is the builder of this temple, no one will ever become a part of it, without being prepared for it by him.

(2.) As the Spirit of the Lord is the builder of this temple, his materials will all be perfectly prepared. However unsightly, or dark, or distant, and totally unfit to form a part of such an edifice, " God, who commanded the light to shine out of darkness," will shine down, not only upon them, and around them, but " into their hearts, to give them the light of the knowledge of the glory of God in the face of Jesus Christ," 2 Cor. iv. 6. And they shall not only see light, but themselves become light in the Lord, Eph. v. 8.

(3.) As the Spirit of the Lord is the builder of this temple, any individual to whom he is made known, and who is in a state of probation, may himself become a part of it. Wherever he may live, and under whatever circumstances he may be placed; however long he may have been in rebellion against God, and however deeply he may have sunk in degradation and guilt; he may, nevertheless, be transformed into the Divine image, and live.

(4.) As the Spirit of the Lord is the builder of this temple, we see what each one must do, in order to be prepared for it. He must become acquainted with the Holy Spirit, and must look to him for what he needs. He must attend to his communications—must understand, believe, and obey them. They will thus be spirit and life to his soul.

(5.) As the Spirit of the Lord is the builder of this temple, and he operates by the truth, we see the reason why a knowledge of the Spirit, and of his truth, should be communicated, in the least possible time, to all people. All people need this knowledge. They are in imminent danger of perishing eternally without it. It is suited to their condition; and adapted to meet their wants. Nothing else will do it. We have this remedy! freely we have received, and freely we are bound to give. God commands, " Go ye into all the world, and preach the gospel to every creature," Mark xvi. 15.

(6.) We see, in view of this subject, that the missionary of the cross is engaged in a great and glorious work. Men may, if they will, view him with pity or contempt— as a wild enthusiast, or blind fanatic. God views him as a co-worker with himself, in preparing his own eternal habitation.

(7.) As the Spirit of the Lord is the author and finisher of this work, all are bound to be instant, sincere, fervent, and persevering, not only in labours, but in supplication to him, that their efforts, and the efforts of others, may not be in vain in the Lord. Without his influence, though you put a Bible into every family, and preach the gospel to every creature, not a blind eye will be opened, not a deaf ear be unstopped; nor a hard heart will be softened; nor a distant soul be brought nigh by the blood of Jesus. Not a living soul will ever shine in that living temple; but all be cold, motionless, and dead.

(8.) As the Spirit of the Lord is the builder of this temple, it will be completed. For four thousand years he was preparing to lay the foundation; and that is now done. For six thousand years, he has been preparing the materials, and taking them on to the spot. And has HE begun, and will he not make an end? Shall any of his enemies ever taunt him, and say, " He began to build, and was not able to finish?" No. Let difficulties accumulate till they fill the whole earth, and rise up to heaven. " Who art thou, O great mountain? before Zerubbabel thou shalt become a plain; and he shall bring forth the head-stone thereof with shoutings, crying, GRACE, GRACE UNTO IT," Zech. iv. 7.

SKETCH XLV.

NATURE AND IMPORTANCE OF CHRISTIAN ZEAL.

"And your zeal hath provoked very many."—2 COR. ix. 2.

THE apostle is pleading the cause of Christian liberality. He exhibits a delightful instance of this in the case of the Macedonian church. Their liberality is described as abounding to the extent of their power—beyond their power: their contributions were urged upon the apostles, yea, urged with much entreaty. But you say, doubtless they were rich; but if so, they could only do according to their ability. But the truth is, they were poor, in great trials, and yet they were ensamples of liberality to all the other churches. The apostle commends the liberality of the Corinthians in the verse preceding our text; and then states the influence of their zeal on others. If the maintenance of Christianity in our own souls, and its diffusion in our own churches, be greatly dependant on the spirit of zeal, how much more the dissemination of the gospel among the perishing heathen, where obstacles of an almost insuperable kind seem to impede the advancement of the kingdom of Christ!

I. LET US, THEN, CONSIDER THE NATURE OF CHRISTIAN ZEAL.

The word is derived from the Greek, zelos, the root of which, zeo, signifies to boil, to be hot, etc. Therefore, when

o

applied to the mind, it signifies fervour—an impassioned, ardent state of mind. It is the opposite of listlessness, apathy, and coldness.

1. *Christian zeal is spiritual in its origin.*

It is not natural for man to be religiously zealous. A man may be so in sin, as was Manasseh; a zealous Pharisee, as Saul of Tarsus. Or a man may have sectarian zeal, and be an ardent bigot; or superstitious zeal, as the devotees of idolatry. But, unless a man have the spirit of God, he cannot have the zeal of the Christian. This flame must be enkindled by the fire of the Holy Ghost. It must descend from heaven on the altar of our souls.

2. *It is intellectual in its character.*

The Jews had a zeal, but it was not "according to know-ledge;" so, the apostle Paul was a zealous persecutor, but he did it ignorantly, etc., 1 Tim. i. 13. Now, Christian zeal is not like the fire and smoke which issue from the volcano; but like the burning rays of the noontide sun—bright, clear, and glorious. A Christian has a reason for his zeal, as well as his hope. It is associated with a why and a wherefore. A principle based on sanctified reason.

3. *It is modest and humble in its pretensions.*

There is a zeal of show, and glare, and pretension. A zeal, which only aims at the exaltation of its possessor, like that of Jehu of old, when he said to Jehonadab, " Come with me, and see my zeal for the Lord," 2 Kings. x. 16, etc. It is essential to this kind of zeal that it must be seen and be applauded, or it will expire. The Pharisees were clad in this. Peter, in his early profession, was characterized by it. "Though all men shall be offended because of thee, yet will I never be offended," Matt. xxvi. 33. How dif-ferent afterwards—"Simon, son of Jonas, lovest thou me? Yea, Lord; thou knowest that I love thee," John xxi. 16.

Christian zeal is diffident and retiring, seeking to exalt Christ only.

4. *It is consistent and enduring in its influence.*

The Galatians were zealous, but they ran well only for a time, Gal. iii.   The zeal of many is merely spasmodic—a disease, and not health.   Or, in many cases, it is like the flaming forth of the eccentric comet, attracting general attention, and then passing away.   But Christian zeal is the healthy action of the heart, indicating vigour of spirit.   It is like the morning light, "that shineth more and more unto the perfect day," Prov. iv. 18.

5. *It is diligent and active in its efforts.*

A man may have a creed in which zeal is an item.   Zealous profession—zealous desires—zealous principles and intentions—zealous prayers.   But let us see these carried out—carried out " in works of faith, and labours of love." Christian zeal toils and labours, etc.   Zeal is embodied. It has an ear to hearken to God's commands; feet to run in the way of usefulness;   the hand to work, and the shoulder to bear burdens; and a spirit of noble activity and enterprise in the things of God.

6. *It is kind and affectionate in its spirit.*

Christian zeal is not the fire of wrath to hate, of anger to curse, or of presumption to anathematise; but of heaven to warm and to bless.   It is always in company with the chief of the graces, "charity;" and therefore "envieth not," and "thinketh no evil," 1 Cor. xiii.   It does not dwell on Sinai, but in Zion.   It does not love the tempest, and the thunderings and earthquake; but the calm serenity of Tabor or Olivet.   It has the eagle's eye, and soars upwards; but the nature and gentleness of the dove.   It has the power of the ox, and the courage of the lion; but the nature of the lamb.   It hates sin, but yearns over the sinner; it denounces vice, but tries to rescue its victim.   It deplores the misery of the world, and ardently prays and labours for its removal. It ascends, and brings the live coal from the celestial altar, and with it labours to provoke others to love and good works. Consider,

II. THE SPHERES IN WHICH IT MAY BE EXERCISED. These are numberless, but they may be compressed in two.

1. *In securing all the good within its power.*

Zealous in attaining the gifts and graces of the Spirit of God. In seeking knowledge—spiritual power—conformity to Christ, and meetness for the Divine glory. It must be exercised in mortifying sin—self-denial—growth in grace, etc. All that is included in spiritual, practical, and experimental religion.

2. *In communicating all possible good to others.*

Exerting a beneficial influence on society. Imitating Christ, "who went about doing good." Removing ignorance, reclaiming the vicious, exhorting the careless, reproving the wicked, guiding the inquirer, and comforting the afflicted. This is its motto—" Let us do good unto all men," etc. What a sphere is the missionary field, where untold millions are " living without God, and without hope in the world!" Where the avenues of death are eternally crowded with deathless beings, who are hurrying, in a state of ignorance and pollution, into the eternal world !

III. THE PRINCIPLES ON WHICH IT SHOULD BE CULTIVATED.

1. *It is an essential characteristic of true religion.*

The poet has well said,

> " Religion, without zeal and love,
> Is but an empty name."

Look over the record of the saints, the excellent of the

earth : Noah, Abraham, Jacob, Moses, Caleb, and Joshua ;
Samuel, David, Elijah, Isaiah, the Baptist, Paul, the early
Christians, the Corinthians, etc.   It is the spiritual heat of
the new life.   The sustaining principle in labours, etc.

2. *It is a distinguishing trait in the most excellent order
of beings.*

" Who maketh his angels spirits, and his ministers a
flame of fire," Heb. i. 7.   Seraphim are described as burning
ones—they are all ardour, intensity, etc.   But I refer Christians especially to the world's Redeemer.

" And he saw that there was no man, and wondered that
there was no intercessor : therefore his arm brought salvation unto him ; and his righteousness, it sustained him.
For he put on righteousness as a breastplate, and an helmet
of salvation upon his head ; and he put on the garments of
vengeance for clothing, and was clad with zeal as a cloke,"
Isa. lix. 16, 17.   He enters on his incarnate state.   At
twelve years of age, he exclaimed, " Wist ye not that I must
be about my Father's business ?"   He commences his life of
sorrow, etc.   He sees the tempest before him—the whole
was palpable to him, yet he exclaims, " I have a baptism
to be baptised with, and how am I straitened till it be accomplished," Luke xii. 50.   He crowds a long life of labours into the limits of three years.   He then treads the
winepress alone—stands in the fearful gap—and ends his
toils and sufferings and life together.

3. *It is essential to the triumphs of the church.*

We believe in the final overthrow of sin, and Satan's
kingdom.   In the millennial glory of the church of Christ.
But can it be without zeal on the part of Christians.   Three
things are essential : the diffusion of unmixed truth—the
maintenance of evangelical purity—and the cultivation of
intense zeal.   Think of the difficulties ; of the opposition ;
of the warring elements, etc. ; and say, can we dispense with

zeal? Political parties cannot—commerce cannot—science cannot—the cause of.freedom cannot,—much less religion.

APPLICATION.

1. Let me urge you to seek after the attainment of this Christian principle. Let me provoke you to zeal. Look at the zeal of Pagans, Mohammedans. Look at the zeal of the worldly. Look at the zeal of the Romish church. Look at the zeal of the infidel

2. Think of the magnitude of the objects you contemplate. Your designs have to do with the everlasting interests of your own souls, etc.; of those around you; and all the unenlightened heathen—you act for eternity

3. Think of the limited period of your opportunities. Where are the first friends of the gospel in this island? Where the puritans? Where are our friends? "Your fathers, where are they?" Go to the grave-yard, there lie their sleeping remains; their record is on high—though dead they yet speak to us. Remember, "Whatsoever thy hand findeth to do, do it with thy might; for there is no work, nor device, nor knowledge, nor wisdom, in the grave, whither thou goest," Eccl. ix. 10. Think of the zeal of those who consecrate themselves to the missionary work. What self-denial they endure, and what sacrifices they make! What enjoyments they surrender! What trials they encounter! What sufferings they sustain! A true missionary must hazard his life for Christ, and for the souls of the heathen. Then let our zeal at home sustain, and cheer, and encourage them; yea, let our "zeal provoke very many."

SKETCH XLVI.

JESUS THE TRUE MESSIAH.

BY REV. ANDREW FULLER.*

" Sacrifice and offering thou didst not desire ; mine ears hast thou opened : burnt offering and sin offering hast thou not required. Then said I, Lo, I come : in the volume of the book it is written of me, I delight to do thy will, O my God : yea, thy law is within my heart."—Psa. xl. 6—8.

No Christian can doubt whether the passage relates to the Messiah, seeing it is expressly applied to him in the New Testament, Heb. x. 5—10; and, if a Jew should raise an objection, he will find it difficult, if not impossible, to give a fair exposition of it on any other principle. Who else, with propriety, could use the language here used ? Certainly, David could not. Whether the Messiah, therefore, be already come, as we believe, or be yet to come, as the body of the Jewish nation believes, it must be of his coming that the prophet speaks. The question at issue between them and us, is not whether the Scriptures predict and characterize the Messiah; but, whether these predictions and characters be fulfilled in Jesus ?

That we may be able to judge of this question, let it be observed, that there are three characters held up in the passage I have read, as distinguishing the Messiah's coming: viz., that the sacrifices and ceremonies of the Mosaic law would, from thence, be superseded; that the great body of Scripture prophecy would be accomplished; and that the

* Preached in the Jews' Chapel, Church Street, Spitalfields, 1809.

will of God would be perfectly fulfilled. Let us calmly and candidly try the question at issue by these characters.

I. IT IS INTIMATED THAT WHENEVER THE MESSIAH SHOULD COME THE SACRIFICES AND CEREMONIES OF THE MOSAIC LAW WERE TO BE SUPERSEDED BY HIM.

" Sacrifice and offering thou didst not desire;—then said I, Lo, I come." I am aware that modern Jewish writers contend for the perpetuity of the ceremonial, as well as of the moral law; but in this they are opposed both by Scripture and by fact. As to Scripture, it is not confined to the passage I have read, nor to a few others. It is common for the sacred writers of the Old Testament to speak of sacrifices and ceremonies in a depreciating strain, such as would not, I presume, have been used, had they been regarded for their own sake, or designed to continue always. Such is the language of the following passages: see 1 Sam. xv. 22; Psa. l. 7—15; li. 16, 17; Isa. i. 11, 12; Jer. vii. 21—23; Dan. ix. 27.

Is it not, then, in perfect harmony with the tenor of these Scriptures, that Messiah, when described as coming into the world, should say, " Sacrifice and offering thou didst not desire; mine ears hast thou opened: burnt offering and sin offering hast thou not required. Then said I, Lo, I come?"—plainly intimating that he would come to accomplish that which could not be accomplished by sacrifices and offerings; and that, as these were but the scaffolding of his temple, when that should be reared, these should, of course, be taken down. See also Jer. xxxi. 31—34; Heb. viii. 13; x. 17, 18.

II. IT IS SUGGESTED THAT WHENEVER MESSIAH SHOULD COME, THE GREAT BODY OF SCRIPTURE PROPHECY SHOULD BE ACCOMPLISHED IN HIM.—" In the volume of the book it is written of me." That the prophetic writings abound in predictions of the Messiah, no Jew will deny; the only question is, are they fulfilled in Jesus?

In trying the question, whether the prophecies be fulfilled in Jesus? it will be necessary, for the sake of perspicuity, to class them under different heads, such as time, place, family, etc.

I. *The time when Messiah should come is clearly marked out in prophecy.* It was said by Jacob, when blessing the tribes, " The sceptre shall not depart from Judah, nor a lawgiver from between his feet, until Shiloh come; and unto him shall the gathering of the people be," Gen. xlix. 10. All this was true in respect of Jesus. Till he came, though the ten tribes were scattered, Judah continned a people; and retained the government. But soon after his death, they were dispersed among the nations; and have been so ever since. " Kings and princes," says one of your own writers, " we have none !"

If, therefore, Shiloh be not come, he can never come within the limits of time marked out by this prophecy. Again; it is clearly intimated in the prophecy of Haggai, for the encouragement of the builders of the second temple, that the Messiah should come during the standing of that temple ; and that the honour that should be done it by his presence, would more than balance its inferiority in other respects to the first. " For thus saith the Lord of hosts; Yet once, it is a little while, and I will shake the heavens, and the earth, and the sea, and the dry land; and I will shake all nations, and the desire of all nations shall come : and I will fill this house with glory, saith the Lord of hosts. The silver is mine, and the gold is mine, saith the Lord of hosts. The glory of this latter house shall be greater than of the former, saith the Lord of hosts," Hag. ii. 6—9. All this was literally fulfilled in Jesus. But soon after his death, the second temple was reduced to ashes. If, therefore, Jesus was not the Messiah, it is impossible that this prophecy should ever be accomplished.

Again. The prophet Daniel was informed by the angel Gabriel as follows, Dan. ix. 20—27. Whether Christian writers agree as to the exact time when these seventy sabbatical weeks, or four hundred and ninety years, began, or not, thus much is certain, that they must have been fulfilled about the time that Jesus appeared and suffered, or they never can be fulfilled. Such was the effect of this, and other prophecies, upon the minds of the Jewish nation, that about that time there was a general expectation of the Messiah's appearance.

2. *The place where Messiah should be born, and where he should principally impart his doctrine is determined.* " But thou, Beth-lehem Ephratah, though thou be little among the thousands of Judah, yet out of thee shall come forth unto me that is to be ruler in Israel; whose goings forth have been from of old, from everlasting," Micah v. 2. Speaking of Galilee of the nations in connexion with the birth of the child, whose name should be called " the mighty God," it is said, " The people that walked in darkness have seen a great light: they that dwell in the land of the shadow of death, upon them hath the light shined," Isa ix. 2. These prophecies were literally and manifestly fulfilled in Jesus; and it is scarcely credible that they can be fulfilled in any other.

3. *The house, or family, from whom Messiah should descend, is clearly ascertained.* So much is said of his descending from David, that I need not refer to particular proofs; and the rather, as no Jew will deny it. The genealogies of Matthew and Luke, whatever varieties there are between them, agree in tracing his pedigree to David. And though, in both, it is traced in the name of Joseph,

yet this appears to be only in conformity to the Jewish custom, of tracing no pedigree in the name of a female. The father of Joseph, as mentioned by Luke, seems to have been his father by marriage only; so that it was, in reality, Mary's pedigree that is traced by Luke, though under her husband's name; and this being the natural line of descent, and that of Matthew the legal one, by which as King, he would have inherited the crown, there is no inconsistency between them.

4. *The kind of miracles that Messiah should perform is specified.* Isaiah, speaking of the coming of God to save his people, says, " Then the eyes of the blind shall be opened, and the ears of the deaf shall be unstopped. Then shall the lame leap as an hart, and the tongue of the dumb sing: for in the wilderness shall waters break out, and streams in the desert," Isa. xxxv. 5, 6. That such miracles were performed by Jesus, his enemies themselves bare witness, in that they ascribed them to his connexion with Beelzebub, Luke xi. 15. When his Messiahship was questioned, he could say, in the presence of many witnesses, " The blind receive their sight, and the lame walk, the lepers are cleansed, and the deaf hear, the dead are raised up, and the poor have the gospel preached unto them," Matt. xi. 5.

5. *It was predicted of the Messiah, that he should as a king be distinguished by his lowliness,* entering into Jerusalem, not in a chariot of state, but in a much humbler style. " Rejoice greatly, O daughter of Zion; shout, O daughter of Jerusalem: behold thy King cometh unto thee: he is just, and having salvation; lowly, and riding upon an ass, and upon a colt the foal of an ass," Zech. ix. 9. To fulfil this prophecy, it was necessary that the Messiah should descend from parents in low circumstances; and that the leading people of the land should not accompany

him. Had they believed in him, and introduced him as a king, it must have been in another fashion. But it was reserved for the common people and the children to fulfil the prophet's words, by shouting, "Hosanna, to the Son of David. Blessed is he that cometh in the name of the Lord; Hosanna in the highest," Matt. xxi. 9.

6. *It is predicted of the Messiah, that he should suffer and die by the hands of wicked men.* "Thus saith the Lord, the Redeemer of Israel, and his Holy One, to him whom man despiseth, to him whom the nation abhorreth. —As many were astonished at thee; his visage was so marred more than any man, and his form more than the sons of men: so shall he sprinkle many nations," etc., Isa. xlix. 7; lii. 14, 15; liii.; Dan. ix. 26.

7. *It was foretold that the Messiah, after being cut off out of the land of the living, and laid in the grave, should rise from the dead.* Nothing less can be implied by all the promises made to him as the reward of his sufferings; for if he had continued under the power of death, how should he have seen his seed, or prolonged his days? If his kingdom had been that of a mortal man, how could it continue as long as the sun and moon? How was he to "see of the travail of his soul and be satisfied," unless he survived that travail? But more than this, it is foretold that he should rise from the dead at so early a period as not to see corruption. The argument of Peter, from this passage, has never been answered. David said, "Thou wilt not suffer thine Holy One to see corruption," Psa. xvi. 10: but David did see corruption; he refers to Him, there-fore, of whom it is witnessed that he saw no corruption.

Lastly. *It was foretold that the great body of the Jewish nation would not believe in him; and that he would set up his kingdom among the Gentiles.* Such is evidently the meaning of the prophet's complaint, "Who hath be-

lieved our report?" and of the Messiah's words, in another
part of the same prophecies,—"Then I said, I have laboured in vain; I have spent my strength for nought, and
in vain; yet surely my judgment is with the Lord, and my
work with my God!" etc., Isa. liii. 1; xlix. 4, 6.

III. IT IS DECLARED THAT WHEN THE MESSIAH SHOULD
COME, THE WILL OF GOD WOULD BE PERFECTLY FULFILLED
BY HIM.

" I delight to do thy will, O my God : yea, thy law is
within my heart," Psa. xl. 8. Agreeably to this, the
Messiah is denominated God's servant, whom he would
uphold; in whom he would be glorified; and who should
bring Jacob again to him, Isa. xlii. 1, etc. The will of
God sometimes denotes what he approves, and sometimes
what he appoints. The first is the rule of our conduct,
the last of his own; and both we affirm to have been fulfilled by Jesus.

(1.) In respect of the Divine precepts, his whole life
was in perfect conformity to them. All his actions were
governed by love.

(2.) But it was not merely to fulfil the Divine precepts
that the Messiah was to come; but to execute his purpose
in saving lost sinners. Even his obedience to the law was
subservient to this, or he could not have been "the Lord
our righteousness." He was God's servant, to raise up the
tribes of Jacob, to give light to the Gentiles, and to be
his salvation to the end of the earth. In accomplishing
this, it behoved him to endure the penalty, as well as obey
the precepts of the law. His soul must be made an offering
for sin; he must be cut off out of the land of the living—
cut off, but not for himself; and this that he might "make
reconciliation for iniquity, and bring in everlasting righteousness," Dan. ix. 24.

I have lately looked into some of the modern Jewish
writings. It would be going beyond my limits to attempt
an answer to many of their objections to the gospel; but
I will touch upon a few which struck me in course of
reading. They find many things spoken in prophecy of
the reign of Messiah, which are not as yet fulfilled in
Jesus; such as the cessation of wars, the restoration of the
Jewish nation, etc.; and argue from hence, that Jesus is
not the Messiah.   But it is not said that these effects
should immediately follow on his appearing.   On the contrary, there was to be an increase of his government; yea,
a continued increase. Jesus may be the Messiah, and his
reign may be begun; while yet, seeing it is not ended,
there may be many things at present unfulfilled.

But they object, that the doctrine taught by Jesus was
not of a pacific tendency—that, on the contrary, it was,
by his own confession, adapted to produce division and
discord.   " Think not that I am come to send peace on
earth : I came not to send peace, but a sword.   For I am
come to set a man at variance against his father, and the
daughter against her mother, and the daughter-in-law
against her mother-in-law.   And a man's foes shall be
they of his own household," Matt. x. 34—36.

(3.) They further object, with their fathers, that Jesus
pretended to be the Son of God, and so was guilty of
blasphemy.   But, if he were the Messiah, he was the Son
of God.   Did not God, in the second psalm, address him
as his Son; and are not the kings and judges of the earth
admonished to submit to him under that character?

(4.) Some of the precepts of Jesus are objected to, as
being impracticable; and Christians accused of hypocrisy
for pretending to respect them, while none of them act up
to them; that is, when they are smitten on one cheek,
they do not offer the other.   But this is perverseness.

Jesus did not mean it literally; nor did he so exemplify it
when smitten before Pilate. Nor do the Jews so understand their own commandments. If they do, however, it
will follow that they break the sixth commandment in
every malefactor whose execution they promote, and even
in the killing of animals for food. The manifest design of
the precept is to prohibit all private retaliation and revenge;
and to teach us, that we ought rather to suffer insult, than
to " render evil for evil."

But I shall conclude with a few words to professing
Christians. I can perceive, by what I have seen of the
Jewish writings, how much they avail themselves of our
disorders and divisions to justify their unbelief. " Let every
" one that nameth the name of Christ depart from iniquity."
Let us beware of valuing ourselves in the name, while we
are destitute of the thing. We may yield a sort of assent
to the doctrine just delivered, while yet it brings forth no
good fruit in us. These are the things that rivet Jews in
their unbelief. " He that winneth souls is wise," Prov.
xi. 30. I hope all the measures that are taken for the
conversion of the Jews, will be of a winning nature. If
they be malignant and abusive, they must not be opposed
with the same weapons.

SKETCH XLVII.

APOSTOLIC BENEVOLENCE.

BY REV. EDWARD WILLIAMS, D.D.*

"Brethren, my heart's desire and prayer to God for Israel is, that they might be saved. For I bear them record, that they have a zeal of God, but not according to knowledge. For they being ignorant of God's righteousness, and going about to establish their own righteousness, have not submitted themselves unto the righteousness of God. For Christ is the end of the law for righteousness to every one that believeth."

ROM. x. 1—4.

HERE, my Christian friends, we have a pattern highly worthy of our imitation. And with a view to recommend it, I call your attention to reflect with me on,

I. THE PROPER NATURE OF THAT BENEVOLENCE WHICH WAS EXEMPLIFIED BY THE APOSTLE PAUL, AND WHICH IS NOW RECOMMENDED TO YOUR NOTICE.

It was not a transitory flash of light, without heat; it was not a weak wish, devoid of energetic efforts; it was not a selfish desire to acquire fame, or to increase a party; nor was it hasty and abrupt, liable to be shaken with every blast of opposition, either from those whose best interests it sought, or from others who took wrong views of the subject. But the temper of mind now recommended had the following characters :—

* Preached in the Jews' Chapel, Church Street, Spitalfields, 1811.

1. *It was deeply seated in the heart.* A benevolence which is not a rooted principle, will finally die away. Love, benevolent love, is the very essence of all real religion, and of all true virtue.

2. *It was the effect of knowledge.* The wise king of Israel observes, " That the soul be without knowledge, it is not good," Prov. xix. 2. No specific truth can be loved, while we remain ignorant of its character. Conviction is the fruit of knowledge; and so is all acceptable devotion. When the mind is divinely enlightened, and consequently well informed, the religious tenets we contemplate appear in their due proportion and importance.

And thus, my brethren, let it be our constant endeavour to possess more Divine light, that all our efforts may be strengthened by knowledge, derived from the Spirit and word of God, and directed by that wisdom which is from above.

3. *It was an operative principle, manifesting itself in substantial acts of kindness.* This principle, resembling its Divine Author, not only partakes of goodness, but also imparts it. Christian benevolence cannot manifest bitterness and wrath, envy and strife. The kindness exercised is like that of a faithful shepherd to a wandering sheep; like that of a firm friend in the season of adversity; or like that of a loving parent interested for the welfare of his child.

4. *It was a disinterested and self-denying principle.* As this is the proper nature of Christian benevolence, so it is an eminent part of its excellence. It stands directly opposite to that odious vice called selfishness. It is indeed perfectly consistent with some regard to ourselves, but it does not rest there. A man without real religion, would fain bring every ray to centre in himself, as the common focus; but benevolence moves in a contrary direction—love and kindness diffuse themselves as from a radiant point, to

enlighten and to cheer every capable object. Selfishness
is a vortex in which everything within its power is ingulphed;
but benevolence expands itself, like circling waves.

5. *It was a patient and persevering principle.* It was
not only kind, as exemplified by Paul, but it " suffered
long," it was not weary in well-doing; it coped with unparalleled difficulties, and surmounted stupendous obstacles.
He endured all things for the elect's sake, that they also might
obtain eternal salvation, which he knew could be obtained
only in Christ Jesus, 2 Tim. ii. 10. We come now to
consider,

II. The peculiar objects of that benevolence which
was exemplified by Paul, and which is now recommended for imitation.

Though in its aim it was unbounded, and the Gentile
world was Paul's peculiar province, while his brethren in
the apostleship laboured professedly among the Jews; yet
his kinsmen, however disaffected to him, had the warmest
affections of his heart. " I say the truth in Christ, I lie not,
my conscience also bearing me witness in the Holy Ghost,
that I have great heaviness and continual sorrow in my
heart. For I could wish that myself were accursed," or
excommunicated " from Christ, (*i.e.* the Christian assembly,) for my brethren, my kinsmen according to the flesh,"
Rom. ix. 1—3.

1. *The persons he had peculiarly in view were the Israelites, or Jews.* Of these none were excepted; his loving
heart included them all: the learned and the ignorant, the
rich and the poor, the old and the young.

2. *Their highest, their eternal welfare.* " My heart's
desire and prayer to God for Israel is, that they might be
saved." Paul had thoroughly learned, that all men,
through sin, are become obnoxious to the curse denounced

on transgressors by the righteous law of God; and that if Christ be rejected, "there is none other name under heaven given among men whereby they can be saved," Acts iv. 12. Heaven or hell must be the final receptacles of all mankind. Paul felt the momentous influence of such considerations.

III. The powerful obstacles which the benevolence of Paul, when directed to the Jews, had to encounter.

1. *The prejudices of education.* God had revealed himself to Abraham, Isaac, and Jacob, their ancestors, and especially to Moses and the prophets, in a very signal manner. They were strenuous in maintaining that the Jewish religion was a temple, while the Christian was a needless appendage to it; or, rather, an insulting and injurious altar against altar. But Paul, on the contrary, was fully convinced, that Judaism, in its Divine institution, was but a porch, leading to the Christian temple; and that all the Levitical and Mosaic institutions were but shadows of better things.

2. *Another powerful opposition arose 'from their zeal and jealousy for the peculiarities of their profession,* which is common to all religious parties prior to impartial examination. Witness the Egyptians, in favour of their idols; the Philistines in favour of Dagon; the Ephesians for their Diana; the Romans for their demi-gods; and the Mohammedans for their pretended prophet. In fact, a strong and resolute adherence to the religion in which we are brought up, is no certain test of either truth or falsehood.

These principles, common to all mankind, while governed by example and selfish interests, at the expense of reason, of reflection, and of truth; in connexion with higher pretensions—pretensions, indeed, well established—of a revelation from heaven contained in the Hebrew Scripture; may fully account for that zeal and jealousy with which Paul had to contend. " For I bear them record," says he, " that they have a zeal of God." Not only a zeal which is common to all devotees, whatever be the object of their worship ; but a zeal which has the true God for its object, strengthened by a revelation of his will, contained in writings committed to their care. But then, he was constrained to add, that their zeal was " not according to knowledge." This leads me to notice another obstacle.

3. *Their ignorance of God's righteousness.* " For," says the apostle, "they being ignorant of God's righteousness," went "about to establish their own righteousness." If this were eminently indicative of the character of the Jews about eighteen hundred years ago, it is but too applicable to those of the present day until they embrace the gospel.

4. *A mind not religiously submissive.* " They have not," says the apostle, " submitted themselves to the righteousness of God." Submission to God is essential to all true religion. But prejudice, false zeal, and ignorance of God's righteousness, are decided enemies to this humble temper of mind. Pride, a want of submissive resignation to the will of God, was the condemnation of the devil ; and will ever prove, when unsubdued, the condemnation of men. Until the spirit of humility be felt, enmity and opposition to the truth will prevail.

5. *False notions of the Messiah.* " For Christ," says Paul, " is the end of the law for righteousness to every one that believeth." The Jews looked for a deliverer very different from the one whom we preach. They expected— and their descendants of the present day fatally imitate them—they expected a deliverer of a temporal and splendid aspect ; one whose office it would be to rescue the seed of Abraham from civil bondage ; one who would not set aside Levitical services, but restore them to their pristine form.

6. *The supposed incompatibility between the religion of Moses and that of Jesus.* The Jews did not perceive how the Messiah could be " the end of the law to every one that believeth." Had they not been ignorant of this principle, a principle, however, which is abundantly implied in their own Scriptures, they would have seen that no other Messiah but one resembling Jesus, could possibly do them any essential service.

7. *Many cities of refuge, or, more properly, unauthorized subterfuges.* These are provided by men, and not by the institution of God. They are imaginary modes of obtaining the remission of sin. Such as pleading relation to Abraham, repeating prayers, being punctual in the observance of ceremonies, paying implicit submission to the rules of their pretended guardians, and the traditions of the ancients.

8. *The fear of man and the rod of discipline.* The inspired Solomon tells us, that " the fear of man bringeth a snare: but whoso putteth his trust in the Lord shall be safe," Prov. xxix. 25. These two things are contrasted, and they cannot consist together. No one can put his trust in the Lord aright, but as he is delivered from the fear of man. Odious names, anathemas, exclusion from the communion of the body, and from all temporal favours, to be treated as excommunicated persons, to be stripped of all religion, (according to the principles of their education,) and to be deprived of all common civility,—form a snare of no small power. But the fear of the Lord, if real, though but in a small degree, would break the snare, and bid defiance to the fear of man and the puny rod of human authority, when unsupported by the will of God.

What sacrifices the apostle Paul was called to make in maintaining his profession, and preaching the gospel of the grace of God! Yet he could aver, " None of these things move me," Acts xx. 24

IV. THE MANNER IN WHICH THE BENEVOLENCE RECOM-
MENDED OUGHT TO BE DIRECTED AND EXERCISED IN PRE-
SENT CIRCUMSTANCES.

1. *Let your benevolence be exercised in a manner consistent with liberty.* This, I know, is your avowed principle; and on this principle you have acted. But it is proper
that others also should know it.

2. *Treat the poor Jews, on all occasions, as you would
wish to be treated, supposing yourselves in their circumstances.* This comprehends both benevolence and justice.
Keeping this sacred rule in view, you will seek their attention by conciliatory means, by the meekness of wisdom, by
an ardent wish for their improvement, ever tempered with
candour and justice.

3. *Let every effort of benevolence be in subservience to
their eternal welfare.* In some cases, owing to peculiar
circumstances, they may need temporal aid; but the greatest need is that of their immortal souls. Let, therefore,
your "doctrine drop as the rain, and your speech distil as
the dew" upon their minds.

4. *Let prayer be united with benevolent commiseration.*
" My heart's desire and prayer to God," says Paul, " for
Israel is, that they might be saved." If he does not save
them, they are lost for ever. " Except the Lord build the
house, they labour in vain that build it : except the Lord
keep the city, the watchman waketh but in vain," Psa.
cxxvii. 1.

5. *Let intelligent zeal, and vigorous exertion, accompany
your prayers.* I have endeavoured to show that Christian
benevolence is an operative principle. But, like every other
principle, it requires continually to be excited and strengthened. In the present imperfect state of our existence, we
are 'apt to lose sight of our best privileges and greatest
obligations.

I have endeavoured to point out to you particular objects of your benevolent exertions, after the example of one whose character you deservedly revere. Paul, to manifest the purity of his love to souls, devoted his time, his talents, his incessant and unparalleled labours for their salvation. And a man who did this continually to the day of his death, would have thought little of silver and gold, if possessed of it, to accomplish his god-like design. But what has Paul done, compared with his Lord and ours? " For ye know the grace of our Lord Jesus Christ, that though he was rich, yet for our sakes he became poor, that we through his poverty might be rich," 2 Cor. viii. 9,—rich in grace and glory. He gave himself, his body and soul, to humiliation, to labours, to poverty, to insult, to excruciating pain, and an ignominious death, " for us men, and for our salvation."

> " This was compassion like a God,
> That, when the Saviour knew
> The price of pardon was his blood,
> His pity ne'er withdrew."

SKETCH XLVIII.

THE GLORY OF ISRAEL.

BY REV. WILLIAM BENGO COLLYER, D.D.[*]

" The glory of thy people Israel."—LUKE ii. 32.

I AM well aware that the text, unsupported by other autho-rity, will have no weight, in the present discussion, with some part of this numerous auditory.   It is of moment that we should settle the basis of our reasoning, by determining the parts of the Scripture, which will be respectively regarded as a standard of truth.   The former part of the subject must deduce its evidences from Moses and the prophets : these every Jew, who deserves the name, admits to contain a revelation of the will of God.   The latter part of our en-gagement, may, perhaps, be better established by an appeal to the New Testament ; not that Christians reject the old covenant, but that it seems right to stimulate them to acts of benevolence towards the remnant of Israel, by the prin-ciples of their most holy religion ; and by demonstrating that our attentions to his " brethren after the flesh" are strictly in conformity to the spirit of our Master.   Simeon announced Jesus, the reputed son of Joseph, as the Messiah, by declaring him " the glory of his people Israel."

* Delivered at the Jews' Chapel, Spitalfields, before the London Society for Promoting Christianity amongst the Jews.

I. WE ARE TO ESTABLISH THE FACT, IN ADDRESSING THE DESCENDANTS OF ISRAEL.

1. *The nature of the fact advanced is to be established.*

The Messiah was to be " the glory of his people Israel." The evidences of this fact are to be brought from the Old Testament. The prophet Isaiah, the clearness of whose predictions is rivalled only by the sublimity of his language, kindles into more than ordinary fire, when he contemplates the restoration of Israel under the Messiah. He says, "In that day there shall be a root of Jesse, which shall stand for an ensign of the people; to it shall the Gentiles seek: and his rest shall be glorious," Isa. xi. 10. When the prophet Haggai, in speaking of the second temple, writes— "The glory of this latter house shall be greater than of the former, saith the Lord of hosts," Hag. ii. 9; he explains himself as referring to the splendour which it should derive from the Messiah. " For thus saith the Lord of hosts; Yet once, it is a little while, and I will shake the heavens, and the earth, and the sea, and the dry land; and I will shake all nations, and the desire of all nations shall come: and I will fill this house (that is the second temple) with glory, saith the Lord of hosts," Hag. ii. 6, 7. Again, in respect of the latter day glory, Zechariah writes—"Thus speaketh the Lord of hosts, saying, Behold the man whose name is The BRANCH; and he shall grow up out of his place, and he shall build the temple of the Lord: even He shall build the temple of the Lord; and he shall bear the glory, and shall sit and rule upon his throne; and he shall be a priest upon his throne: and the counsel of peace shall be between them both," Zech. vi. 12, 13. These predictions, and a variety of others too numerous to produce, correspond with the testimony of the text—that the Messiah is to be the " glory of his people Israel."

P

2. *That the glory predicted was not confined to a temporal splendour.*

Here, as it appears to us, is the root of the mistake of the Jews. In saying, that the glory predicted was not confined to a temporal splendour, it becomes my duty to justify this assumption by the testimony of the prophets. In order to do this, I must direct your attention to predictions which seem to have been altogether forgotten, or, to say the least, disregarded by the Jews when they formed their estimate of the character of Jesus Christ: they did not take into the account, that he was to suffer as well as to reign; and that humiliation was to precede his glory. Yet so was it predicted respecting the promised Messiah; and the prophecies, which relate to his depression, are as explicit and as ample as those which describe his triumphs. If this be true, it will follow that the indignity offered to the Messiah was as essential to the evidence of his character, and to the establishment of his claims, as any future glory can be. See Isaiah liii., etc. The next remark which I have to make, will explain why I have said, that the glory of the Messiah was not confined to a temporal splendour; for, it is certain, the existence of the Jewish nation, as such, depended upon the Messiah; and this also constitutes a powerful argument in favour of Jesus of Nazareth as the Messiah. We observe,

3. *The Jews lost their distinction as a nation, and their privilege as the people of God, with their rejection of Christ.*

A reference to history would prove all providence bowed to subserve the scheme of redemption; and the obscure carpenter's son, born at Bethlehem, bred at Nazareth, crucified on Calvary, is the Being for whom, and by whom the world was created; and whose mission opens and terminates the period of the existence of the universe. As to the sentiment advanced,—we find certain individuals occupying a place of importance in the volume of inspiration, till they separated their interest from the line of the Messiah, and then punished with merited oblivion. The uncertainty attending the ten tribes of Israel, appears to arise from the formal renunciation of their interest in the Messiah. " What portion have we in David? neither have we inheritance in the son of Jesse : to your tents, O Israel : now see to thine own house, David !" was their cry, 1 Kings xii. 16. The house of David was protected according to the Divine promise, and because of its connexion with the Messiah ; while it is to this day a disputed point, as well with Jews as Gentiles, whether even a remnant of the ten tribes, excepting that which returned with Judah and Benjamin from captivity, exists. It is most certain, that from the time of the rejection of Jesus of Nazareth by the Jews, they ceased to be a nation. " His blood be upon us, and upon our children !" was their imprecation, Matt. xxvii. 25. Upon them and upon their children has it rested to the present hour. " Therefore it is come to pass, that as he cried, and they would not hear; so they cried, and I would not hear, saith the Lord of hosts : but I scattered them with a whirlwind among all the nations whom they knew not," Zech. vii. 13, 14.

4. *Their restoration is predicted in connexion with the Messiah.*

I cannot withhold from you the affecting language of the prophet Zechariah, and it shall be in the place of many passages, which might be produced from the Old Testament to establish the position advanced. "And I will pour upon the house of David, and upon the inhabitants of Jerusalem, the spirit of grace and of supplications : and they shall look upon me whom they have pierced, and they shall mourn for him, as one mourneth for his only son, and shall be in bitterness for him, as one that is in bitterness for his first-born," Zech. xii. 10. Two things are apparent here: there must be, on the part of Israel, a deep and unfeigned sorrow for the wrongs done to the Messiah; and, in connexion with the homage which they shall be induced to pay to their injured Saviour, is their restoration to their pristine dignity. It follows, that so long as they reject Christ, they are the authors of their own ignominy; and that he is waiting to manifest himself, " The glory of his people Israel."

II. The claims of this Society upon your cordial support: and in so doing we shall endeavour to point out your duty, as Christians.

(1.) This Institution deserves your patronage from its spirit. It is not the tool of a party. It moves not in a narrow, sectarian circle. It is open to all " those who love our Lord Jesus Christ in sincerity." It proceeds upon the broad basis of universal co-operation, among good men of every denomination.

(2.) As the spirit of the Society recommends it to your benevolent patronage, so especially does its object. " The lost sheep of the house of Israel" are sought by its measures; and Jesus commanded his disciples to go first to them, Matt. x. 6. As Christians, we are bound to pay a particular regard to the Jewish nation.

I. *Gratitude to them for the oracles of truth.*

They were the ark in which God deposited his law and his ordinances : and to the care which they took of the inspired records do we owe the accuracy, extent, and variety of our knowledge of inspiration.

2. *Love to Christ and to the first preachers of the gospel, ought to teach us to love the Jewish nation.*

The hatred of mankind exercised towards that afflicted people, can be accounted for only on the ground of their own imprecation. Their own desire is accomplished, and the blood of Jesus pursues them every where—the rejection of the Messiah is visited upon them in every nation under heaven.

3. *Faith in the Divine promises should stimulate our efforts.*

The restoration of the Jews is the subject of many animated predictions both in the Old and in the New Testaments. Now, if the fall of them be the riches of the world, and the diminishing of them the riches of the Gentiles; how much more their fulness?

4. *Concern for their condition—connected with a sense of our obligations and our happiness.*

Should we not pity the branches, which, because of unbelief, were cut off? and should we not recollect that we occupy their place in the living Vine? They perish through unbelief—and we stand by faith: let us not be "highminded, but fear," Rom. xi. 20. Shall we not, exulting as we do in our privileges, remember those who once possessed, but who have sadly forfeited them? especially when we know "that blindness (only) in part is happened unto Israel, until the fulness of the Gentiles be come in; and so all Israel shall be saved." Rom. xi. 25. Then the "light to lighten the Gentiles," shall also be "the glory of his people Israel."

SKETCH XLIX.

OBLIGATIONS OF CHRISTIANS TO LABOUR FOR THE CONVERSION OF THE JEWS.

BY REV. EARL GIBBEE, D.D.*

"I will bring thy seed from the east, and gather thee from the west; I will say to the north, Give up; and to the south, Keep not back: bring my sons from far, and my daughters from the ends of the earth."

Isa. xliii. 5, 6.

THIS prophecy looks far beyond the deliverance of the Jews from their former captivity. It evidently points to that great and glorious deliverance which still awaits them. A deliverance that will eclipse, and infinitely outshine, their former deliverances from Egypt and from Babylon. In applying the passage before us to the recall and conversion of the Jews, I would direct your attention to the following particulars.

I. OUR OBLIGATIONS, AS CHRISTIANS, TO ENGAGE IN THIS WORK.

II. OUR ENCOURAGEMENT TO PROCEED AND PERSEVERE IN IT.

III. THE GLORIOUS CONSEQUENCES THAT WILL PROBABLY RESULT FROM IT.

And may the Lord God of Israel, the God of Abraham, the God of Isaac, and the God of Jacob, look down from heaven and visit us! May he graciously be pleased to

---

* Preached at the Church of Kettering, Northamptonshire, before the Bedford Auxiliary Society for promoting Christianity amongst the Jews.

animate our hearts, and to strengthen our hands, in this work and labour of love!

I. OUR OBLIGATIONS, AS CHRISTIANS, TO ENGAGE IN THIS WORK.

It would not be difficult to show that many are our obligations to seek the salvation of the Jews; but I shall content myself with stating only a few.

1. *Gratitude for the inestimable benefits which we have derived from them.*

Should it be asked, What advantage or benefit have we derived from the Jews? we answer, " Much, every way: and chiefly because that unto them were committed the oracles of God," Rom. iii. 2. They were entrusted with that invaluable treasure, which was to enrich the church of God through every succeeding age. To them " pertained the adoption," into which we are admitted; " the covenants," with the privileges of which we are favoured; " the promises," of which we are made partakers; and " of whom," let it never be forgotten by Christians, " as concerning the flesh Jesus Christ came, who is over all, God blessed for ever," Rom. ix. 4, 5.

Here let us pause, and contemplate the immensity of the debt which we owe to this despised and outcast people : and let us remember that most of this debt remains to this day unpaid. Ought we not to be ashamed of our culpable neglect? Ought we not to feel a portion at least of the apostle's spirit, who could wish himself cut off and separated from Christ, for his brethren and for his kinsmen's sake, Rom. ix. 3. Surely the Jews have claims upon us far beyond any heathen nation; and yet for the heathen have we chiefly employed our labours.

2. *As a reparation of the cruel wrongs and injuries which we have inflicted upon them.*

It would be as shocking, as it would be endless, to re-
count the terrible oppressions which this unhappy people
have suffered in every age of their dispersion.   Dreadful
as have been the persecutions which the church of God
hath experienced in former times, I apprehend they have
been far exceeded by the persecutions which even Christian
nations have inflicted on the Jews.   Every Christian country
is deep in this guilt, and every Christian country requires
a national expiation of it.   And let us not fondly suppose,
that England is, in this respect, less criminal than other
nations.   No: the pages of our history are stained with
our cruelty and injustice.   How often has this miserable
people been fined and pillaged by the former governments
of this land!   How often have they been compelled to
redeem their lives at the expense of all their treasures!
Did our monarchs want money to carry on their wars?
The Jews were sure to be the first objects of their rapacity.
Judah's wickedness is no exculpation of England's sin.
Rather, have we not reason to fear, that the Lord may
have a controversy with us, both for our past and present
oppressions of his ancient people?   Have we nothing to
dread in the prospect of the day, which the prophet emphatically calls, " the day of the Lord's vengeance, the year
of recompences for the controversy of Zion?" Isa. xxxiv. 8.
Is it nothing to us, that that great and notable day of the
Lord is at hand, when Jerusalem shall become " a cup of
trembling," and ": a burdensome stone," to all the nations
that have afflicted her? Zech. xii. 2. ` Would we avert
from us the indignation of the Lord, and escape his threat-
ened judgments?   Let us undo the bands of wickedness.   Let us turn to Israel with compassion, and with repentance.

3. *From an ardent desire to promote the glory of God.*
An earnest desire to promote the glory of God is a pro-

minent feature in the character of a true Christian; and we may reasonably doubt the profession of those who do not feel the constant influence of this principle. My brethren, the conversion of the Jews is indisputably an object most intimately connected with the glory of God, and with the honour of Christ. I am fully persuaded, that we can never expect any particular enlargement of the Redeemer's kingdom till the veil be removed from Israel. If, therefore, we would indeed promote the glory of God, and extend the triumphs of the Redeemer, let us turn our attention primarily to the Jews—let us gladly spend and be spent for them. Having thus stated our obligations to engage in this work, let us consider,

II. Our encouragement to proceed and persevere in it.

To some, the attempt to convert the Jews may appear visionary; to others, it may appear inexpedient; but they, who are acquainted with their Bibles, must know that it is not hopeless. We are encouraged to attempt this work,—

I. *From the testimony of prophecy.*

The restoration of the whole house of Israel is so plainly and expressly foretold in Scripture, that it may properly be called an article of our faith. " Thus saith the Lord God; Behold, I will take the children of Israel from among the heathen, whither they be gone, and will gather them on every side, and bring them into their own land.—Moreover I will make a covenant of peace with them; it shall be an everlasting covenant: and I will place them, and multiply them, and will set my sanctuary in the midst of them for evermore. My tabernacle also shall be with them: yea, I will be their God, and they shall be my people," Ezek. xxxvii. 21, 26, 27. See also Hosea iii. 4, 5; Zeph. iii. 14, 15. We are also encouraged to proceed,

2. *From the very great attention which has already been excited among the Jews.*

Arduous as is the work in which we are engaged, and unpromising as it may to many appear; yet we can confidently declare, that our Society hath hitherto no reason to repent of its laudable efforts; on the contrary, its exertions have already produced very striking effects. A spirit of inquiry has been stirred up among the Jews; which is, of itself, a most favourable circumstance: for, if the Jews can only be brought diligently to search and study their own Scriptures, we may reasonably hope that the most important consequences will result from their inquiries. Not a few of the Jews have already been brought to abjure their errors, and openly to confess Jesus of Nazareth, as their Messiah and Redeemer. Several others have evinced an earnest desire to know more of the Friend and Saviour of sinners. Another ground of encouragement may be drawn,

3. *From the present signs of the times.*

That a day will come, when both the house of Judah and of Israel shall be brought home to the fold of Christ, is a truth grounded on the express promise of God: and many reasons may be assigned which induce us to think that this day is at hand. Of late years, the attention of Christians has been very remarkably turned to the study of prophecy; and especially to those prophetic parts of Scripture which directly treat of the conversion of the heathen, of the restoration of the Jews, and of the glories of the millennial era. The strenuous exertions which are making, on every side, to diffuse the knowledge of the gospel of peace, are the surest pledges of the approaching triumph of our Redeemer. Already do the mists of heathen darkness begin to be dissipated; already do the benign rays of the Sun of righteousness begin to illumine those regions of the earth, which have long " sat in darkness and in the shadow of death." Every thing is preparing for the solemn inauguration of Christ, as King and Lord of all: when both Jew and Gentile shall be given to him " for an inheritance, and the uttermost parts of the earth for a possession," Psa. ii. 8.

III. THE GLORIOUS CONSEQUENCES THAT WILL RESULT FROM THE CONVERSION OF THE JEWS. Great will be its consequences both to the world and to the church of God. Consider,

1. *Its glorious consequences to the world.*

Among other blessings, which will result to the world at large from this grand event, we are particularly taught to expect, from the sure word of prophecy, that there will be an universal diffusion of religious knowledge, and an universal enjoyment of uninterrupted peace. " Nation shall not lift up sword against nation, neither shall they learn war any more," Isa. ii. 4. When the Lord shall bring again the captivity of Israel, the whole face of the earth will be changed : it will be the commencement of a new and blessed era to all nations. See Jer. xxxi. 34; Psa. lxxii. 7, 8, 10, 11.

2. *Its glorious consequences to the church of God.*

Inexpressibly magnificent is the description of the happiness and glory of the church, in that day when " the Lord shall bring again Zion," Isa. lii. 8. The conversion of the Jews shall be the means of bringing in the whole fulness of the Gentiles. Then shall the name of Christ be known " from the rising of the sun even unto the going down of the same:" his praises shall be heard and celebrated in the uttermost parts of the earth. See Isa. lx. 1, 3, 5.

(1.) To God's covenant with Abraham and with his

seed, you owe all that you are, and all that you hope to be. . You that are the younger brother of your Father's house, have risen to your present pre-eminence on the ruin of your elder brother.

(2.) My brethren, when Christ sent forth his apostles to preach the gospel of the kingdom, he particularly charged them to " begin at Jerusalem." Let me not be misunderstood, when I humbly hint, that in our attempts to convert the heathen, we should follow this rule, and begin at Jerusalem too. Did Christ command his apostles to " go rather to the lost sheep of the house of Israel," Matt. x. 6 ; and shall we seek them last? O, no! we will remember that as we " have now obtained mercy through their unbelief," so it is the Divine appointment that " through our mercy they also may obtain mercy," Rom. xi. 30, 31.

SKETCH L.

THE VISION OF THE CHURCH OF CHRIST.

" And there appeared a great wonder in heaven ; a woman clothed with the sun, and the moon under her feet, and upon her head a crown of twelve stars."—REV. xii. 1.

MANY of the prophecies of this highly figurative book are deeply mysterious; and some of the hieroglyphics employed by the sacred writer are extremely difficult of interpretation. Now, these observations apply to the latter part of the prophecy we have selected for our present consideration. The views of expositors have widely varied, and have even been directly opposed to each other.   By the Child brought forth, some have referred it to the Messiah; others, to Constantine.   By the dragon, some have understood Pagan Rome; others, Mystical Babylon, or Papal Rome.   The text, however, is of clear and evident interpretation, and to that we shall confine our attention.   The whole subject is that of magnificent and striking metaphor,—representing the church of God in her divine glory, spiritual and celestial character, and ministerial dignity.   Observe,

I. THE FIGURATIVE REPRESENTATION OF THE CHURCH.

It is represented under the similitude of a woman.   This metaphor is frequently exhibited both in the Old and New Testament scriptures : see Psa. xlv. 10, 11, 13, 14; Isa. lxii. 5.; Jer. iii. 14.   Thus, also, in the parable of the marriage of the king's son, the bride is evidently the church. Also, in all those representations were Christ is styled the Bridegroom and the Husband of the church. See John iii. 29; Eph. v. 24, 32; Rev. xxi. 9. Weakness, dependance, and fruitfulness, are the chief ideas associated with the metaphor of the church being likened to a woman. Observe,

II. HER DIVINE GLORY.

" Clothed with the sun." Christ is evidently intended by this magnificent figure. He is the " Sun of righteousness." He proclaimed himself as "the Light of the world," John viii. 12. Christ may be thus represented on account,

1. *Of his greatness.*

Christ is " Most High."—"The Prince of the kings of the earth," Rev. i. 5. "King of kings, and Lord of lords," 1 Tim. vi. 15. "Lord of glory,"—possessed of all the attributes and perfections of Deity. "Over all, God blessed for ever," Rom. ix. 5. Infinitely greater than angels, or seraphim, or cherubim.

2. *On account of his oneness.*

Hosts of stars, but only one sun, the centre of the solar system. So but one Messiah—one Mediator—one "only begotten Son of God." Without fellow or compeer in his mediatorial work, etc.

3. *As the Fountain of light.*

The rays of the sun illumine our world, and make day. So Christ is " the Day-spring," and the great Source of mental and moral light to mankind. He is the true Light —the Light of heaven, and the Light of the earth: His beams make spiritual day in the soul.

4. *For his fertilizing influences.*

Where his rays are not, there frigid winter reigns; there are everlasting mountains of ice; there sterility and barrenness sway their enduring sceptre. The sun softens, fertilizes, gives vegetating power to nature, makes the earth to appear as " the garden of the Lord." So with the influence of Christ on the hearts of men. Where he shines not, is pagan gloom, heathen night, with all its attendant vices and misery! No moral verdure, selfish apathy, cruelty, death. When He shines, goodness, purity, and joy reign, etc.

5. *For his magnificence and glory.*

We cannot do justice to this view of the natural sun. How radiant his light, how grand his rising, how overwhelming his meridian altitude, how gorgeous his setting, how resplendent his circuit, how mighty his attraction, how universal his influence! Now, these things we say of the creature, the natural sun; and what shall we say of the Orb of celestial day? Filling heaven and earth with his glory; exercising his almighty power over all worlds; seated on the throne of the universe; attracting to himself all that is holy on earth and in heaven; and the great Source of all light and joy, and bliss and glory, to angels and men. Now, the church is clothed with this Sun—he surrounds her, overshadows her, throws upon her all his light, and purity, and glory. If she has life, beauty, light, and fertility, he is the Source of the whole,—she owes all to him; and without him would be impotence, and could do nothing.

II. HER SPIRITUAL AND CELESTIAL CHARACTER.

These are indicated by her being in heaven, and having the moon under her feet. The church of God is of heavenly origin,—often called "the kingdom of heaven." Her spirit, principles, aims, and destinies, are all heavenly. She is the "Jerusalem which is above," etc., Gal. iv. 26. But her spiritual character is exhibited in having the moon under her feet. By this,

1. *May be represented her superiority over the Jewish dispensation.*

That was a subordinate economy, borrowing all its light and glory from the Christian, of which its sacrifices and offerings were all typical, " the shadow of good things to come," Heb. x. 1. It was a dispensation of ever-varying rites and ceremonies. Nothing appeared fixed or permanent. This dispensation is obsolete—it has passed away. The Christian church may, therefore, be represented as standing above it—having it under her feet. But, perhaps,

2. *The world may be more especially intended.*

She may be the emblem of the world in the dimness of its light, whether of science, art, philosophy, etc., as compared with the light of the gospel; or, on account of its variableness—ever changing. The pómp and glory of the world are always passing away. Kingdoms, states, etc., exemplify this—Babylon, Tyre, Egypt, all confirm this. Its laws and customs are all transitory. Now, the church of Christ is not of the world—it is elevated above it : called out, separated from, and superior to it. It tramples its honours, distinctions, riches, and gaudy scenes under its feet. She forsakes it, as represented in the Song of Solomon, " leaning on her Beloved." She has the victory over it. " This is the victory which overcometh the world, even our faith," I John. v. 4. " By whom the world is crucified unto me, and I unto the world," Gal. vi. 14. Observe,

IV. HER MINISTERIAL DIGNITY. " Upon her head a crown of twelve stars."

By the stars are evidently meant the twelve apostles, as representing the whole body of the faithful ministers of Jesus Christ. We find the same titles given to the seven angels, or messengers, of the Asiatic churches, Rev. i. 20.— Now, the metaphor teaches us the radiant character of the Christian ministry—they are to shine, in their respective spheres, in the gifts and graces of the Holy Spirit. The metaphor also indicates their connexion with the Sun of righteousness. He is the great source of their light, and the centre of union and order to the whole. This figure also exhibits the diversity of talents and gifts which they possess, " as one star differeth from another star in glory."

Now, these stars are a crown to the church—they are to exercise rule and order and government in the church. They are to enforce the doctrines and laws of Jesus Christ; and thus the church is resplendent when she shines forth in the dignity of gospel truth and holiness. Observe,

1. *The true character of the church of Christ.*

Spiritual, heavenly; clothed with the magnificence of her Lord; raised above the world; and dignified in the radiant purity of her holy ministry. Take away any of these distinctions, and her glory departs. Without the Sun, she becomes dark and frigid. Without her spiritual and celestial elevation, she becomes a mere earthly hierarchy. Without a holy, radiant ministry, she becomes formal and uninfluencial.

2. *The honour and happiness of those identified with her.* ·Her citizens are truly great and glorious.

3. *Her final triumphs are matters of Divine certainty.*

To her the world shall bow. Her " dominion shall be from sea to sea, and from the river unto the ends of the earth," Psa. lxxii. 8.

SKETCH LI.

CHRISTIANITY A SYSTEM OF TRUTH AND PEACE.

"Therefore love the truth and peace."—Zech. viii. 19.

TRUTH and peace are very important elements of moral worth and power in the world. They are essential to man's moral elevation, and real welfare. Are characteristics in the blessed Deity; and leading principles of true religion. And when the religion of the cross shall be universal, they will be the great pillars of the Redeemer's millennial kingdom and glory. Consider their nature; our duty with respect to them; and the reasons on which that duty is grounded.

I. THE NATURE OF TRUTH AND PEACE.

1. *Truth.* This signifies,

(1.) Veracity—the opposite of falsehood. Hence, we often read of speaking the truth, etc. "I speak the truth in Christ, I lie not," 1 Tim. ii. 7.

(2.) *Sincerity*—the opposite of dissimulation. "Worship God in spirit and in truth," John iv. 24. Paul prays that the Philippians may be sincere, etc., Phil. i. 10.

(3.) It is put for the testimony of the gospel. "Grace and truth." "Who hath bewitched you," etc., Gal. iii. 1.

(4.) It is put for the pure doctrines of Christianity, in opposition to error. "I have no greater joy," etc. See also 2 Thess. ii. 10; 2 Tim. iii. 8; iv. 4.

(5.) For the experimental knowledge of the gospel, or religious experience, in opposition to the form of godliness. "Ye shall know the truth," etc., John viii. 32. Hence, the Spirit guides into all truth, John xvi. 13, etc.

(6.) For the Lord Jesus Christ, "He is the way, the truth, and the life," John xiv. 6. The Prince of truth.

2. *Peace* is the opposite of war, strife, perturbation, and contention, etc. Gospel peace implies,

(1.) A pacific state of mind towards God. No longer enemies, etc., but reconciled to God, etc. Rom. v. 10.

(2.) The peace God imparted to the soul. "Peace be unto you," Luke xxiv. 36. "The peace of God, which passeth all understanding, shall keep your hearts and minds through Christ Jesus," Phil. iv. 7.

(3.) A peaceable spirit towards our fellow-men. "The fruit of the Spirit is peace," etc., Gal. v. 22. "Follow peace with all men," etc., Heb. xii. 14.

II. Our duty to love the truth and peace.

1. *What does this imply?*

(1.) That we understand them. Many are ignorant of them. It implies that we have heard, pondered, and understood their nature—that we have chosen them!

(2.) Received the truth. Had its principles implanted, etc. Welcomed peace; given them a residence in our hearts, etc.

(3.) That we delight in them, cultivate them, grow in them, give them their right prominence.

2. *How will love to truth and peace be evidenced?*

(1.) There will be the exhibition of them in our character and lives; words, conduct, profession, etc.

(2.) There will be the earnest maintenance and defence of them—cannot be indifferent; and "earnestly contend for the faith," etc., Jude 3. Witnesses for them—"Truth and Peace," motto. Support them—denying ourselves, etc. Buy them at any price, nor sell at any offer.

(3.) We shall diffuse them. By effort, by prayer, "O send out," etc.

III. Notice the reasons on which this duty is grounded.

1. *On account of their intrinsic excellency.* *Truth* is one of the brightest jewels in the crown of Deity. One of the pillars of the moral world, the girdle of the Christian warrior. It is like the light of heaven, etc. *Peace* is the very element of enjoyment—the sunshine, the repose of the soul, the atmosphere of heaven, the mind of God.

2. *On account of our Christian prdfession.* We are called to " love the truth and peace," it is a main part of our religion. If we do not, who ought, and will?

3. *Our love to Christ and his church.* He died for their establishment in the hearts of his people; and for their embodiment in his kingdom. His church cannot be pure or prosperous without them.

4. *Our compassion to the world.* The world is apostate; deceived, dark, and wretched. *Truth* only can extricate and exalt it. *Peace* only can bless it, and make it happy.

Observe, in carrying out the spirit of the text,

1. *The order prescribed.* *Truth,* and then *Peace.* This order must not be inverted—one is the basis, the other the superstructure; one the life, the other the spirit; one the principle, the other the emotion of the Christian character.

2. *Some love truth and not peace.* Hence they are bitter, intolerant, bigotted; to whom the words of Christ are strikingly applicable, " Ye know not what manner of spirit ye are of," Luke ix. 55.

3. *Some appear to love peace and not truth.* These live under the influence of a false and morbid liberality. Hence they are ready to sacrifice any thing for what they denominate *peace :* such *peace* is valueless, harmonizes with sinful compromising—gratifies the flesh, and is acceptable to Satan.

4. *Truth and peace must go together :* they constitute the very essence of the gospel; and, when universally diffused, will introduce the world's millennial purity and bliss.

SKETCH LII.

THE WILLING CHURCH.

"Thy people shall be willing in the day of thy power, in the beauties of holiness from the womb of the morning : thou hast the dew of thy youth."
PSA. CX. 3.

THIS psalm contains one beautiful and continuous prophecy of the person, work, and kingdom of the Messiah. The text evidently refers to Christ subsequent to his resurrection. It begins with the authoritative yet gracious mandate of Jehovah, " Sit thou on my right hand, until I make thine enemies thy footstool." This seems to be a direct reply to Christ's sacerdotal prayer—" Jesus lifted up his eyes to heaven, and said, Father, the hour is come; glorify thy Son, that thy Son also may glorify thee," John xvii. 1. " I have glorified thee on the earth," etc., ver. 4. God replies to the prayers of his Son,—" Thy engagements have been faithfully executed, thy humiliation is past, thy sufferings are over; thou hast redeemed a fallen world to thyself; thou hast a right to reign."

The prophecy then reveals the means by which his kingdom is to be set up, and his triumph effected:—" The Lord shall send the rod of his strength." Here is a manifest reference to the gospel. It coincides with the apostle's description, " The power of God unto salvation," Rom. i. 16. It is to be sent " out of Zion." The gospel is to be first preached at Jerusalem, and to go forth from thence to all the nations. " Thus it was written, and thus it behoved Christ to suffer," etc., Luke xxiv. 46.

Then the immediate results of preaching the gospel are

brought before us. " Rule thou"—or, thou shalt rule—" in the midst of thine enemies." And so it was in the city of Christ's death, his kingdom was set up. In the city where dwelt Pilate, the high priests, the council, the soldiers, and the people, he began his gracious triumphs. Then follows our text. " Thy people"—those who are subjugated by the power of thy gospel, who bow down before the sceptre of thy grace, they " shall be willing ;" or, " they shall be volunteers ;" or, as in the margin of some Bibles, " A people of willingness." They shall devote themselves to thy cause. They shall be thy cheerful, and faithful, and uncompromising followers and friends. And " in the beauties of holiness," or arrayed in holy vestments, they shall appear as a " holy nation," a " royal priesthood ;" clothed in the garments of salvation, they shall adorn their profession, and show forth thy praise. Also, in point of number, they shall appear as the dew-drops of the morning ; and that, too, in thy youth, or in the beginning of thy conquests, or as soon as thy dominion is established in the world. How literally was all this accomplished. The first converts, clothed in the habiliments of gospel purity, gave themselves fully to the Lord ; and by two sermons of the apostle Peter, on the opening of the kingdom of heaven, five thousand souls were converted, and every where the " word of the Lord ran and was glorified." Such we conceive to be the spirit and meaning of the text. Now, we cannot dwell on all the points which the text contains. For instance, in fully elucidating the text, we might dwell on the beauty and propriety of the figure, wherein the gospel dispensation is likened to a " day"—to " Christ's day"—the " day of Christ's power ;" that is, of his royal authority, of his right to reign and rule, and sway over all the earth, the sceptre of his truth and love. But we wish to confine ourselves to two things :—

I. To the devotedness of the church.

II. The connexion between such devotedness and the spread of the gospel and kingdom of Christ.

. I. To the devotedness of the church.

I do not pass over the holy vestments of the people of God as of minor importance; but because we are now speaking only of the spiritual members of Christ's body, we only design our remarks to bear on those who are renewed in their minds, and who are professedly partakers of the Divine nature, and in heart and conversation are holy ·to the Lord. Such, in reality, are the Church of Christ, and such only. These are "Christ's people," and these are the cheerful volunteers and consecrated followers of the Lamb. Observe, then,

I. *The extent of the willingness, or the devotedness of the church.*

It clearly involves the devotedness of themselves—their hearts, souls, minds, and bodies. " I beseech you, brethren, by the mercies of God, that ye present your bodies," etc.; Rom. xii. 1. It is to give our approbation, our esteem, and our love to Christ. It is to give him our desires, our joys, and our delights; our thoughts, our admiration, and our praise; our conversation, and loyal obedience to his commands. It is to place his interests and claims first and highest. It is to speak and act, to eat and drink, to move and live, so as to glorify him. It is to recognize his will as our only rule—his commands as our one directory. Now, is this beyond Christ's claims? And when this, all this, is yielded, can anything else be withheld? Can talents, however splendid? Can powers, however mighty? Can influence, however extensive? Can wealth, however ample? If we have given Christ our souls, our entire selves, without reservation, shall we not be ready for health or sickness, for riches or poverty, for freedom or bonds, for life or death; for anything to suffer or do, which he requireth of us? We see, that devotedness to this extent, yea, and beyond all we can say or even conjecture, was yielded by the early disciples, the first churches of Christ. Consider,

2. *The principle of such devotedness.*

This is one simple element—not miraculous influences, or gifts; but the indwelling, operative love of Christ. The language of the apostle was the language of every disciple. Wherefore do we abandon the faith of our fathers? Wherefore become the followers of the slandered malefactor? etc. Wherefore give up ease and wealth, liberty and life? "The love of Christ constraineth us," 2 Cor. v. 14. It has claims which these have not, and bears us away above all these things. It fills, it captivates, it absorbs our souls. Love so divine, so heavenly, so expensive to its Author, so inexpressibly precious, constrains us. It expands; it causeth us to appear as fools to the world,—as beside ourselves. Oh, yes! This is the principle of true devotedness. Nothing else will accomplish this; this has done it; it cannot fail to do it. This is the hallowed fire which burns up the dross of selfishness; this the hallowed flame, which changes all into its own nature and element. This is the deep and rapid stream which fills the channel of the soul, and sweeps all before it, and bears the man onward to the ocean of eternal love. The Christian exclaims, "I love him, I love his cause, and his gospel, his people, and the whole world, because he first loved me, and because his love is shed abroad in my heart," etc. Consider,

3. *How this devotedness is to be sustained.*

I need not say it will be tried. Our hearts will try and resist, or be indolent. The world will try it, by its fascinations, its maxims; and Satan, too, will try it, and, if possible, suspend or weaken it. Formalists, too, will say,

" Be not righteous overmuch; be prudent—be moderate!"
All these will try it. How is it to be sustained? By faith
and hope in the glories of a blissful immortality. Was it
not that which sustained the devotedness of Moses, of the
prophets, of the apostles, of the early Christians? The
apostle, while looking on the retrospect, exclaimed, "I have
fought a good fight, I have finished my course, I have
kept the faith : henceforth there is laid up for me a crown
of righteousnesss, which the Lord, the righteous judge, shall
give me at that day : and not to me only, but unto all
them also that love his appearing," 2 Tim. iv. 7. The primitive saints were so indifferent to the world, because they
were seeking a better country; to their homes, because
they had titles to heavenly mansions; to their friends, because they had their chief Friend in heaven; to riches,
because of the grandeur of their estate in glory; to life,
because of the better resurrection to immortality beyond the
grave. Oh! this devotedness may and will be sustained
by keeping the eye of faith on the goal, on the prize, on
heaven, and walking as on the precincts of eternity every day.

4. *By whom should this devotedness be evinced?*

By every minister of Jesus Christ; by every elder and
deacon; by every sabbath school teacher, and tract distributer; by every parent; by all the young men of Christ's
sacred army;—yea, in one word, by every Christian! This
devotedness must be the rule and spirit of the church—of
the whole church of the Redeemer; and then, and not till
then, will the truth spread generally and mightily prevail.
But we pass on to notice,

II. THE CONNEXION BETWEEN SUCH DEVOTEDNESS, AND
THE SPREAD OF THE GOSPEL AND KINGDOM OF CHRIST.

1. *The instrumentality for spreading the gospel, and
extending the kingdom of Christ, is committed to the church.*

Q

The world can only be evangelized by the truth. The gospel must be preached in all the world, and to every creature, Mark xvi. 15. " For whosoever shall call upon the name of the Lord shall be saved," Rom. x. 13; Acts ii. 21. Now, the church has the gospel in trust for the benefit of the world. Bearing this standard, they are to extend Christ's domains, and give to him a people out of every nation. This is the work of the church in her collective capacity, and of each member. " Ye are the salt of the earth."— " Ye are the light of the world," Matt. v. 13, 14.

2. *In proportion to the church's devotedness will the cause of Christ prevail.*

Look at the apostolic age. Look at the three earliest centuries. Look at the reformation in our land, in the days of Wesley and Whitfield. Look at churches where there is this devotedness in our own day, and the results are invariably the same. Means are established in the kingdom of grace, as in the kingdom of nature. If our brethren had not gone to India, etc., we should not have had converted Brahmins now preaching, etc. And if the churches had not felt, and devoted their property, too, the missionaries had not gone. Look at the dark ages, when the church was corrupt and faithless, and see the results. Look at churches where there is coldness, and avarice, and self; and see what is their condition!

3. *This devotedness of the church is indispensably necessary to this end, and nothing else is so necessary as this.*

When we look at the world, and see what is requisite for its salvation, where do we begin? With God; with the sacrifice of Christ; with the Holy Spirit; with the gospel. Can you believe any supposable blame rests here? Is there as much piety in our churches—as much zeal—as much love—as much liberality, as God demands? Is the talent and wealth of Christ's professing people given to him?

No; not a tithe of it; not so much as God demanded for the Jewish priesthood. Oh, how unlike the first disciples! We are not willing, not fully, not cheerfully, not entirely. If the church be not faithful in this matter, who shall accomplish this end? Eminent holiness is all-important; but can it exist without this devotedness? We remark,

1. *Let the unwillingness of the church be the subject of solemn reflection.*

I do not say of prayer so much, because the great defect is not there. Christians pray, (I do not say enough,) but much better than they act. Do not pray less, but act more in accordance with your prayers. Pray not less, but differently; so as not to lay the blame with God. Do not speak and pray as though you wanted souls to be saved, and that God was reluctant; that you desired the gospel to be sent every where, but that God did not. Do not pray as if you would arouse Jehovah, but yourselves. Be willing, and every thing shall be effected. Be willing, and every church shall thrust out her sons into the harvest. Be willing, and the converts of our churches, both at home and abroad, shall be as the dew-drops of the morning.

2. *To the unconverted the gospel of the kingdom of Jesus is now come.*

Jesus seeks your return to loyal obedience. He asks your heart's affection, your spirit's devotedness, and your live's obedience. He asks all on the ground of his love to you. Will you bow to the sceptre of his grace? His arms and heart are both open to receive you—

> " Oh that my Jesus' heavenly charms
> Might every bosom move ;
> Fly, sinners, fly into those arms
> Of everlasting love !''

SKETCH LIII.

THE HERALDS OF MERCY.

"How beautiful upon the mountains are the feet of him that bringeth glad
tidings, that publisheth peace; that bringeth good tidings of good, that publisheth salvation; that saith unto Zion, Thy God reigneth."—Isa. lii. 7.

THIS beautiful prophecy evidently refers to the proclama-
tion of the gospel; and is thus quoted by the apostle, Rom.
x. 15. It is the expression of that joy and delight which
the human mind experiences in the annunciation of truths
and blessings so rich and glorious, as those which form the
sum and substance of Christianity. Our text has been
realized in the experience of myriads; and is now strikingly
appropriate to the messengers of salvation, as they visit
the regions of Pagan superstition and cruelty. Consider,

I. THE REPRESENTATION OF THE GOSPEL GIVEN.
II. THE CHARACTER OF ITS MINISTRY.
III. OUR OBLIGATION TO LABOUR FOR ITS DIFFUSION.

I. THE REPRESENTATION OF THE GOSPEL GIVEN.

1. *Glad tidings, or tidings of good.* The gospel does
not announce that which is ordinarily good. It loses sight
of the inferior blessings which relate to the body and time,
although these are generally found in its train; and refers
us to that which is pre-eminently good—supremely good—
eternally good. The good the gospel announces includes,

(1.) The enjoyment of God's favour and love. By sin
this is forfeited. In guilt we are heirs only of wrath, and
are condemned already, John iii. 18. Sin exposes to
death; the gospel reveals to us the Divine mediation, by
which it may be blotted out. It announces remission of

sins in the name of Jesus Christ. " Being justified freely,"
etc. Rom. iii. 24, 25. It calls the sinner, " Repent ye
therefore, and be converted, that your sins may be blotted
out," Acts iii. 19. It points to Jesus and his atoning
death. " In whom we have redemption through his blood,
the forgiveness of sins, according to the riches of his grace,"
Eph. i. 7; Col. i. 14. With the forgiveness of sin is connected
God's favour, and the rich communications of his love.

(2.) The restoration of the Divine image. Sin defiles
the soul; it mars its beauty, impairs it health and vigour.
It perverts its powers, and deranges all its dignified energies
and attributes. The gospel directs to the means of purity.
It refers to the " blood of Jesus Christ," which " cleanseth
us from all sin," 1 John i. 7. To the Spirit of God which
renews the mind, and by which the sinfulness of the heart
is subdued, etc. To the Divine word, by which the mind
is led to the sanctifying knowledge of " the truth as it is
in Jesus." Hence the gospel is both the charter of mercy,
and the renovator of the heart—for it both brings salvation,
and teaches men to deny ungodliness, Titus ii. 11, 12.

(3.) The offer of eternal life. Man is destined to endless being. His guilt exposes to endless punishment. "The
wages of sin is death; but the gift of God is eternal life
through Jesus Christ our Lord," Rom. vi. 23. It opens
to men the gates of everlasting felicity.

2. *It publishes peace.* The cessation of hostilities on
the part of God towards the sinner, and the gracious terms
on which he makes peace with him. And this comports
with the essential character of the gospel, which delivers
from the power and works of the devil, and which brings
into holy harmony with the will of God, all the passions
and feelings of the soul. This peace is the peace of God
in us, as well as towards us; and our hearts are swayed, by
his word and Spirit, into absolute obedience and love.

But peace often signifies every good; and, with the acceptance of the gospel, every good is received and enjoyed:—all the graces of the Spirit; all the plenitude of Divine love; all the regards of a benign Providence; all spiritual blessings in heavenly places in Christ Jesus, Rom. viii. 32.

3. *It affirms the reign of God.* God reigneth; not Baal, nor Ashtoreth, nor Juggernaut. Not the sun, or the moon, etc. But Jehovah—the Creator of the world—the Ruler of the universe. He reigneth in the exercise of wisdom, almightiness, benevolence, purity, and mercy. What a contrast to the senseless idols of heathen lands! His reign is coeval with time, and shall be universal and eternal!

II. THE CHARACTER OF ITS MINISTRY. "How beautiful upon the mountains are the feet of him," etc. Observe,

1. *This ministry is human.* Not angelic: angels are deeply interested; they hailed the advent of the Messiah, and rejoice in its success, etc.; but they do not constitute its ministry. This celestial treasure is put into "earthen vessels, that the excellency of the power may be of God, and not of us," 2 Cor. iv. 7. God sanctifies and calls men to go forth in this embassy of mercy and love.

2. *This ministry is benevolent.* It is emphatically an offer of goodness—a message of mercy—an exhibition of love. The subject is the benevolence of God; the design is benevolent—human happiness; the spirit is to be such—love of Christ, and love to souls constrain. A messenger will produce little effect unless his heart overflows with it.

3. *This ministry is active and diligent.* "Feet upon the mountains," etc.—following the benighted wanderer—seeking the lost. Oh, see the field of effort, and the extent of labour. "Go ye into all the world, and preach the gospel to every creature," Mark xvi. 15.

4. *A ministry which should command attention.* The

attention of men is demanded. "How beautiful," etc. Observe, and attend, and hearken. Here are depths of love. Here are subjects of sublime grandeur. Here are concerns of great importance. Here are facts and truths in which we are eternally interested. To attention to this we are called, and for it we are responsible; and what shall the end of those be who obey not the gospel? "Who hath ears to hear, let him hear!" Matt. xiii. 9.

III. OUR OBLIGATIONS TO LABOUR FOR ITS DIFFUSION.

1. *There is the obligation arising from our possession of it.* We have it for ourselves, and next for the world. Monopoly is iniquitous to our dying race, etc.

2. *Obligation of gratefulness.* To God, who sent it to us. To the memories of the missionaries, who introduced it. To our martyred reformers, who rescued it from corruption. To our immediate predecessors, from whom we received it.

3. *Obligation of the Divine command.* Our Divine Saviour is now reiterating, "Go ye therefore, and teach all nations," Matt. xxviii. 19. It is his royal will—his divine mandate. To refuse or neglect, is disloyalty and rebellion.

APPLICATION.

1. Rejoice in the glad tidings of the gospel. Make it your boast, etc. Glory in it—secure its consolations.

2. Value and support its ministry. Do so with your influence, your prayers, and your lives.

3. Be solicitous for its consummation. Oh think of the universal reign of goodness, and peace, and joy, throughout our world; and hasten it on by an ardent love and strong faith, and by increasing toil in the great vineyard of the Saviour!

SKETCH LIV.

WHAT CHILDREN SHOULD DO FOR CHRIST'S CAUSE AMONG THE DYING HEATHEN.

"And the children crying in the temple, and saying, Hosannah to the Son of David."—MATT. xxi. 15.

IT is not well to overlook the influence of children, or to neglect them in making our efforts for the universal diffusion of the gospel. Samuel ministered before the Lord when a little child, 1 Sam. ii. 18. The captive little maid of Israel directed the leprous Naaman, her master, to the prophet Elisha, who was the instrument in the hands of God of recovering him of his leprosy, 2 Kings v. 3. Josiah very early gave himself to the Lord, and did good service in the cause of pure religion in the land, 2 Kings xxii. 1, 2. And on the interesting occasion to which the text refers, the children mingled their songs of joy with those of the multitude, who did homage to Christ; and cried in the temple, saying, " Hosannah to the Son of David." Let us,

I. ASCERTAIN WHAT IS REQUISITE IN CHILDREN IF THEY WOULD PROMOTE THE CAUSE OF JESUS.

1. *That they should have a correct knowledge of the state of the heathen.*

This is necessary to give correct views of their condition, and also to excite emotions of compassion for their miseries. This knowledge is given in some portions of God's blessed word : " The dark places of the earth are full of the habitations of cruelty," Psa. lxxiv. 20, etc. ; and they are amply supplied by the accounts furnished by modern missionaries.

2. *That they should have just views of the gospel as adapted to save them.*

If the heathen are dark, miserable, and perishing, how can they be rescued? We reply, By the communication of the gospel, which enlightens the eyes, pronounces blessings on the miserable, and offers everlasting life, through Jesus Christ, to all who believe. See Acts xxvi. 16—18. It is indispensable,

3. *That they should have right conceptions of the value of immortal souls.*

Human life is precious; but how much more the soul that will never die—the soul that will think, and feel, be wretched or happy for ever!—be exalted to heaven, or consigned to hell!—dwell with angels, or be the companion of devils through all eternity! See Mark viii. 36; ix. 44—50.

4. *That they should experimentally know the love of the Lord Jesus Christ.*

If we are ignorant of this love, how can we truly feel for those who are without God and without Christ, and "without hope in the world?" The love of Christ must produce true pity for the dying heathen. When we love Jesus we shall have his spirit, and we shall ardently long that all men may know and love him too. " God is love," 1 John. iv. 8. " The love of Christ constraineth us," etc., 2 Cor. v. 14, 15.

II. WHAT CHILDREN MAY DO FOR CARRYING ON THE BLESSED CAUSE OF JESUS IN THE WORLD.

1. *They can contribute of their means.*

Most children have halfpence and presents given to them. Now, they can lay by a part of these, to enable missionaries to go and preach; and to provide teachers, and books, and schools for those who are " perishing for lack of knowledge." A hundred children, giving only a halfpenny a week, would raise nearly eleven pounds a year for this good work.

2. They can collect from others.

They can respectfully lend missionary tracts and quarterly papers; and seek of their friends to assist them in this benevolent undertaking. I know a school where about fifty children have given and collected as much as sixty pounds, in one year, to send missionaries and teachers to Orissa, in India.

3. They can pray for God's blessing to attend their efforts and give success.

Every night and morning, when they kneel down to pray for themselves and friends at home, they should think of the heathen, and pray that God would send out to them His light and His truth. And children, who fear God, should meet and converse, and read and pray together, in reference to this blessed and holy cause. See Psa. lxxii. 15; lxxiv. 22; 1 Thes. iii. 1.

4. Some children might seek gifts and talents for missionary work.

All the missionaries, at present labouring, will soon die. Others must supply their places; and, therefore, pious children who love the heathen, should ask God to raise up labourers for his vineyard; and, if it be his will, to qualify and send them. See Isa. vi. 8. And now,

III. WHAT SHOULD INDUCE CHILDREN THUS TO FEEL AND WORK IN THE CAUSE OF CHRIST?

1. Gratitude to God for his goodness to them.

How he has distinguished them! Given them their existence in a land of gospel light, and religious mercies. Given them pious parents, pastors, teachers, and friends who love them. Given them sabbath schools, books, etc.

2. From the remembrance that good men once came as missionaries to this country.

The people of this country were once savages, and gross

idolaters. But the servants of Jesus came, and brought the gospel to them; and by it they were civilized and saved. Now, ought we not to do the same to those countries which are still ignorant of Jesus Christ and everlasting life?

3. *Because God has commanded it.*

He has ordered that the gospel must be preached in all the world, and to every creature. Now, to keep the gospel to ourselves would be disobeying God, and be extremely cruel to the pagan nations of the earth.

4. *Because we shall have an increase of happiness by thus doing good to others.*

In doing good we always get good. In doing good we always increase our own happiness. And besides, if we do good from love to God and love to men, the Lord Jesus Christ will reward us at the last day. The poor heathen may not be able to reward us, but we shall be recompensed at the resurrection of the just, Matt. xxv. 21.

APPLICATION.

1. How many children have given their hearts to the Lord Jesus Christ? Let this be the first concern of each and all of you.

2. How many are labouring for the poor benighted people in pagan lands! Oh! feel for them, and try to help them. Think of the poor children without schools, without ministers and good books, and without any knowledge of the blessed Redeemer.

3. How many will now enrol themselves under the missionary banners of King Jesus?—from this day, serving Christ personally; and also praying, and giving, and labouring for the welfare of the millions who know not God, nor Jesus Christ, whom He hath sent! John xvii. 3.

SKETCH LV.

EZEKIEL'S VISION OF DRY BONES.

BY REV. J. WEITBRECHT, MISSIONARY AT BURDWAN.*

"The hand of the Lord was upon me, and carried me out in the Spirit of the Lord, and set me down in the midst of the valley which was full of bones, and caused me to pass by them round about: and behold, there were very many in the open valley; and lo, they were very dry. And he said unto me, Son of man, can these bones live? And I answered, O Lord God, thou knowest," etc.—EZEK. xxxvii. 1—6.

THIS remarkable vision which the prophet Ezekiel relates, was shown to him at a peculiar time, and under peculiar circumstances; which it is proper to point out, in order to render the meaning of it more clear and intelligible. He lived with the remnant of his brethren, far away from the land of his fathers, in Chaldea, a captive and an exile. The Jews had lost their political existence as a nation; king Nebuchadnezzar having transported those who survived the sword of the Chaldeans to his own land, to people its uninhabited parts. They had also lost their religious constitution and ordinances; for their temple was destroyed, and the beautiful service of Jehovah was abolished.

Thus this unfortunate nation suffered for their unfaithfulness to God and their propensity to idolatry, and appeared on the point of being entirely annihilated—struck out, as it were, from the list of nations; and, what must have been more painful to those who still preserved a sense of religion, their very *name* appeared to have been wiped out from the remembrance of the Lord. In their sadness and desolation,

* From a Sermon, preached in the Church of St. John, Upper Holloway, May 29, 1842.

they uttered the mournful complaint, which the prophet records : " Our bones are dried, and our hope is lost : we are cut off for our parts," Ezek. xxxviii. 11. As a nation, as a religious society, and likewise in reference to their spiritual state, they looked upon themselves as dead in the sight of God and of their fellow-creatures; so entirely deprived of life and energy, and all hope of recovery, as to resemble a body in the grave, of which nothing remains but the dry bones, disjointed and broken. Ah, my hearers! how sad is the state of a sinner, who, after repeated and fruitless invitations of Divine mercy, is at last forsaken by God, and left to feel all the consequences of his rebellion! Considering their situation as it then was, their cries of despondency, and almost despair, were not ungrounded.

But hopeless as their case was in the eyes of man, it was different in the eyes of God : and to assure them that *He* had still a time of gracious visitation in reserve for them,— to revive them as a nation, and more especially to create a new spiritual life and energy among them,—the prophet Ezekiel was shown the vision of a valley, strewed all over with dead bones, which, by the breath of the Almighty, were to become re-united to bodies, and endowed with life, so as to constitute, after this miraculous resurrection, " an exceeding great army."

It is not my intention to unfold this impressive scene in its exclusive application to the Jewish Church. We shall recognize in it a striking resemblance to the heathen world at large—and to this subject I desire to direct your particular attention ; but we shall find, likewise that the vision points out the real state of a great portion of the *Christian* world, as far as formal religion, in its spiritually lifeless and dead aspect, is still prevailing among *us*. And my earnest prayer to the Lord and Giver of life is, that this feeble testimony to the truth may, in more than one respect, resemble that of the prophet, who, in obedience to the Divine command, prophesied to dead bones; but whose prophecy became, by the manifestation of the Spirit, instrumental to their revival. We will consider,

I. The appearance of the valley.
II. The Divine command given to the prophet.
III. The effect produced by his prophesying.

I. The vision of the valley.

'Ezekiel relates the scene he witnessed, in a very lively and interesting manner. "The hand of the Lord was upon me, and carried me out in the Spirit of the Lord, and set me down in the midst of the valley which was full of bones."

(1.) Considering what this earth, a perfect master-piece of God's creation, was intended for, when first it came from His skilful and omnipotent hand—viz., a dwelling-place for immortal beings—we can form some idea how ill it has answered the end proposed. The workmanship, indeed, was perfect—"God saw every thing that he had made, and, behold, it was *very good*," Gen. i. 31; but man caused the confusion, and defiled it by his transgression. The earth has now become a place of suffering and distress. What with the ravages of war, which in almost every age has devoured its millions; the scourges of pestilence; and the diseases of every description, which, like a deadly atmosphere, have followed the commission of crime and sin in their train; this world has been turned in a *Tophet*, a valley of dead bones, a charnel-house and a grave, where the dead are cast away from the sight of the living. *We* are walking upon the dust of the departed, and ere long shall be ourselves numbered amongst them.

(2.) But the vision points out *spiritual death* in a more prominent manner. It is very desirable that we should obtain a correct view of the real state of man. We must hear what the Searcher of hearts says; and then we find, at once, that the vision which was shown to the prophet is a true and faithful picture of the fallen beings who people this world. A valley of dead bones it presents to this day. Sinners are dead in the sight of God, because they have lost the true life—the life of holiness, the life of love, the life of immortality, with which a merciful Creator had endowed the being he made in his likeness.

The prophet was greatly struck by the *immense number* of dead bones: the valley was strewed over and covered with them. And what else can this fearful sight point out, but the *universal* desolation which sin and apostasy have caused in this world? " Behold, there were very many in the open valley." The whole human family has been poisoned by the venom of " the old Serpent." " Wherefore, as by one man sin entered into the world, and death by sin; and so death passed upon all men, for that all have sinned," Rom. v. 12.

I can speak from experience, dear friends, as to the millions of human beings in India. Moral and spiritual death is indeed reigning among *them*. Often, when I saw the masses moving before me, did the thought strike my mind— " Oh, what are these creatures doing in the world, leading little more than an animal life; for the gratification of their bodily wants and desires is all they care for;—and yet they are belonging to the same family whose original destiny was heaven and immortality!"

Another remark of the prophet, as he was gazing at the scene before him, was, "And, lo, the bones were *very dry*." The moisture which they had derived from the circulation of the blood, while the body was alive and covered with skin and flesh, was dried up; every sign of vitality had disappeared. What does this signify?—*hopeless ruin*—a condition irremediable and forlorn. So lifeless and dry, so entirely past recovery, or, as we should call it, re-animation, in a *spiritual* point of view, is the condition of those who have fallen from God and eternal life, into the death of sin and ignorance! As a branch cut off from the tree withers, and its sap is dried up, so lifeless and senseless to every thing divine and spiritual is the natural man, and especially the dark soul of the idolatrous heathen. Consider,

II. THE COMMAND TO PROPHESY.

There are two things which deserve our particular notice in this passage : first, the command to prophesy; and, secondly, the agency by which the thing prophesied was to be accomplished. A most wonderful operation was about to be performed; the millions of dead bones were to be united to bodies, and endowed with life and energy. The address, of itself, was not likely to produce this effect; but the Lord engaged to accompany it by the power of His Spirit.

A wise and merciful God has so decreed it, that His sovereign power of awakening and converting sinners is to be manifested in the use of means which He has appointed. The work is not entrusted to angelic beings; but sinners are made the instruments of converting sinners: the man who has been enlightened from above is commissioned as the most suitable agent for prophesying, *i.e.* bearing testimony to the love and mercy of God, and thereby to become a fellow-worker with God, in His wonderful operation upon the heart of man.

Here, then, you perceive the importance of the ministry of the gospel. The prophet had to address a host of dead bones in the valley. This might have appeared to *him* a hopeless task. To speak to one who has no life, no mind, no perception, no understanding of Divine things!—a person of a sceptical and philosophising disposition would have been apt to rebel against such a command. But the prophet was obedient : though he could not perceive what his agency was to avail, he believed that God could raise the dead ; and the very giving of such a command satisfied him that He WOULD accomplish the thing. Now, in this light we consider the preaching of the gospel to the most hopeless sinners. The gospel is a message of mercy to fallen man, of whatever race, language, or complexion he may be. As in Adam all are fallen, so in Christ are all to be raised up again, 1 Cor. xv. 22.

What is the grand subject of our ministry ?—nothing more or less than a Divine declaration to fallen dying sinners, that God, by the power of His grace, *will* cause the dead to live. While *we* use the means, God works effectually through *our* instrumentality : therefore, what *He* has commanded *we* must do, and what *He* has promised *we* must expect. And here I may mention one encouraging fact : throughout the length and breadth of our Indian empire the impression has gained ground among the natives, that the Christian religion will eventually supersede their idolatrous worship. The Brahmins, who are the most bitter opposers of the labours of the Missionaries, cannot help acknowledging that this will be the case. They feel convinced of it, being acute enough to discern the superior beauty and adaptation of the gospel to man's spiritual wants : they are aware of the approaching fall of idolatry, from the success we have already met with, in the conversion of Hindoos of all castes : and, what is very remarkable, they feel sure of it from a certain prophecy in their own books, foretelling that the present religious system will be destroyed at the end of this age, by a foreign nation. And often have I heard the declaration from the mouth of the haughty Brahmin, " We know that you will eventually succeed in destroying our religion ; for it will be nothing less than a proof of the truth of our Shasters."

III. The effect of the prophesying.

" So, as I prophesied," etc. Here we see the result of the prophet's ministry. An unexpected, an astonishing change took place among the bones : they were formed into natural bodies, according to their original creation.

The spiritual import of this part of the vision is obvious, and confirms our previous views. The Lord has committed a glorious power to His church :—oh, what could not be effected, if we all did but truly appreciate it! When her ministers go forth upon His command, declaring his word faithfully, not adding thereto nor diminishing aught from it, it *will* effect the thing for which he sent it.

The shaking of the dry bones signifies the awakening of sinners : this is the first great act in a sinner's conversion. When the arrows of the word touch the heart, a concern is manifested. A sinner who effectually receives the word, though he were before dead and insensible to Divine things, will be moved, and tremble with fear, in listening to the message of the Almighty. ·

After this, the bones were covered with flesh and sinews. Here we recognise a further progress; the body is preparing for a new and active life; all the different parts which are necessary for constituting such a body are one by one joined and prepared for exercise. Here we have a significant description of the wise and wonderful process by which the faculties of the human mind are raised, drawn out from sin and error, and brought into the obedience of the gospel.

Though the bodies were formed into their natural state, the prophet perceived that there was no breath in them. The Lord commanded him again to prophesy :—" Prophesy, son of man, and say to the wind, Thus saith the Lord God, Come from the four winds, O breath, and breathe upon these slain, that they may live. So I prophesied as he commanded me, and the breath came into them, and they lived, and stood up upon their feet, an exceeding great army." You all understand the meaning of this, my hearers: this breath bestowed with the prophesying signifies the *Spirit of God*, who is alone the Creator of spiritual life.

This earth, degraded as it has been by the Fall, is not to resemble for ever a valley of dead bones;—they must be, they will be "made alive." Look at this field, my hearers! Do you not hear a sound at a distance? Is there not a shaking of bones perceptible in every part of the world?

Now, before the prophet prophesied, the dead bones could not be raised to life; and without the knowledge of the gospel, no sinner can be converted. God always works through means and instruments, in the spiritual as well as in the natural world; though the display of power in conversion is his own prerogative. Difficulties should never deter us in this holy work; the success depends on and is secured by Him who "inhabiteth eternity," before whom the "nations are as a drop of a bucket."

Should not every Christian consider himself bound, by the love of Jesus, to do more for His glory; and strengthen the hands of his brethren who labour in foreign lands, until in every heathen town and village the Redeemer is adored, and souls rejoice in his salvation?

When the Almighty is about to do an important work, He raises up instruments by which it is to be performed. A century ago, the thought of preaching the gospel to the Heathen scarcely entered the mind of any Christian in England. What has the Lord wrought amongst us since!

Oh, let us work while it is day—work and pray, that we may, in the day of His appearance, be among the great army who shall grace His triumph; and that we may become instrumental in gathering to the host of the redeemed many who shall rejoice in His salvation!

SKETCH LVI.

THE UNIVERSAL REIGN OF CHRIST.

"And the seventh angel sounded; and there were great voices in heaven, saying, The kingdoms of this world are become the kingdoms of our Lord, and of his Christ; and he shall reign for ever and ever."

REV. xi. 15.

THIS world was made by and for Christ. He was the Logos by whom all things were made, whether they be things in heaven, or things on earth, Col. i. 16, 17. He made it to be the theatre of his goodness—the place of the especial manifestations of his power, and wisdom, and love. By the introduction of sin it became rebellious, and revolted from its rightful owner. Satan, the usurper, established his tyrannical and wicked dominion over it; and under his hellish control it has been the scene of crime, and pollution, and woe, and death; and one immense yawning passage has been opened from it to the horrible regions of despair and of everlasting woe. But Divine mercy has appeared on its behalf; a system of renovation has been set up; and its ultimate destiny is one of universal righteousness, peace, and glory.

The text prophetically anticipates the period when angelic voices shall make the courts of heaven to reverberate with loud hallelujahs, and when the burden of the song shall be —"The kingdoms of this world have become the kingdoms of our Lord, and of his Christ; and he shall reign for ever and ever."

I. BRIEFLY GLANCE AT THE PRESENT CONDITION OF THE KINGDOM OF THIS WORLD.

II. WHAT THE STATEMENT OF THE TEXT INVOLVES.

III. The certainty of its realization.

IV. The claims which this subject has upon the friends of the Saviour.

I. Let us briefly glance at the present condition of the kingdoms of the world.

1. *Many of these kingdoms are totally enveloped in Pagan darkness and superstition.*

Idolatry of the grossest description prevails. Imaginary deities of gold, silver, iron, brass, wood, and clay, are adored and worshipped. Animals and vegetables are deified. Demon vengeance is deprecated, and demon mercy supplicated. Some of these kingdoms have a moral darkness resting on them as dense and fearful as that of Egypt.

2. *Many of these kingdoms are in a state of servile debasement to the power of the false prophet.*

Mohammed is their only saviour—the koran their only polar star—delusion their only solace. There waves the crescent, not the cross. There triumphs impurity, commingled with superstitious rites, not Christian intelligence and purity.

3. *Many of these kingdoms are spell-bound by the influence of corrupt forms of religion.*

How true this is of Papal nations, where antichrist reigns, and where the " Mother of harlots," sways her corrupt influence without let or hinderance. The picture is little brighter in reference to the gross superstitions of the Greek church, and her pompous array of unmeaning ceremonies.

4. *In the most enlightened nations where a purer form of Christianity prevails, practical iniquity abounds.*

Look at so-called Christian Britain, which is the literal Goshen of religious privileges; yet, what profanity! what intemperance! what sensuality! what contempt of God! what disregard of sabbaths and ordinances! what infidelity! what crime, and moral degradation and misery!

How few are really walking in the narrow path of spiritual purity; and how densely crowded the broad way of death! Not more than two hundred millions of the human race know anything correctly of God, or Divine revelation; while from six to eight hundred millions are perishing for lack of scriptural knowledge.   We proceed to show,

II. WHAT THE STATEMENT OF THE TEXT INVOLVES.

1. *The universal diffusion of Divine knowledge.*

That the beams of gospel-day shall illumine every nation, and people, and tongue;—that all men shall know the Lord, from the least of them unto the greatest of them, Jer. xxxi. 34; and that the darkness of ignorance and error shall be banished from the face of the wide earth.

2. *That all false systems of religion shall be overthrown.*

That the idols of the heathen shall be given " to the moles and to the bats," Isa. ii. 20; that, from Juggernaut to the smallest household god, they shall all be abandoned and abhorred—that the long reign of Polytheism shall come to an entire, universal, and eternal end.

3. *Corrupt forms of Christianity shall be annihilated.*

That antichrist shall fall to rise no more—that the clay of human inventions shall be separated from the gold and the silver; that the wood, hay, and stubble, shall be consumed by the mouth of the Lord; and that the one foundation of hope only shall be known, even Jesus Christ.

4. *The universal surrender of every heart to love and obey the Lord Jesus Christ.*

Religion is ever personal; and it is only when all the persons of a kingdom are pious, that such a kingdom, in reality, becomes the kingdom of Christ; so that all men, of all kingdoms, must personally know and believe in Jesus Christ, before the sublime and holy consummation of the text can be fully accomplished.   Observe, then,

III. The certainty of its realization. This cannot be reasonably doubted when you consider,

1. *That all kingdoms are in reality the right of the Lord Jesus.*—His right as their Creator, their Governor, and Benefactor; but expressly by their redemption through his infinitely precious blood.

2. *The terms of the Divine covenant assure it.* Jesus is to see of the travail of his soul until he is satisfied, Isa. liii. 11. All flesh are to see his salvation, Luke iii. 6. " And men shall be blessed in him: all nations shall call him blessed," Psa. lxxii. 17.

3. *We are directed on the highest authority to pray and labour for it.* " Thy kingdom come!" Matt. vi. 10. " Prayer also shall be made for him continually, and daily shall he be praised," Psa. lxxii.15. " And this gospel of the kingdom shall be preached in all the world for a witness unto all nations, and then shall the end come," Matt. xxiv. 14, etc. " The glory of the Lord shall be revealed, and all flesh shall see it together," Isa. xl. 5. " He shall have dominion also from sea to sea, and from the river unto the ends of the earth," Psa. lxxii. 8. We reason,

4. *From the achievements of the past.* Greater difficultíes do not impede the course of Divine truth; viler hearts do not remain to be converted and sanctified. The untold myriads of the saved of past generations, as the first fruits, indicate with certainty the general harvest of the universal family of man. Now, these, with the promises of the eternal and unchangeable Jehovah, place the subject beyond all doubt and disputation.

IV. The claims which this subject has upon all the friends of the Saviour.

1. *It demands their solemn consideration.* A world to be saved! An all-sufficient Saviour—a universal gospel—

an efficient Spirit—a God delighting in the exercise of his clemency and love.

2. *It demands our fervent prayers.* O pray for the heathen! Pray that Providence may open effectual doors of usefulness, and afford facilities for Christian missions, etc. That God would raise up more labourers, and send them forth into his vineyard. That God would smile on the efforts employed; especially that he would shower down the gracious influences of his Spirit on the church.

3. *It demands our individual influence.* Plead for missions—collect for missions—give to missions; and do all these heartily and liberally, and with persevering constancy, and devotedness of heart.

4. *It demands a revival of pure religion in the churches at home.* We want more light, and more purity, and more moral power, and more of the mind of our Divine Master: more zeal for God's glory, and more pity for a dying world. Who will enter on this hallowed crusade? Who will rally round the standard of mercy? Who will labour for Christ and for souls? " Who will consecrate himself this day unto the Lord?" O think of the final issue— the universal triumph of truth, and love, and mercy! O anticipate the day when the song shall be sung, ". The kingdoms of this world are become the kingdoms of our Lord, and of his Christ; and he shall reign for ever and ever." Amen.

THE END.

LONDON : PRINTED BY KNIGHT AND SON, UPPER HOLLOWAY.

BOOKS LATELY PUBLISHED.

MISSIONARY ENTERPRISES in MANY LANDS. With a Brief History of Missionary Societies. By Jabez Burns, Minister of Ænon-Chapel, St. Mary-le-bone. Royal 32mo., pp. 416. Illustrated by Twenty fine Engravings. Cloth, gilt edges, 2s. 6d. A liberal allowance to Ministers and Schools.

Opinions of the Press.

" This little compendium of missionary institutions, missionary toils, and missionary results, will be a most suitable present to put into the hands of young people beginning to take a lively interest in the kingdom of Christ. It contains much information on missionary subjects; and many striking anecdotes illustrative of the progress of Divine truth."—*Evangelical Magazine, May.* 1845.

" This is a most interesting little volume for the young. It is a gem-book of brief records, exemplifying the faith, energy, enterprise, and success of missionaries of various Societies in all parts of the globe Sufficient notice is taken of the scene of labour to give a good general idea of it, and facts are sketched with so much rapidity and life, that the least attentive have scarce time to tire before the narrative is complete."—*Primitive Church Magazine, March,* 1845.

" After a brief history of the principal Missionary Societies, the author presents his readers with a number of well-selected and well-told incidents, illustrative of the difficulties and successes of missionary labour in all quarters of the globe. No special prominence is given to any denomination, and we feel confident that it will prove to be a work universally popular, and especially welcome to the young. It cannot fail to increase, by its interesting details, the spirit of missions where it exists, or to produce it where as yet it may unhappily be wanting. The volume is adorned with numerous engravings on wood, is neatly got up, and very cheap; we wish it may obtain, as it certainly deserves, a wide circulation."—*Baptist Record, March,* 1845.

" A beautifully got up book, full of matter, and all matter of fact. A rich store of information is furnished respecting Missions, Missionaries, and the result of Missionary labour. We hope that the work will be widely circulated, especially amongst the young."—*Methodist New Connexion Magazine, March,* 1845.

" A Missionary History for the young, and its contents are well adapted to inform and interest their minds. It is written in a clear style, so as easily to be understood by the juvenile reader, who may in its pages trace the rise and progress of Christian missions in nearly every part of the globe. The progress of the gospel in heathen countries is a theme on which Christians delight to dwell, and this sketch of missionary proceedings may serve the purpose of giving correct ideas and notions to young persons, concerning the nature and importance of missionary enterprises, and may tend greatly to enlist their sympathies in these noble designs of Christian philanthropy. This volume ought to find a place in lending libraries for Sunday and day scholars."—*Sunday School Teachers' Magazine, March,* 1845.

" This is really a beautiful little book, and as valuable as it is beautiful. Mr. Burn's has done many things in book publishing, but he never did better than this. We predict it will become an universal favourite, and find a rapid and extensive sale. It contains above twenty neat engravings. Gilt edges and ornamented cover."—*Baptist Reporter.*

" Parents and guardians of youth! take our counsel, and place this beautiful volume in the hands of the children you love. It will interest them at once, and interest them throughout. We thank the excellent compiler for so suitable and so seasonable a present. The publishers have creditably done their part."—*Christian Examiner, February,* 1845.

" This is a judicious compilation, from various authentic sources, of missionary facts and anecdotes. Though but a small volume, it contains a large amount of matter, and is illustrated with numerous engravings The volume is full of important information, and is pregnant with interest in every part of it. We regard it as a great boon to the public, and as a valuable contribution to the cause of missions. Every religious parent should place it in the hands of his children, as a means of exciting their interest in the missionary enterprise, and no Sunday school library should be without it It is very neatly bound in cloth, with gilt edges, and its price is a mere trifle."—*General Advertiser, April,* 1845.

' This is an interesting manual for children; and now that they are actively engaged in contributing their pence to aid in the diffusion of the gospel, it cannot fail, if carefully read, to keep alive in their hearts those sympathies for heathens which have been happily awakened."—*Primitive Methodist Magazine, March,* 1845.

AN INQUIRY INTO THE ORGANIZATION AND GO-VERNMENT OF THE APOSTOLIC CHURCH: particularly with reference to the claims of Episcopacy. By ALBERT BARNES. Reprinted verbatim from the American edition. Fine paper, 18mo., pp. 270; cloth, 2s.

" Who will not rejoice to meet Albert Barnes, who has laid the church of Christ under such a weight of obligation by his numerous and invaluable Biblical labours, on the present occasion ? Himself a Presbyterian, he has demolished the claims of Episcopacy in a manner as satisfactory as can well be conceived. The book is an exquisite specimen of Scriptural controversy. As this very cheap Pocket Edition was mainly undertaken at our recommendation, we cannot but wish for it the most extensive circulation."
Christian Witness, Feb. 1845.

" This is a very able and dispassionate Treatise, triumphantly disposing of the unscriptural claims and pretensions of the *soi-disant* apostolical successionists."—*Patriot.*

" The fame of Albert Barnes, of Philadelphia, has become European. As a writer, he has few competitors in his own land, and not many in ours. His present volume will extend his fame. We know no volume in which the great controversy between Presbyterians and Prelatists is more ably discussed; and none, certainly, in which the argument against the assumptions of Prelacy is more triumphantly conducted. We regard *this* part of his book as literally unanswerable.—The volume is one of great value—it is just suited for the times; and it ought to be extensively circulated in these lands."—*Christian Examiner.*

" Mr. Barnes justly contends that questions as to the constitution of the Church should be tried not by appeal to the *Fathers,* but by appeal to the *Bible;* and he has accordingly turned away from the consideration of church antiquities, and confined his inquiry to an examination of Scriptural evidence. The mild and Christian spirit in which it is conducted is deserving of great commendation."—*Watchman.*

" The name of " ALBERT BARNES" is known favourably in England as that of an able commentator on various portions of holy writ. He appears to advantage in this work as a controversalist. He writes with temper as well as ability. He examines the exclusive claims put forth by some American Bishops, and shows them, as we think, to be, so far as Scripture is concerned,—and on such a question the appeal must be made to Scripture, —utterly groundless; so that both labour and dexterity are required to find even the shadow of a reason for them. The true question is, not whether Episcopacy be a form of church government which *may be* adopted, but whether it is made by our Lord Jesus Christ the only channel through which ministerial authority can flow, so that communion with it is ordinarily necessary for the *regular* attainment of covenant blessings. Many volumes have been written on the subject: the small one now before us is one of the most useful manuals we have met with.
Wesleyan-Methodist Magazine Jan. 1845.

SELF-CULTURE. By WILLIAM E. CHANNING. An elegant Pamphlet, in neat wrapper, intended for the pocket. Price 4d.

" It should be the pocket companion of every young man in the country, and to be found on every lady's centre table."

" A gem of English composition, of sound, vigorous thought, and pure wisdom."

FAMILY AND PRIVATE DEVOTIONS, SERMONS, ETC.

HAWKER'S MORNING AND EVENING PORTIONS: being a selection of a Verse of Scripture, with Short Observations, for every Day in the Year. By Robert Hawker, D.D., Vicar of Charles, Plymouth. In one thick volume, ROYAL 18mo., LARGE TYPE. Cloth, only 4s. The Morning and Evening separate, cloth, lettered, 2s.

JENKS' FAMILY DEVOTIONS; with Prayers for Particular Persons on most occasions. New edition, by the Rev. Charles Simeon. 12mo. Large type, cloth, lettered, 3s.

FAMILY WORSHIP; a course of Morning and Evening Prayers for every Day in the Month: with Prayers for special occasions, and a discourse on Family Religion. By the Rev. James Bean. New edition, 18mo., cloth, lettered, 1s. 6d.

VILLAGE SERMONS; OR, FIFTY-TWO PLAIN AND SHORT DISCOURSES on the Principal Doctrines of the Gospel; intended for the use of Families, Sunday Schools, and Companies assembled for Religious Instruction in Country Villages. By the Rev. George Burder. A new Edition, with a Life of the Author, by the Rev. Ingram Cobbin. The only cheap edition ever published. 12mo., cloth, lettered, 3s.

SERMONS on the LEADING DOCTRINES OF THE GOSPEL. By the Rev. Edward Cooper, late rector of Hamstall Ridware, etc. Complete edition, 12mo. Cloth, 2s. 6d.

SERMONS, PRACTICAL AND FAMILIAR; designed for Parochial and Domestic Instruction. By the Rev. Edward Cooper. 12mo, cloth, lettered, 3s.

FIFTY-TWO DOCTRINAL AND PRACTICAL SERMONS: being a Sermon for every Sunday in the Year. Selected from the Vols. of the Rev. Edward Cooper. Designed for Village and Domestic use. Cloth, lettered, 3s. 6d.

THE SERMONS OF THE REV. RICHARD CECIL, late of St. John's Chapel, Bedford Row, London. Now first collected, and printed verbatim from the Author's works. 12mo., 2s. 6d.

AN UNIVERSAL HISTORY OF CHRISTIAN MARTYR-DOM. Originally composed by the Rev. John Fox, M.A.; with Notes, Commentaries, and Illustrations by the Rev. J. Milner, M.A. A new Edition, greatly improved and corrected, complete in one large volume, 8vo., upwards of 1000 pages; with 16 original designs. Cloth, lettered, 10s. 6d.

ORATIONS, LECTURES, AND ADDRESSES: to which is added, NATURE: AN ESSAY. By Ralph Waldo Emerson. Handsomely printed in a large type; 12mo., pp. 180. Elegantly bound in cloth, lettered, 1s. 6d.

Third Edition, Price 2s. 6d.,

THE BIBLE READER'S HAND-BOOK:

COMBINING MANY OF THE ADVANTAGES OF

A DICTIONARY, INDEX, CONCORDANCE, NATURAL HISTORY, GEOGRAPHY, COMMENTARY; EXPLAINING THE TERMS AND PHRASES, AND ELUCIDATING SOME OF THE MOST DIFFICULT PASSAGES OF THE HOLY BIBLE.

CHIEFLY ARRANGED IN ALPHABETICAL ORDER.

BY THE REV. INGRAM COBBIN, A. M.

Pocket Volume; plate and vignette.   Cloth, gilt edges, 2s. 6d.
An allowance to Ministers and Schools.

Opinions of the Press.

" This is a most valuable volume ; and its worth, in our esteem, is exceedingly enhanced by its extraordinary cheapness, which renders it accessible to the poorest boy in England."—*Christian Witness, Feb.* 1845.

" Mr. Cobbin has afforded very important and valuable aid to the Biblical student, by the publication of his ' Condensed' and ' Portable' Commentaries.   The little volume before us will in no way detract from his reputation.   It is, what its title indicates, a Hand-book to the Bible, explaining terms and phrases, and elucidating some of the most difficult passages.   As a book of easy reference, it will be found very useful, the subjects being *Alphabetically* arranged; and it will, we think, supply, as the author desires, ' the place of a Biblical friend, capable of replying to many questions which will naturally arise in the inquiring mind while perusing the sacred pages.'   Sunday-school teachers will find it a useful companion."—*Patriot.*

" An invaluable companion to Scripture reading.   It is a small volume, prepared by one of the most useful Biblical writers of the day, and published in his usual style of elegance and cheapness, by Mr. Thomas Arnold.   It really combines most of the advantages of a Dictionary, Index, Concordance, Natural History, Geography, and Commentary of the Holy Scriptures.   We consider that the combined exertions of Ingram Cobbin as a compiler, and of Thomas Arnold as a publisher, will be a special blessing to many generations."—*Sunday School Magazine.*

" This little volume contains a variety of useful and interesting matter, illustrative of Holy Scripture.   It is arranged in Alphabetical order, under several heads.   It would be impossible, in the small compass which we can assign to this notice, to give anything like an adequate idea of its contents : but we feel certain, that it will constitute an interesting and valuable companion to the readers of Scripture in general ; *and will form a very suitable assistant to the young in particular.*"—*Christian Guardian.*

" Professedly designed for Bible readers ; an examination of the contents of this volume has convinced us that it is equally well adapted for *Scripture teachers.*   Many of those who are benevolently engaged in the instruction of the young, possess but limited means and opportunities for the acquisition of a correct and extensive supply of facts, explanations, and illustrations, together with historical, geographical, and chronological information needful for their work.   To such, the volume before us will be found very serviceable, as containing these requisites to a considerable extent, and in an *arranged form,* so as to be rendered easily subsidiary to the intelligent teaching of Scripture truth.—*Sunday School Teachers' Magazine.*